THE RED
CIRCLE

THE RED CIRCLE

MY LIFE IN THE NAVY SEAL SNIPER CORPS AND HOW I TRAINED AMERICA'S DEADLIEST MARKSMEN

BRANDON WEBB

WITH JOHN DAVID MANN

ST. MARTIN'S PRESS ✹ NEW YORK

www.stmartins.com

Design by Omar Chapa

Library of Congress Cataloging-in-Publication Data

Webb, Brandon.
    The red circle : my life in the Navy Seal Sniper Corps and how I trained America's deadliest marksmen / Brandon Webb with John David Mann.
       p. cm.
    ISBN 978-0-312-60422-6 (hardback)
    ISBN 978-1-250-01840-3 (e-book)
    1. United States. Navy. SEALs—Biography.   2. Snipers—United States—Biography.   3. Snipers—Afghanistan—Biography.   4. United States. Navy. SEALs—Physical training.   5. United States. Navy—Commando troops—Training of.   6. Afghan War, 2001—Personal narratives, American.   7. War on Terrorism, 2001–2009—Personal narratives, American.   8. California, Southern—Biography.   I. Mann, John David.   II. Title.   III. Title: My life in the Navy Seal Sniper Corps and how I trained America's deadliest marksmen.
   VG87.W43 2012
   359.0092—dc23
   [B]

                                        2012001375

First Edition: April 2012

10 9 8 7 6 5 4 3 2 1

For my three children

AUTHOR'S NOTE

All the events in this book are true and are described herein to the best of my recollection; however, some details have been altered. With the exception of historical figures (e.g., Admiral Bob Harward, President George W. Bush, Harmid Karzai), close friends, and fallen comrades, I have changed most of the names; in some instances I have provided only the first names of friends who are still on active duty. Some dates, locations, and particulars of certain operations have been modified; and I have at all times sought to avoid disclosing methods and other sensitive mission-related information.

CONTENTS

FOREWORD

I first met Brandon Webb when I was a student in the Naval Special Warfare Sniper Course.

Sniper school was one of the toughest things I've ever done, in some ways even more difficult than the infamous ordeal known as BUD/S, or Basic Underwater Demolition/SEAL training, that every SEAL undergoes. The sniper course starts with a stalking phase, which is all about stealth and concealment, training us to crawl painstaking inches and yards undetected across enemy-held territory. I have to be honest: This was not easy for me. The shooting part came naturally. The stalking part did not. I'm a pretty big guy, and trying to make myself look like an ice plant or manzanita bush instead of a six-foot Texan . . . it just wasn't happening. I don't know how I would have gotten through it, if it weren't for Brandon being my instructor.

Brandon and his cadre were incredibly tough on us.

They were intent on making us some of the best Special Operations forces in the field, and I have to admit: In that they succeeded. As I say in my book, Brandon's standards were so high they would have made an Apache scout gasp. It wasn't just a matter of making our lives hard. Brandon went beyond the call. He set aside time after course hours to answer questions and work with all the students; he mentored me, did whatever it took to make sure I knew my stuff.

Graduating sniper school was one of the proudest achievements of my life.

I went from sniper school almost directly to Afghanistan. Not too many months after being under Brandon's care I found myself in the soaring Hindu Kush mountains, a subrange of the Himalayas, not far from the Afghanistan-Pakistan border on June 29, 2005. Everyone else in my recon team was gone, including my brother Morgan's best friend, Matt "Axe" Axelson—all killed by the same couple hundred Taliban forces who were now doing their level best to kill me, too. If it had not been for Brandon's patience, care, and skill with me in the sniper course not long before, I can promise you this: I would have left these Texan bones bleaching on the Afghan hillside.

My story, the story of Operation Redwing and the brave men who gave their lives in the battle for Murphy's Ridge, is chronicled in the pages of the book *Lone Survivor*. Brandon's story is chronicled here in the pages you hold in your hands. And it's about time. His training saved my life then, just as it would again several years later in a very different environment, fighting house to house on the hot, muggy streets of Iraq.

And I know I'm not the only one. There are a lot of people out there, people whose names you'll never hear, who are alive today because of the efforts, skill, and dedication of Brandon and others like him. What you're about to read is not just the story of the making of a Navy SEAL sniper but the story of one guy who went on to help shape the lives of *hundreds* of elite Special Operations warriors.

It was a great honor to serve on and off the battlefield with the men of the U.S. Navy SEAL teams and U.S. SOCOM (Special Operations Command). Brandon and I have both lost many great friends over the years, and it's comforting to know that the memories of these great warriors will live on in the stories we share with you. My hope is that you will come to know them as intimately as we did, and that you continue to pass on their stories of heroism so that we may never forget the ultimate sacrifice they made for the freedom we enjoy today.

Brandon has a great story to tell, and it is living proof that you can achieve anything you put your mind to. It's an honor to introduce his memoir.

Never quit.

Marcus Luttrell (USN Ret.), Navy SEAL and
No. 1 national bestselling author of Lone Survivor

THE RED CIRCLE

INTRODUCTION

Four of us—Cassidy, Osman, Brad, and I—went out before dawn to patrol a site where a C-130 gunship had engaged some forces the night before, to see if we could find any bodies. We reached the coordinates we'd been given just moments before the indistinct grays of predawn resolved into the pastels of daybreak. Before we could do any serious searching, we heard voices coming from some nearby caves above us. The four of us instantly hit the ground and waited. As we watched, a spill of enemy fighters started pouring out of one of the caves—twenty, at least, and all armed.

If this were happening in the movies, we would all just leap to our feet and blow these guys away, but in real life it doesn't work that way. We were outnumbered at least five to one, and we were not exactly armed with machine guns. This was not the OK Corral, and if we leapt to our feet we would all be mowed down in short order. There was no hiding until they were gone, either: These guys were headed our way. We would have to call in an air strike, and do it fast.

There was a B-52 nearby; Brad got it on the radio. It was my job to give him the coordinates—but there was a snag. The only way to ensure that the team in the B-52 dropped their fireworks on the other guys and not on us was to give them exact coordinates. Typically we would do this using a high-powered laser range finder hooked into a GPS so that when it ranged the target it would give us not only distance but also the target's GPS coordinates, which we could then pass on up to whoever we were calling for air support. These bombers are extremely accurate with their ordnance, like vertical snipers in the sky.

We'd only planned for a simple twelve-hour mission and didn't have all our usual equipment. Typically, for a full-on recon mission, I'd have at least a good sniper rifle. We didn't have even a decent range finder.

Training, training. As a SEAL sniper I'd been taught to estimate distances on the fly even without all the usual tools, using only my five senses and my gut, but typically I'd be shooting a 10-gram bullet from the muzzle of a rifle. In this case, we were shooting a 1,000-pound "bullet" out of a 125-ton aircraft, flying 20,000 feet above us at near the speed of sound, at a target less than 500 yards away from where we sat—and I had to get it right.

Range estimation. This was something else we covered in sniper school: You visualize a familiar distance, say, a football field. *That's one football field, two football fields, three football fields* . . . but this can be risky when you're not on level ground. Here I had to sight up a rugged, rocky incline. And daybreak lighting can play tricks with distances.

Those twenty-plus al Qaeda, or Taliban, or who the hell knew who, were trickling down the slope heading straight for our position. They hadn't seen us yet, but it would be only seconds before they did. If we were going to do this thing, it had to be *now*.

"Brandon!" Cassidy hissed. "You need to Kentucky-windage this drop!" "Kentucky windage" is a term that means basically this: *Wing it.* *Give it your best shot.* I gave Cassidy a bearing I estimated as 100 meters *past* the group. If I was going to be off at all, better to guess long than short, and if I was balls-on accurate, a drop 100 meters behind them should at least buy us a few seconds to adjust and drop a second time.

Now the enemy cluster was so close we couldn't wait any longer. We were concealed but not covered; that is, they couldn't easily see us, but once they knew where we were, our concealment would give no protection against incoming fire. We quickly moved to cover—and that's when they spotted us. There were a few alarmed shouts and then the sounds of small-arms fire.

There is nothing quite so galvanizing as the distinct *crack! snap!* of semiautomatic weaponry being fired over your head, the *crack!* being the sound of the initial shot itself and the *snap!* being the bullet breaking the sound barrier as it zings past you.

We returned fire. I sighted one guy wearing a black headdress, dropped him. Quickly resighted and dropped a second, this one wearing the traditional Afghan wool roll-up hat. Sighted a third—then glanced up and saw vapor trails in the sky. The B-52 was flying so high it was invisible to us, but I knew exactly what was happening up there: They were dropping the first bomb.

When you are this close to a big explosion it rocks your chest cavity. You want to make sure your mouth is open so the contained impact doesn't burst your lungs. Brad got the call: We were seconds from impact. We opened our mouths, dropped and rolled.

The Joint Direct Attack Munition is a big bomb and extremely accurate. When the first set of JDAMs hit, it shook the mountain under our feet, throwing rubble everywhere.

I whipped around and glanced back up the incline to assess the strike. Perfect—about 100 yards behind the target. I rolled again, adjusting numbers in my head, and quickly shouted the new coordinates to Cassidy, who gave them to Brad to relay up to the bird. In moments like this your senses go into hyperacute mode and seconds seem to stretch into minutes, hours, a timeless series of discrete snapshots. I focused on my breathing, making it slow and deliberate, feeling the cool morning air mixed with the distinct smell of explosives teasing my lungs. I knew my numbers were accurate and that the men shooting to kill us would themselves be dead in seconds. For a brief moment, I was at peace. And then an unexpected sound sliced through the strange silence: the wail of a baby crying.

My stomach twisted. I had a five-week-old baby boy at home whom I'd not yet held in my arms; hopefully I would survive this war to meet him face-to-face. Someone up on that hillside had a baby they would never see or hold again.

I knew these people had made the decision to bring their families out here to this godforsaken fortress, knowingly putting them in harm's way. Sometimes, I'd heard, they even did this intentionally, using their own children, their flesh and blood, as living shields to prevent us from attacking. *It was their choice,* I told myself, *not ours.* But I'll never forget the sound of that baby's cry.

We opened our mouths, ducked and rolled. The second drop took them all.

The pages that follow provide a rare look into the most difficult, elite sniper training in the world and the traits it takes to produce a successful graduate: a sniper capable of stopping another man's beating heart without hesitation at distances of over a mile.

These accounts and descriptions may read like reports from an alien land. It is a unique existence of brutal conditions, extreme pressure, and hair-trigger judgment. I have never second-guessed decisions made in the field; combat is no place for Monday-morning quarterbacking, and a SEAL sniper can't afford to indulge in the luxuries of uncertainty or ambivalence.

This doesn't mean that those of us occupying this unusual world shed or lose connection with our humanity. If anything, the opposite is the case. In a way, living in the crosshairs of split-second decisions with life-or-death consequences makes you *more* acutely attuned to the truest, grittiest realities of human fragility and the preciousness of life. It also puts you face-to-face with our deepest potential for idiocy and senselessness, and the consequences of those failings.

I am clear that the people we killed that day in the hills of Afghanistan would have employed any and all means to kill me, my family, and my friends without an instant's hesitation. In all honesty, though, I have seen similarly fanatic attitudes within our own American culture and even at the highest levels of our military. There is nothing simple about war, and there are plenty of extremists on all sides.

These pages also chronicle an extraordinary shift that has taken place in the fundamental nature of military strategy over the past decade. The October 2000 attack on the USS *Cole* in the Gulf of Aden was the signal event in this radical shift: a guided missile destroyer, crewed by nearly 300 sailors and costing more than $1 billion to put in the water, was crippled and nearly sunk by two men in a small powerboat. Seventeen American servicemen were killed and another thirty-nine injured.

We had entered the age of asymmetrical warfare.

I was part of the detail assigned to guard the USS *Cole* immediately after the attack and soon became involved in a complete restructuring of Naval Special Operations and its role in war.

Up through the end of the twentieth century, our approach to combat was still shaped by the Cold War and great land wars of our past. Even as late as Desert Storm, we waged war by unleashing massive ground forces to roll across the desert. In that world, Special Ops was the bastard child, called upon occasionally for unusual missions but mainly there to support our conventional forces.

Now that picture has completely flipped on its head. Since the events of 9/11 we have reconfigured our conventional forces—nuclear subs, aircraft carriers, destroyers, all our major assets—to support small units much like the one we took into the caves in Afghanistan that day. From being a special-case accessory, we have suddenly become the vanguard of military strategy.

In April 2009 we all watched entranced on CNN as a Navy SEAL sniper team fired three simultaneous shots, instantly executing the three pirates who had kidnapped a U.S. shipping captain off the Somali coast. From the moment they were mobilized, it took that sniper team less than ten hours to deploy, get halfway around the world, parachute with full kit at 12,000 feet into darkness and plunge into the deep waters of the Indian Ocean, rendezvous with waiting U.S. Naval forces, and complete their mission, start to finish.

As a former Navy SEAL sniper, sniper instructor, and eventually course manager (called head master) of the U.S. Navy SEAL sniper course, I know exactly what those ten hours were like—and also the last few seconds before the perfectly coordinated shot. The twenty-first-century sniper is trained to take into exacting account such variables as wind, ambient temperature, barometric pressure, degree of latitude, bullet velocity, even the deviation caused by the earth's rotation known as the Coriolis effect. Firing at such long range, with so much riding on the accuracy of the first shot, it is critical to account for all environmental and ballistic factors. At the instant before making the 1-centimeter movement of their fingers that would end three lives and save a fourth, their minds were going through dozens of calculations.

Two years later the world was stunned when we learned that a team of Navy SEALs had entered an innocent-looking suburban compound in

Pakistan and in moments eliminated the man who had been America's Public Enemy No. 1 for nearly a decade. The killing of Osama bin Laden, like the rescue of Captain Phillips off the coast of Somalia, signaled to the world that something fundamental had changed in the way we wage war and keep the peace.

In the wars of our fathers and their fathers, the decisive victories were won by tank battalions and overwhelming air support. In today's world of suicide bombers, decentralized terrorism, and rampantly adaptive piracy, the fortunes and well-being of nations rest increasingly in the hands, reflexes, and capabilities of individual warriors like the Navy SEAL sniper.

Not surprisingly, the public suddenly wants to know more about the traditionally secretive world of Special Operations, and rightly so. I hope my own story will provide an instructive window into that unseen world.

ONE
RITE OF PASSAGE

Every culture has its rites of passage.

Native American adolescents journeyed into the wilderness for days on end in vision quests aimed at gaining life direction from an animal spirit, or totem, through a fast-induced dream. For Australian aborigines it was the walkabout, young males trekking the outback for as long as six months to trace the ceremonial paths, or dreaming tracks, taken by their ancestors. Mormon boys ages nineteen to twenty-five are sent around the world for two years to do full-time mission work.

For me, it was shorter and simpler. My rite of passage came when I was thrown off a boat in the middle of the Pacific Ocean by my dad, a few weeks past my sixteenth birthday. I had to find my own path home from that oceanic wilderness, and it turned out to be a path that ultimately led to the most elite sniper corps in the world.

I don't know if you'd call that a dreaming track, exactly,

but you *could* say it was a path taken by my ancestors, at least in one sense: My father was thrown out of the house at age sixteen by *his* father, too. And I suppose the only way to make sense out of my story is to start with him.

Jack Webb grew up in Toronto, short, strong, and stocky. A talented hockey player and avid drummer, he was always a bit of a wild man. A true child of the sixties, Jack grew out his full black beard as soon as his hormones would cooperate. His father hewed to old-fashioned values and threatened to kick Jack out if he didn't cut his beard and long hair. When my father refused, out he went.

My grandfather may have thrown his son out, but he didn't succeed in changing his mind. To this day my dad still sports a full beard, though its black is now flecked with gray.

Now on his own, Jack made his way from Toronto to Malibu, where he picked up landscaping jobs and soon had his own company. Driving home from a job one day, he picked up three young hippie girls hitchhiking. One of them, a free spirit named Lynn, became his wife.

After they married, my parents moved up to British Columbia to the little ski town of Kimberley, just north of Vancouver, where he took a job as a guide at a hunting lodge, despite the fact that he knew absolutely nothing about hunting. The guy who hired him said, "Look, don't worry about it. Stay on the trail, and you'll be fine." He was. His first time out, he took a small group into the Canadian Rockies, pointing out all sorts of wildlife along the way. When they got back, the group told my dad's boss he'd hired the greatest guide in the world. They didn't know he was flat-out winging it.

Soon Jack was working construction, and on the job he taught himself everything there was to know about building houses. In those days, if you were a builder you did it all—pouring the foundation, framing, wiring, drywall, plumbing, roofing, everything from *A* to *Z*. Jack had never graduated high school, but he was a resourceful man with a big appetite for learning, and he soon became an accomplished builder with his own company, High Country Construction.

It was about this time that I came into the picture, followed a few years later by my sister, Rhiannon, and once I arrived on the scene my mother's life became considerably more complicated.

Free spirit though she may be, my mother has always been fiercely loyal to me and my sister, and to my dad, too, as far as that was possible. I always felt completely loved and supported by her, even through the difficulties to come.

My mother has also always been very entrepreneurial. She opened up a restaurant with my dad's sister, and later, when we lived in Washington for a while, she had her own boat maintenance business, sanding and varnishing the boats and keeping the woodwork in good condition. She wrote and published her own cookbook for boaters, *The Galley Companion*. Later still, when I worked on a California dive boat in my teens, she held a job there as head cook.

One more thing about my mom: She has always had a great sense of humor.

She would have had to, to cope with me.

I was born on June 12, 1974, screaming at the top of my tiny lungs, and I screamed for weeks. For the next ten months I stayed awake every night from ten till seven the next morning, yelling my head off, at which point I would sleep blissfully through the day while my mom recovered from the night's battle fatigue. My parents did everything they could to keep me awake during the day so they would have a shot at getting me to sleep at night. Didn't matter. It wasn't going to happen.

According to my mom, I was as wild as the Canadian landscape. I started crawling at six months and crawled *everywhere*. My mom talks about a study she heard about, where they put babies on a glass counter to see how far they would crawl. Nearly all the babies would stop when they got close to the edge—but the last 1 percent went crawling off into thin air every time.

"That 1 percent?" she says. "That was Brandon."

I started walking at nine months, and there was not a gate or door that could hold me. My mom bought every childproof lock she could find, but evidently "childproof" did not mean "Brandon-proof." She had doorknobs that even she couldn't open, but I always managed to get through them. She would lock me into my high chair, but if she stepped into the bathroom for even a moment, I'd be gone when she returned.

By eighteen months I discovered the joys of climbing and found I could climb up, over, and into pretty much anything. This ability, combined with my easy friendship with locks and predilection for drinking anything I could get my hands on, added up to quite a few visits to the emergency room to have my little toddler-sized stomach pumped. Among the beverages I sampled during those early years were kerosene, bleach, and Avon honeysuckle after-bath splash. I'm not saying this is a method I would endorse or recommend, but I am convinced that this is why I have always been able to hold my liquor and have never had a problem with addiction. By the time I was three, the hospital emergency room staff and my mom knew each other on a first-name basis.

When my mom was pregnant with my sister, my dad built an enclosure with a swing and what he thought was a Brandon-proof gate. (There's that term again: "Brandon-proof." Hadn't they learned?) My mom still doesn't know how I got out, since she was sitting right there reading a book—but she looked up and I was gone: I had crawled under a barbed-wire fence, scooted down a steep hill, and was out of sight.

My mother was wild with fear. Seven months pregnant, she knew there was no way she could get under that barbed-wire fence, and she didn't have any wire cutters. The night before, she and my father had seen a pack of coyotes ranging around, and now all she could think of was how her tiny son would make a tasty little coyote meal. The only reason she spotted me was that I was wearing a red sweatshirt. Somehow she managed to coax me back up the hill and under the fence so she could grab me, crying hysterically and at the same time wanting to beat me.

From my earliest years, I always had a penchant for danger and physical extremes, and it made my poor mother's life a living hell. She likes to say that when I was little, she was the victim of parent abuse. She once called Social Services on herself when I had driven her to the edge with my behavior. She explained to the poor lady on the phone that her two-year-old son was driving her so crazy, she was about to hurt him. The social worker spent a week at our house observing, but I behaved like an angel for those seven days, and she left thinking my mom must *be* crazy.

It didn't take long for my parents to figure out that while they couldn't control my wild energy, they *could* channel it. Once they saw how madly in love I was with skiing, they knew they'd stumbled on the parenting strategy that would serve us all well for years to come: If they could get me involved in every sports activity possible, maybe it would keep me out of trouble. It did, too—at least for a while.

By age five I was on a ski team, and by age seven I had piled wrestling, football, baseball, swim, and track teams onto my athletic schedule. Later, as an adult, I found I have a love of extreme sports. The steeper the ski slope, the larger the wave, the higher the cliff, the more difficult the jump from the plane or helicopter—the more danger and adrenaline involved, the more I want to try to conquer it. In my thirties, I would channel that same impulse into a drive to conquer huge goals in the entrepreneurial world. At the age of five, my Mount Everest was a 2,500-foot hill called North Star Mountain.

My earliest memories are of the crisp cold in my face and the sibilant *schuss* of the snow under my skis as I flew down the face of North Star. Every day, during the long months of ski season, my mom would pick me up from kindergarten and drive us straight out to the slopes. We had a season pass, and we used up every penny of it.

Less than half the height of its more famous neighbors, Whistler and Blackcomb, North Star is not really much of a mountain, but I didn't know that. To me, it seemed vast and inexhaustible. When I think back on my early childhood, what I remember most are the countless afternoons on my bright yellow Mickey Mouse K2 skis, exploring every trail and out-of-the-way patch of what seemed to me an endless world of snow and adventure.

My best friend at the time was a kid named Justin, who was as devoted to skiing as I was. We would spend every afternoon we could exploring North Star together. Justin and I got into ski racing and joined a team. By the time we were in first grade, our team was competing in tournaments at Whistler, and I was winning those races. My mom still has some first-place ribbons I took at Whistler at the age of six.

I don't think my mom was joking when she called Social Services, but the truth is, she would never have hurt me, no matter how bad I got. With my father, it was a different story.

I was not exactly scared of my dad, but I knew he was in charge and not afraid to whip out his belt and get after me when he thought I needed it. Over the years, my backside and my dad's leather belt really got to know each other. Today, now that I'm a parent myself, I believe in discipline just as much as my dad did—although instead of a spanking, my kids' punishment is push-ups. My ten-year-old son can knock out more push-ups than most adults I know.

Although my dad was very strict, he was also not afraid to hug me and tell me he loved me. He was a good father, and I have a lot of happy memories of him from those early years.

When my dad went out on construction job site visits, he often took me with him, and I loved it. It always felt like an adventure, just me and my dad going on trips to these serious grown-up work sites—and they were great places to pick up colorful new ways of using the English language. I also went along when he played gigs with his country rock band, Jack the Bear, of which he was the drummer and principal sponsor. Jack the Bear played to a pretty rough-and-tumble crowd in the rural backcountry taverns of the Canadian Rockies. By the age of five I had the mouth of a sailor. Typically I would stay in the bar for the first set, and then Dad would tuck me in for the night in our VW Westphalia van outside with the family dog, Shy, where I would lie awake listening to the music and voices until finally fading off into sleep.

Best of all, there was hockey.

My dad has always been an outstanding hockey player. During those early years he was captain of his hockey team, and I would go with him when they would play their games, which were typically pretty late at night. It was a working league and the players all had their full-time jobs, so that was the only time they could play.

I was only five, but no matter how late it was, I never got tired at my dad's hockey practice. I would go through the place looking for lost pucks or fish for quarters and play the big, brand-new Atari Asteroids video game console they had there. Crawling around, exploring every inch of the place, it felt a lot like being up on the mountain, only in a way this was even better, because I was there with my dad. After practice we would go hang out in the locker room, surrounded by sweaty hockey players who were cursing and laughing and cracking beers. I thought it was the coolest thing ever. It was just us, just the guys.

I could tell my dad really enjoyed having me there. I looked up to him, and in many ways, he was my hero.

Then, about the time I turned six, our lives changed.

•   •   •

My father had always been into sailing. My parents had a dream of sailing around the world, and business was now doing so well they decided it was time to take a few years off and hit the water, just the four of us, to make that dream into a reality. We owned a beautiful 60-foot Sparkman & Stephens ketch, which he kept moored on the California coast; why not let that become our new home as we circled the globe?

Just as we were getting ready to leave, my dad decided to do one more big project. My mother objected, but my dad prevailed: One last gig, he said, and that would really set us up. A group of investors was going to put up the money, so he took out a large construction loan and built the place. Then the recession of 1980 hit—and the project collapsed. My dad was left with the bill and no investors. He tried to negotiate with the bank. He kept trying for two years. They came and took our house. My dad declared bankruptcy and we lost everything.

Being so young at the time, I didn't quite grasp what was happening, and nobody ever sat me down and said, "Brandon, we're ruined, wiped out." Even so, there was an ominous undercurrent that I couldn't have missed.

I remember going into the bank one day with my dad to close our accounts—the same bank he'd been wrestling with for the past year—because we were about to move away from Kimberley. One of these was a savings account he had opened for me some two years earlier.

This had been quite a big deal for both of us when we opened it. "Look, Brandon," I remember him telling me, "this is your first savings account. We're opening it in *your* name—this is going to be *your* money." He showed me the passbook and the first line, where he had entered the initial deposit. "Now you get to watch it grow." I was so excited about it, and I could tell he was, too.

Now, when we asked where it stood, my dad was informed it had a zero balance.

"What?" he practically shouted at the teller. He was livid. "How is that possible?"

I don't remember how much he had put in there in the first place, but it wasn't much, and whatever it was had been wiped out by monthly fees, without my dad realizing it. He had wanted to teach me a life lesson about how you can invest and save—but the only lesson I learned that day was about how you can get wiped out without even realizing it.

When I was seven we left Canada for good, moving to a little town called Blaine, jammed right up into the northwest corner of Washington state, where we began the painful process of starting over.

As huge a change as this financial collapse was for my parents, it crept up on Rhiannon and me only gradually. It was only now, when we picked up and moved to Washington, that I began to realize that something pretty serious was going on here. No more Jack the Bear gigs or late-night hockey practices, and no more skiing the North Star face with my friend Justin. All of a sudden I was yanked out of the life I loved and we were living in a strange place in a smaller house. Now, when my mom took me shopping for new school clothes, we were hitting the thrift shops instead of going to the big department stores. It wasn't just that we were living in a different place. Our *lives* were different. I never saw Justin again.

My dad was different, too. He became moodier and angrier, and tougher on me. The whole thing had devastated him. Today, thirty years later, he is still getting over it, and I can't say I blame him. As a seven-year-old, though, I didn't understand any of that. All I knew was that before, I would go with him everywhere—and now I didn't see him all that much. I always loved my dad, but I think it was during these years that a wedge started quietly building between us, one that would have life-changing consequences in later years.

It was in Blaine that I started getting into trouble, getting into fights with other kids and raising hell. Fortunately, my parents already had a formula for dealing with that, and they got me as involved in athletics as they could. Soon I was doing sports again year-round.

What I remember most about Blaine is baseball and wrestling. I was crazy about wrestling, and it was also one of the few places where I would still regularly connect with my dad. My mom was at all the baseball games, but at the wrestling matches it was always my dad cheering our team on. I could tell he was proud of me. I especially loved going on trips with our wrestling team to compete in matches. In fourth grade I placed second in the regionals and made it to the state championships.

Another thing that made life in Blaine better was that making new friends, even in tough circumstances, has always come pretty easy to me. I had three especially good buddies there, Chris Bysh, Gaytor Rasmussen, and Scott Dodd; we all stay in touch to this day. Chris became my best friend, and as with Justin back in Vancouver, we got into lots of athletics together—especially baseball.

On our Little League team, Chris played catcher and I was the pitcher. We did pretty well and made All-Stars. We even got invited to attend a special baseball camp being hosted by the Orioles. I was so excited about going. This was going to be a blast!

It never happened. Instead my parents shipped Rhiannon and me off to Toronto to stay with relatives for that whole summer. I was absolutely furious at my dad. What was wrong with him? I could not believe he was going to take away this incredible opportunity and ruin my summer, and for no good reason whatsoever!

He actually had a very good reason; it was just one he couldn't tell us. At the time, my parents' marriage was on rocky ground. I don't know the details of what happened, but I'm sure that whatever it was, the financial stress didn't help. They were making a serious effort to reconcile and put things back on an even keel and thought they would have a better shot at it if they didn't have to tiptoe around Rhiannon and me for a few months.

But of course, I didn't know any of this until many years later, and it wasn't easy to find anyplace in me that could forgive him for taking this prize away from me.

While we were living in Blaine, my father started picking up the pieces of his career. He found a job as foreman for a large construction company and was soon building houses again. He and my mom had never given up on their dream of sailing around the world, and by the time I entered fifth grade we were able to purchase a 50-foot ketch.

Soon we were leaving Blaine behind and moving 100 miles or so south to Seattle, where we began living on our new boat, which we christened *Agio,* Italian for "ease." There were times when life on the *Agio* lived up to its name—and there would be times when it most definitely did not.

My parents were excited about the move and hopeful about the future. Me, I was pissed. This was the sixth time we had moved since I was a baby, and I was starting to seriously resent it. It seemed like as soon as I would make some new friends and start to settle into a social group, we'd be up and moving yet one more time, and I'd have to go through the whole process all over again. Even though I was pretty good at easing my way into new situations and making new friends, this was getting old. I was tired of being uprooted, tired of being picked on as the new kid. It probably served to build character and develop in both Rhiannon and me the ability to adapt to new circumstances, but at the time, it just felt hard. I was jealous of the kids who got to stay in one town and have friends they'd known since preschool. We never had that.

No matter how much we moved around and how difficult things sometimes got, one thing Rhiannon and I always did have was each other. Like any typical brother and sister, we'd fight sometimes and get on each other's nerves, but we were close all through these years. Sometimes we'd talk together about how we felt about it all. Typically, I would be angry, and she would cry.

After a few years in Seattle, we pulled up stakes and moved yet again, sailing down the coast to head for Ventura, California. The trip was not an easy one. To me, it felt like the weather pretty accurately reflected my mood: 100 miles off the coast of Oregon, we hit the tail end of a hurricane. For more than twenty-four hours we struggled with the full force of nature, beating into the gale-force winds, until my father finally dropped our sails and put out a sea anchor. We hove to and waited for the storm to pass.

The next few dozen hours left a deep impression. I remember my mother gripping Rhiannon and me close to her, life jackets donned and survival raft at the ready, wondering which would turn out to have more staying power—us or the hurricane. In the end, after nearly two days, the storm must have decided we were not worth it: It finally released its grip and moved on. We found we had been pushed almost 200 miles in the wrong direction.

When we finally pulled into Coos Bay, Oregon, a crowd of locals had gathered on the docks to hear about the family that had been out there on the ocean's angry face and survived the storm. Everyone loves a good sea story.

I was ten when we arrived in Ventura, and California has been my home ever since. My father's great passion in life was sailing, and the next few years involved plenty of it. We continued to live on the *Agio* for the better part of the next six years, and while we each had our own stateroom, it was still tight quarters and I looked for every opportunity to escape. A few times I tried to run away from home.

Life in California revolved around the water. All my new friends surfed, and I soon joined them. I also started getting into trouble again. My mom, who went to work for a few years on California's offshore oil platforms, never knew what to expect when she would come home. Once she found me and a few friends hunting down squirrels with homemade blowguns.

Another time she saw the boat's mast swaying as she approached. She broke into a run, and when she reached the boat she saw that my friends and I were taking turns pushing off and swinging around the mast high above the deck on a harness I'd rigged.

During most of this time, my father and I might as well have been living on separate planets. He was working his tail off. He would leave early in the morning and come back at five o'clock—briefly—for dinner. My mom was pretty good about corralling us inside for family dinner together, but as soon as we pushed back our plates we would all head off to do our own thing.

There was a period there, in eighth grade, when my dad made an extra effort to get me into ice hockey. The closest rink was in Thousand Oaks, nearly an hour's drive away. During hockey season he would get up every Saturday at 5:30 A.M. to drive me out to Thousand Oaks for practice. He even helped coach our team. Throughout that hockey season the two of us had an opportunity to bond again, just as we had when we were back in Kimberley. That soon came abruptly to an end, and my sports career with it.

I'd noticed that my knees were starting to ache, and toward the end of that hockey season it got pretty severe. I could play through it, but after practice I would have two swollen bumps on my knees, and if you tapped it in just the right spot, it felt like someone was jamming an ice pick into my knee.

My folks took me to the doctor, and he knew what it was right away.

"Your boy has Osgood-Schlatter syndrome. He's been so involved in sports, so constantly and for so long, his knees haven't had the chance to develop properly."

In rare cases, he told us, surgery was indicated. He didn't think that would be necessary for me, but I would have to wear a brace for a while.

"Of course," he added, "he'll have to cut out the sports."

My mom nearly gasped. "What do you mean, *cut out the sports*?" She was terrified: Without sports, she knew it would be no time at all before I was getting into worse and worse trouble.

They tried putting my legs in braces, but as soon as the braces were on I was off skateboarding around the harbor. Finally they realized they had no choice but to put me in casts. As much as I hated them, those casts probably saved my life, or at least my knees. Confined to plaster casts, my joints were finally able to grow properly, and I've never had any knee problems since.

At the time, it was also a catastrophe of sorts. I was a freshman in high school, and I desperately wanted to wrestle and play baseball. No dice. I spent my ninth-grade year with casts on my legs. As soon as they were off, so was I—off getting into trouble again.

Without athletics to absorb my time and energy, my mother hit on a new tack: getting me a job. Soon before my thirteenth birthday, she introduced me to a man named Bill Magee, who owned a charter dive boat in Ventura Harbor, the *Peace*. Bill offered to let me work on his boat.

I worked on the *Peace* all summer, every summer, for the next few years. Everything about being on that dive boat, with the tantalizing possibility of adventure outside the harbor and west to the Channel Islands, completely captivated me. It's no exaggeration to say that going to work on the *Peace* changed the course of my life.

Bill Magee was one of the nicest men I've ever known. He and the boat's captain, Michael Roach, were like second fathers to me. They watched out for me and entrusted me with a lot of responsibility. I had not really had that experience before. They showed me a whole new side to the concept of respect and instilled in me the belief that I could *be* somebody and do something special with my life.

Bill had made some money in construction and eventually sold a successful roofing company up in the Bay Area, which had allowed him to fulfill a dream I expect he'd held on to for some time. Sport diving was his hobby, and he had put a chunk of the proceeds from his sale into the *Peace*—cashed in his chips and taken to the sea.

Captain Roach was the perfect complement to Bill, the classic salty Irish sea captain. He taught me how to give a firm handshake and look a man straight in the eye when you are talking to him.

Bill Magee was also pretty wild—the Hugh Hefner of the high seas. Bill had a new girlfriend every week, usually about half his age, and he was always throwing hot tub parties (I believe the *Peace* was the first boat to feature a hot tub) with lots of women, alcohol, and God knew what else. Strictly speaking, the *Peace* was a *dive* boat, which meant that people were paying to be taken out scuba diving. Unofficially, it was also a hell of a party boat. We'd take our passengers on tours of the Channel Islands off Ventura, taking out groups of divers four at a time—and in between dives, when we were anchored up for the night, we would *party*. Bill would front me a few hundred dollars so I could sit down and join the interminable poker games. Here I was, at thirteen, drinking Scotch and playing poker with the guys.

At the same time, the diving was no joke. When you weren't on an anchor watch, it was fine to whoop it up and party, but when you were on, you had to be *on*. You had to know your limits and capacities. I didn't know it at the time, but it was great preparation for the Navy SEALs.

As low man on the totem pole, I often got the chores on the *Peace* nobody else wanted to do. One of these was diving down whenever the anchor got stuck to get in there and free it. This often happened in the middle of the night. Many were the times I was rousted out of a deep sleep to hear, "Wake up, Brandon! We have to move and the anchor is stuck. Get your wet suit on—you're going in."

I'd dive down there with a flashlight, scared shitless. It was a hell of a way to get over one's fear of sharks, let alone fear of the dark.

Sometimes I would get to depth to find the anchor wedged under a 1-ton ledge that was being rocked off the ocean floor by the weight of the boat it was attached to and the pull of sea swell on the surface. With a blast of air, I would signal the guy pulling the anchor to let out some slack in the chain, and then go to work untangling the mess. A second blast of air to the surface signaled that my work was done, and the crew would haul the anchor up while I stayed below, watching to make sure it had come fully clear of the bottom. Often it would stick again, and I'd have to repeat the entire routine. When it was finally clear, I would blast a final jet of air to signal where I was and alert them to my position and ascent. Once back on board, I would run through a fast hot shower and try to get in some hurried shut-eye before the break of the new day. It was terrifying, and I loved it.

I learned how to scuba dive without any pool sessions; it was all open-water Pacific Ocean dives from the start. Pretty soon I found I preferred diving without a buoyancy compensator, a kind of inflatable vest with an air hose plugged into it that most divers wear. I thought it was a crutch. To me, it was like the difference between swimming in a full suit of clothes and swimming in a Speedo. So I never used one. I also found I liked going down with two tanks, instead of the single tank most sport divers prefer. A second tank adds significant weight, so you have to be fit enough to handle it, but you get more bottom time and can swim serious distances. Sport divers typically just drop straight down and goof around for a while. Serious hunters mean business and wear two tanks.

By my second summer on the *Peace* I had logged over two hundred dives and was equipped with twin steel 72s (72-cubic-foot-capacity scuba tanks), no buoyancy compensator—just a single- and second-stage scuba regulator and a large speargun.

It was Captain Mike and James Hrabak, the alternate second captain, who taught me how to stalk and hunt in the reefs and open water—skills that would prove enormously useful later on. Soon I was an accomplished hunter on tanks or free diving (just holding my breath). It didn't matter if it was yellowtail, calico bass, halibut, abalone, or lobster—I was all over it, and nothing was safe.

Usually when we took paying customers out on a dive it would be a pretty mellow thing. There was one group of hard-core divers, though, guys I thought of as the Animals, who would come out with us a few times a year. With the usual passengers, we might dive three times a day. With the Animals, we would do six serious dives every day, hunting for lobster in the winter, halibut or some other fish in the summer. These guys got the biggest kick out of seeing me surface with no buoyancy compensator, two steel tanks, and a 40-pound halibut in my bag.

Eventually I became a rescue diver and an accomplished deckhand. I was often trusted at the helm of the boat from midnight to 2:00 A.M. on a night transit to the islands. As a teenager, manning the helm of a 70-foot dive boat with thirty-two sleeping passengers while transiting through one of the busiest shipping lanes in the world, I knew this was a huge responsibility. I took it very seriously and never had an incident. By the time I approached my sixteenth birthday, I had made more than a thousand dives and had enough hours and knowledge to take the Coast Guard 100-ton Master Captain license.

As wild a lifestyle as Bill Magee lived, with his hot tub and girlfriends and poker parties, I believe it was Bill and Captain Mike who set my ethical rudder toward true north. The phrase "they ran a tight ship" was never more apt: Bill and Captain Mike set a standard of excellence that I would often be reminded of during my time with the Navy SEALs. The guys I worked with on that boat were really good at what they did and took their jobs seriously.

I wish that had been true of everyone we encountered; unfortunately, it wasn't.

There was one guy we especially hated because of his slipshod ways and sloppy attitude. George Borden owned a dive shop in the area. You could tell the dive shop owners and instructors who were genuinely professional, like my friend Mike Dahan, who ran a good class and really taught the fundamentals. Not George. To him, it was all a numbers game: Doesn't matter if these people really know how to dive or not, just push 'em through. Every time George chartered the *Peace,* it would be a mess and create more work for us.

One time he brought a group out to do an advanced certification class. One of the students was an Iranian girl named Mahvash, which means "beauty of the moon"—and she was indeed absolutely beautiful. I was completely smitten with her.

Mahvash was just eighteen and had done only six dives, which was the bare minimum to be certified. We couldn't believe George was allowing her in this advanced class, which included making a few deep dives, deep enough to require decompression stops on the way up. When they boarded the boat, her mother was clearly against it. "I don't know if you're ready for this," she argued, but Mahvash joined the class anyway.

We took the boat out to Catalina Island, a fantastic place with its own little resort town on the southern end. We left at night and anchored at Catalina, then dove all the next day. The following day we went out to a deep diving spot off the back side of Catalina. This area is a preserve; the reefs start at 100 feet out, and the visibility goes on forever. I was not on duty that morning, so I made a dive on my own, just for fun. It was amazing, as it always is.

As I came back up, pausing to do a decompression stop on the anchor chain, I looked down and noticed a whole cluster of George's students down there on a deep dive. *Oh, man,* I thought, *what a mess.* I went all the way up, got on the boat, and took off my gear, then started helping other people with theirs.

A few minutes later, George surfaced with his students and his "assistant." (By regulation, he was required to have a certified dive master with him, but this guy was only a dive master-in-training. As I said, George always cut corners.)

As they helped the students up onto the boat one by one, someone suddenly said, "Hey, where's Mahvash?"

George was only a few feet away from me, and when I saw the look in his eyes I said, "Oh, shit." Mahvash wasn't with them. None of them had a clue where she was. They panicked—but there was nothing they could do. None of them could go back down for her, because when you dive that deep, you can't go back down again for at least twelve hours.

I had just come up from my own dive, so I couldn't go either.

Our dive master, Ivan Fuentes, whipped on his tanks, jumped over the side of the boat, and went down. We waited. A very long five minutes later he surfaced, a couple hundred yards from the boat, and waved for me. I swam a rescue line out to him. When I got close, I saw that he had Mahvash with him. She wasn't moving. As I got even closer, I saw that the girl with the beauty of the moon was dead.

For a moment, my own heart stopped. It was the first time I had ever seen death up close. I wanted to cry and scream at the same time. I wanted to swim back and choke the life out of that idiot George. By his carelessness and disregard for safety, as far as I was concerned, he had caused this girl's death.

Ivan told me he had found Mahvash about 100 feet down, hovering 10 feet off the ocean floor. Apparently she had gotten separated from the group, panicked, spit her regulator out, and drowned. We tried doing rescue breathing with her, but it was too late. She had embolized coming up: That is, her lungs had burst.

That night I tried to cry, but the tears wouldn't come—they were choked off by fury. It was a lesson I've never forgotten: how precious life is, and at the same time, how fragile.

The family wanted to press charges, and I gave a deposition for them, but nothing came of it, and George was never prosecuted. It wasn't the last time I would see innocence and beauty crushed with impunity by what I considered to be arrogance and crass thoughtlessness.

At the close of my freshman year at Ventura High, my parents decided the time was finally right for us to embark on our world-encircling sailing trip on the *Agio*. They had saved enough money, and they knew that the longer they put it off, the older Rhiannon and I would be. They figured, better do it while we were still young enough to go along with the family's plans.

Whenever they would talk about this voyage, I would ignore it and hope the whole idea would go away. I was having a great time working on the *Peace* and enjoying the incredible freedom of my harbor lifestyle. Because of my position as deckhand, most of the shop owners assumed I was much older than I really was, and I was never carded for drinks when the boys and I went out for dinner. I was quite content in my own little world at the harbor. Sailing off to faraway places didn't sound thrilling to me. I had more important things to do—like diving, surfing, chasing girls, and getting my driver's license.

Unknown to me at the time, Captain Bill talked to my parents and offered to let me stay with him on the *Peace* if they wanted to leave me behind. They appreciated the offer, but no, they decided, the time had come, and we were going to make this trip all together as a family. They put Rhiannon and me on independent studies for a year, and we started packing up the boat to leave. The plan was to sail to New Zealand and see how things shook out. If things went well that far, we'd make the rest of the trip around the world, and if things weren't going as well as we hoped, well, we could always turn back at that point.

Just as we were getting ready to leave, we had an unexpected visit from friends we'd known back in Kimberley: Ken and Gail, parents of my childhood pal Justin. I was shocked when I saw them; we all were. They were both a complete mess, especially Gail, and we soon learned why.

In addition to being total ski animals, Justin and I had also been rabid hockey buffs even at the tender age of five. While my knee problems had later benched me, Justin had kept playing competitively right up through high school. Earlier that year, Ken told us, Justin had been in a freak hockey accident. He got body-checked by another player, went down, and hit his head on the ice pretty hard, hard enough to give him a concussion. They took him home, put him to bed.

He never woke up.

When I heard what happened, the bottom fell out of my stomach. I couldn't believe Justin was gone. It had been nearly ten years since I'd seen him, but I'd always known he was there, somewhere, probably doing a lot of the same things I was doing. Only now he wasn't.

Justin had been an only child; now his parents were alone in the world, and I felt awful for both of them, as well as heartbroken and freaked out that my friend was gone. I also felt something else I couldn't quite put my finger on. The words "lost innocence" didn't occur to me at the time, and it was only later on, at the climax of our ocean voyage, that I began to identify that sinking feeling: It was as if Justin's passing had marked the end of an era, a childhood I would never come back to.

Our first stop was San Diego Harbor to stock up on supplies, after which we headed down to Guadalupe Island and Cabo San Lucas. After a few weeks' stay in Cabo, we sailed around the tip of Baja into La Paz, then spent a few weeks in and around the surrounding islands before heading over to mainland Mexico. We hit Mazatlán, Puerto Vallarta, Manzanillo, and finally Acapulco, our last point to resupply before leaving the continent behind. Soon we headed southwest, traversing thousands of miles of open water into the heart of the South Pacific, bound for the sparsely populated Marquesas Islands, not far from Tahiti. It would take us a month to reach our destination.

Thirty days doesn't sound like a lot, but when you're out on the open sea with nothing but water stretching to every horizon, it is an eternity. My sister and I had some good times on that voyage. We would sit up on the bow watching the dolphins jumping and playing in our boat's bow wake. We always had a line out and caught quite a few fish.

A long stretch at sea is an excellent time to get to know yourself. My dad and I split the night watch between us. I would take over from my mom and sister at midnight, watch from then till 4:00 A.M., and then hand it off to my father, who took it till sunrise. The night sky over the South Pacific was amazing. There were times when the sky was so clear and filled with stars it felt like we were floating in space. Every ten minutes or so I would see a shooting star.

These interludes of solitude, with the heavens opened up like the pages of a book before me, began working on my mind. During those long hours I started reflecting on my life, on all the experiences I'd had, and could not help but think about the future and where it might be going.

I think this is something most kids never have the chance to experience, this kind of break in the day when there is nothing to think about but the expanse of time and the possibilities it holds. While my family and I were crossing the South Pacific, all my friends back home were back at school, running around, going to class, chasing girls, going to bed, and then waking up and doing it all over again the next day. Distractions and commotion, and little time for genuine introspection. As an adult, I have met people who grew up on ranches and found they had experiences similar to my ocean transit at sixteen.

I can't say I came to any startling new self-knowledge during that time, but in some way I couldn't have articulated, it felt like my thinking sank a little deeper, and maybe grew bigger. I began getting a sense that I wanted to do something different, something special, with my life. I didn't know exactly what that might be, but I knew that as much as I loved the life of a dive boat captain, which is what Bill Magee and Captain Mike had been grooming me for during the last few years, I would never be content with the harbor. Despite the incredible tranquility of the ocean, there was an impatience growing inside me, an urge that was starting to whisper, *Wherever my life is heading, let's get on with it!*

Those thirty days at sea also provided the time to accomplish a lot. I finished my entire school year (months ahead of schedule), taught myself how to juggle, and read a ton of books. I went through the entire Lord of the Rings series and a carton full of classic novels. Steinbeck was one of my favorites. I liked his direct, in-your-face style, and I identified with his strong connection to California.

I also practiced celestial navigation with my dad. This was in the days before GPS. We had a sat nav (satellite navigation) unit, a precursor to today's GPS devices, but it would take a wait of twelve hours for a satellite to get overhead for us to fix our position that way. So we did a lot of our navigation the old-fashioned way: celestial observation and dead reckoning.

After thirty days at sea we made landfall at Hiva Oa, one of the larger (that is, least tiny) of the remote Marquesas Islands. Shrouded in a nearly constant cloud cover, the Marquesas rise majestically out of the Pacific, with an appearance similar to the north shore of the Hawaiian chain. The local harbor was a thing of beauty with its gorgeous black sand beaches and, high up on the distant cliffs, a panorama of waterfalls. Gauguin spent his last years here, as did the Belgian singer-songwriter Jacques Brel. Both Herman Melville and Robert Louis Stevenson wrote books inspired by visits to Hiva Oa.

We anchored the *Agio* in a cove and took a small boat ashore. The lifestyle of the people we encountered was both amazing and hilarious to me: They lived in fairly primitive, thatched-roof huts—and drove brand-new Toyota four-wheel drives, subsidized by the French government.

On Hiva Oa I met a girl I will never forget. I never knew her name; there was a complete language barrier between us. Somehow, though, we just clicked. We took long walks through the most stunning tropical scenery, past the most amazing waterfalls, and as beautiful as our surroundings were, she was even more so. She was something out of a dream. I never tried anything with her, never even kissed her, but after we left, I missed her badly. Of course, I knew we couldn't stay there and that it wasn't my dad's fault we had to leave, but still, I hated it, and this added fuel to the coals of resentment that were already burning.

Up to this point in our trip, my dad and I had been having a steadily escalating series of disagreements on points of seamanship. So far these had been fairly minor—but things were about to change.

On the open ocean it wasn't that bad. When you're sailing straight in one direction, all you're really doing is taking fixes and monitoring your course. Every time we'd get closer in to land, though, and especially when it came to navigating the coastal waterways, the two of us would start to butt heads. I wanted more of a say in how we managed the boat. I felt like I should be consulted. By this time I'd had a lot of experience in coastal waterway navigation. "Look," I'd say, "I'm no slouch, I know what I'm doing here."

In the South Pacific, because of the nature of the deepwater reefs, it's common to set two anchors. First you set a bow (front) hook, and then you throw a stern anchor off the back and snug the boat up tight. For both anchors, my father was using a type of anchor called a CQR he'd used for most of his cruising life in Seattle, California, and Mexico. A CQR is a plow type of anchor that does an excellent job of holding in sand, clay, or mud bottoms, but it's not the best choice to hold in rocks or coral reef.

We also had on board a multipurpose Bruce anchor I had salvaged from my time on the dive boat, and this was the anchor I favored. The Bruce is designed to function in a wide range of seafloor compositions. Because of its fierce reliability, it is the choice of most commercial boats. The Bruce and I knew each other well, going back to my early days working on the dive boat; in fact, it was the reason for many of those 2:00 A.M. wake-up calls. That frigging Bruce anchor would hold fast in *anything*.

"Look," I said, "we're in a coral reef. I get what the underwater topography looks like here, Dad, I'm a diver. Do you have any idea how many stuck anchors I've dealt with? Trust me, we need the Bruce on the bow."

My father didn't see it that way. "There's only one captain on this boat," was all he'd say, "and you know who that is."

I was so frustrated. At the same time, I was being a cocky smart-ass about the whole thing. I was well aware that my own attitude was not going a long way toward selling the idea, but my heels were dug in. My parents couldn't stop me from screaming my head off when I was two weeks old, and at sixteen I guess I hadn't gotten much easier to persuade.

That first night in port we set our bow and rear anchors, again both CQRs. Of the two, the bow is the more important—and when we awoke the next morning I was delighted to see that we had dragged the bow anchor right along the ocean floor and nearly grounded our boat. I couldn't wait to give my dad an earful about what a useless piece of crap that damn CQR was. Equally well spelled out was this ancillary point: what an obnoxious prick I was being.

Every time we argued, my sister would go to her room to get away from the tension, while my mom would try to be the peacemaker. Of course, she would side with my dad, but then later on she would come to my stateroom privately, sit down with me, and say, "Brandon, you have to chill out. I know you have a lot of experience, but this is your dad's boat." I would vent my frustration to her, and she would be understanding and try to keep the situation from spiraling out of control. For a while, she succeeded.

Our trip continued on through the rest of the island chain to the Marquesas' main northern island, Nuka Hiva, and then on to the Tuamotu Archipelago, a series of coral atolls that comprise the largest atoll chain in the world. All the while, my father and I continued arguing. By the time we pulled into Papeete, the capital of Tahiti, the situation had badly deteriorated.

I don't remember what I said that finally set him off, but whatever it was, it brought to an end not only my trip with my family but also my life with my family. Suddenly my dad had me by the scruff of the neck, his fist curled and ready to lash out, both of us screaming at each other. *My God, my mother thought, he's going to kick the crap out of Brandon.* He didn't hit me, but we both knew we were going to a place that neither of us wanted to. We'd reached a point of no return. One of us had to go—and it wasn't going to be him. With my mom and sister wailing in grief and disbelief, my father threw me off the boat.

He didn't actually hurl me off physically. He just told me that I should take a pack with me and find passage aboard another boat to my destination of choice. He said it like he meant it.

Before I knew it I was off the *Agio* for good—and on my own in the middle of the South Pacific.

In a way, I was relieved. The tension between us had grown unbearable, and I knew that if we hadn't parted ways, something really bad would have happened, and it would have caused irreparable harm to both of us, and for sure to our relationship.

Still, I was somewhat in shock at what *had* happened. I was also scared.

In later years we would reconnect and rebuild our friendship, but for now my father wanted nothing to do with me. My mom knew there was no reconciling us at that point, but she did what she could to make sure I would be okay. She knew that if I could make my way home, Bill Magee would take me in and look after me, and before I left Tahiti she helped me get a radio call patched through to Ventura so we could fill him in on my situation. She also helped me secure passage on the *Shilo,* a 40-foot catamaran headed north for Hilo, Hawaii, a journey of nearly 3,000 miles. My boatmates were a family of three: a couple and their three-year-old boy. The mom's hands were pretty full taking care of their infant son, and they had been looking for crew. I stood the midnight shift, which left me plenty of time to think about the future.

In a way, I didn't blame my father for throwing me off the family boat. It felt like the only possible thing to do. My mom was completely torn up and had pleaded and pleaded with him to relent, and yet I think that she also realized that there was no going back.

During the day on the *Shilo,* I was either asleep or occupied with the practical matters of the boat. During the nights, I was alone with my thoughts. Those nights were rough. Rhiannon and I had been a lot less close since we'd both become California teenagers with our own sets of friends—but she was my sister and had been a part of my life since as early as I could remember. Now she was gone. My whole family was gone. I was alone. Those first few nights on that 40-foot cat, I cried myself to sleep.

As I said, I was scared, too, but I told myself I had to get past being scared, and when I did I found there was also a part of me that was excited about whatever lay ahead. I knew my life had hit a major turning point. I'd had experiences most other sixteen-year-olds had not. Still, I was far from an adult. I didn't even have my driver's license yet.

Often, during those lonely nights, I thought about what had happened with my dad and me back in the harbor off Papeete. On the one hand, it was a hard lesson in the demands of authority. My dad was right: There's only one captain on a ship, just like there's only one person in charge of a mission, or a department, or any venture. At the same time, he *was* making the wrong decision. I had learned how to take orders during my time on the *Peace,* and that sense of respect for the chain of command would become a crucial trait later on during my service in the military. Still, as we shall see, there would be quite a few other occasions when I would feel it was my duty to challenge authority, despite my training, when my gut told me the guy in charge was leading us down the wrong path.

That catamaran was *fast*—way faster than any single-hull boat I'd ever sailed. It took us less than two weeks to make Hilo.

A day before we reached our destination, I came up on deck from my stateroom on the port side of the boat. It was a gorgeous morning. As I stood on deck, something in the hull caught my eye. I bent down to look. Just above the waterline, a swordfish had rammed our boat during the night, spearing himself straight through the hull and breaking off the tip of his snout. That damn fish must have leapt clear out of the water to spear us. I grabbed my camera to take a picture of it. I still have that snapshot. The next day we breezed into the harbor at Hilo with a short length of sword-fish beak jammed through our hull.

The image of that swordfish stuck in my mind as firmly as its beak stuck in the *Shilo*'s flank. What the hell was going on for that fish? What made it leap up out of the water to attack this strange, unknown vessel? Did it know it was going up against something more than ten times larger and heavier than itself?

What future was *I* leaping out of the water to go up against?

Years later I would learn this odd factoid of biology: Although like all fish it is cold-blooded, the swordfish has special organs in its head that heat the eyes and brain as much as 60°F above ambient temperature, greatly enhancing the animal's vision and therefore its ability to nail its prey. The falcon or eagle would probably be most people's choice, but if you were looking for a totem to represent the idea of a sniper—especially a sniper who works in water—the swordfish would not be a bad pick.

Perhaps this *had* been a vision quest, after all.

.   .   .   .

Once we reached Hilo I made my way back to the mainland by plane and met up with my old boss, Bill Magee. As my mom had known would be the case, Bill was happy to see me and said I could go back to work for him and live on board. "Hey," he said, "you've already got your schoolwork out of the way for the rest of the year. Why don't you just settle into boat life?"

I can't even imagine how my life might have turned out if he hadn't made this kind offer.

Soon after I rejoined Captain Bill and the *Peace,* the Animals showed up for a few days of diving. This time one of them, a younger guy, brought a few friends with him. These guys were rugged. I didn't know what they did, but you could see that whatever it was, they knew it inside and out. They weren't muscle-bound showoffs or tough guys with attitude; it was more subtle than that. Being around them, you could just sense that there was something special about the way these guys carried themselves. It felt like they could take on a shark on a bad day and come out smiling.

On our first dive, when these guys saw me, a sixteen-year-old kid diving with no buoyancy compensator and my twin steel 72s, they *noticed.* "Holy shit," said one of them, "who *is* this kid?"

The two of us got to talking. He wanted to know how I'd come to be a deckhand, and I told him a little bit about my background.

"You know," he said, "you should check out the seals."

At least that's what I thought he said. I had no idea what he was talking about. Seals? Was this guy seriously into seals, like whale watching and shit? Was he making a joke?

"No," he said, "not seals—*SEALs.*"

I still didn't get it.

"Navy maritime Special Operations Forces," he explained. "SEALs. It stands for Sea, Air, and Land. SEALs."

I'd never heard of them before.

"To become a SEAL," he added, "you go through the toughest military training in the world."

Now, that got my attention. I didn't know much about the military, but I had always been fascinated with aviation and wanted to be a pilot when I grew up, maybe even an astronaut. What he was describing intrigued me. *I love the water,* I thought, *and I'm a pretty good diver. That sounds like a hell of a challenge.*

The truth was, I knew I needed a plan, somewhere to go and something to aim at. At the time, when I wasn't on the dive boat, I would surf and hang out with some guys around the harbor. They were starting to get into crystal meth. I had no interest in it—I would drink beer and that was the extent of it—but seeing them and where they were heading scared me. I knew that I had to get the hell out of there sooner or later, if I wanted to make anything better out of my life.

From that point on, my goal was fixed: I was going to become a Navy SEAL.

I had no idea how hard it would be.

TWO

BOOT CAMP

Stepping off a cross-country flight from LAX, I walked up the jetway, through the airport, and out into Orlando, land of Disney, Epcot, and the U.S. Naval Training Center. The evening air was still warm from the blistering Florida sun. It was March 1993: I was nineteen years old and about to enter navy boot camp.

I couldn't help wondering why the navy had sent me clear across the country when there was a perfectly good boot camp in San Diego, a few hours from where I live, but what the hell did I know? The ink was still wet on my enlistment contract, and I knew better than to ask the question. Besides, I was excited to finally get out of Ventura and on to bigger and better things.

There were a few other boot camp candidates on my plane. We were met by the local navy representative, who put us on a bus that started crawling north on Route 436. It took about forty minutes to reach our destination. Most of those minutes passed in a silence freighted with thrill, foreboding, and dread.

As we pulled into the training center and parked, we saw a few dozen guys lining the roadway, yelling obscenities at us and telling us how fond of us they were. Our welcome committee. It felt like we were in a bad prison movie.

It was ten o'clock at night, just in time to unload, find out where we were supposed to bunk, and hit the sack. A few of my busmates audibly cried themselves to sleep that first night. I didn't mind. What I really didn't appreciate was the four o'clock wake-up call the next morning with some assholes banging on aluminum trash cans and yelling, "Wake up! Get the hell out of your rack!" Senior recruits, in charge of moving the herd along.

After a trip to the barber to get rid of our hair, we assembled in a room where they staged what they called the Moment of Truth: "Okay, who here lied to your recruiter?" Now was our last chance to tell the navy some dark secret about our sexual preference (these were the don't-ask-don't-tell days) or admit to our drug addiction. When it came to sex, drinking, and carousing in general, I was certainly no angel, but I happened to have the dual advantage of being heterosexual and drug free. If I hadn't been, I would've had the sense to keep my mouth shut. Some admitted that, yes, they'd used on occasion. They were given a piss test. Some of them passed; the others were gone.

Next I learned that I was being assigned to Company I-081 (a company being roughly a hundred people), which was integrated. At the time, the navy had three boot camp facilities: the one in San Diego, another in Great Lakes, Illinois, and the one I was standing in. Of the three, only Orlando had integrated companies.

By "integrated," they didn't mean blacks, whites, Hispanics, and Asians all together in harmony. They meant men and women recruits training together in the same outfit. This was my first exposure to that aspect of military planning we fondly call FUBAR: *fucked up beyond all repair.* In its sociologically progressive wisdom, the navy had recently decided it would force-integrate men and women in boot camp while at the same time forbidding them to develop any sexual interest in one another. It does not take a PhD in behavioral psychology to figure out what's going to happen when you put nineteen-year-old men and women together in close confinement. We had a steady parade of grab-assing going on throughout boot camp, from start to finish. I was guilty as charged, though never caught or convicted.

Talk about a waste of resources. A men-only or women-only company would have one barracks room for sleeping and inspection. In our integrated company we needed *three:* one for group inspection, and then two more so the men and women could sleep in separate quarters. It was crazy. We assembled in one common area, with beds and lockers for inspection, where we stood at attention by our lockers while instructors screamed in our faces, just like you've seen in the movies. Then we all filed off to separate berthing places to sleep, guys to one and girls to another. Which meant I had two beds to make every day, and we had three separate locations for one purpose. Your tax dollars at work.

Still, I could hardly complain. I have always been a big fan of the fairer sex.

Now, I am the first to admit that with a shaved head, I am not a handsome man. People tell me I look mean. As my hair started growing in, though, my bonus points started going up with some of the women. "Wow," said one. "You know, you're kind of cute with hair." I had a crush on her and got a few great back massages the first week in.

Hey, maybe this boot camp stuff wasn't going to be so bad after all.

No—it *was* that bad. Back rubs and grab-assing notwithstanding, boot camp was long days of hard training. I've been a physically active person all my life, and I thought of myself as being in pretty good shape.

Ha. Boot camp kicked my ass. Doing the physical training (PTs) was one thing: push-ups and more push-ups. But that wasn't what really got to us. It was the endless hours of marching drills.

Picture a mob of one hundred green recruits, from all over the country, from all walks of life and all levels of preparedness—and unpreparedness. They had to teach us how to step in step, pivot and turn, march right, march left, pivot and turn . . . and every time *anyone* screwed up, which was practically every second of every minute of every hour, they would yell at us to drop to the pavement, hot and sweating, and push out another ten, or another twenty—then back on our feet to *get it right this time*. Which, of course, we would not.

The hours and weeks it took to whip this motley bunch into some kind of cohesive quasi-military force was grueling. Any chance we could grab to lie down flat on the concrete and rest, even for just half a minute, felt like heaven. When night came, I was dog-tired and hit that cot like a dying desert wanderer stumbling upon an oasis. Still, I was no stranger to hard work, and I was one of the better equipped people there. There were others who suffered a whole lot more than I did.

Petty Officer First Class Howard was my first experience with leadership in the navy, and he exemplified both the best and worst of what I would encounter in the years to come. He was smart, sharp, and very professional in both manner and appearance. There was never a ribbon out of place, not a stain or wrinkle in his working whites and crisp navy Dixie cup. He ran a damn good company.

And he was profoundly unfair.

Petty Officer First Class Howard was a black man who had grown up on the mean streets of a tough inner-city neighborhood, and apparently he was out to single-handedly set the race record straight during his tenure as a recruit company commander. Right away he handed out all the leadership positions in the company to all the black recruits. Of the hundred or so people in Company I-081, maybe ten were black, and they got all the cherry appointments. The two laundry spots, which came at the bottom of the totem pole, he assigned to a white guy and a white girl.

Petty Officer First Class Howard was, in fact, a first-class racist. This was not hard to see. It also wasn't hard to see that he was going to press his agenda at every opportunity. This was my first exposure to discrimination from the underdog's perspective, and my goal was simple: stay out of the man's way and off his radar. In this goal, I had an ally: my night-time-barracks bunkmate Rouche Coleman.

Coleman was a street-smart African American kid from the meaner neighborhoods of Chicago who had joined the navy to escape the gang violence that permeated his home turf. He had been shot once and had the scar to prove it. He was soft-spoken, articulate, and blazingly intelligent.

Coleman and I hit it off right away, and he made it his mission to watch out for me. True to Petty Officer First Class Howard's program, Coleman was assigned to be the starboard watch section leader. As section leader he was responsible for managing a nightly watch bill and met every night with Howard and the pin staff (recruit leadership). He would come back to our bunk and tell me about the meetings.

"He doesn't like white people much," said Coleman.

"Yeah," I said. "I'd kind of noticed."

"In fact," he went on, "he is one racist sonofabitch."

I couldn't disagree.

"In fact, you're lucky you got me looking out for your white ass."

He was dead right. I *was* lucky to have him looking out for my white ass. Later on we were broken into groups to work at various assignments on base. Sure enough, all us white folks were sent to the galley for kitchen duty. Coleman interjected on my behalf and requested that I be sent to help him in his duties back at our barracks. His request was granted, and we whiled away a lot of hours diligently playing cards and shooting the shit.

Coleman was one of the nicest people I've ever met. We became genuinely close friends and stayed close throughout boot camp. We kept in touch for a few years afterward until our assignments sent us off in different directions and life drew us further apart. Eventually we lost touch. I often wonder about him and how he's doing.

At boot camp I discovered that the military experience does a great job breaking down racial barriers and forcing you to learn about people from different racial, ethnic, and cultural backgrounds. This proved to be one of the top fringe benefits from my time in the navy, and over the years to come I would make quite a few of the best friends one could hope for in a lifetime.

Soon after we arrived in Orlando, they gathered us all in a big circle and went around asking each of us in turn, "What do you want to do in the navy?"

Some of my campmates hesitated at the question, stumbled in their answers, or appeared not sure what to say. Not me. When my turn came, I didn't have to think about it. "I want to be a SEAL."

I knew what reaction to expect, too, and was not surprised when it came. "Good luck with that," one guy sneered, and a line of snickers and wisecracks rippled around the circle.

It has always amazed me, when you tell people about something big you aspire to accomplish, how many try to shoot it down, throw out obstacles, tell you it'll never happen. I think they don't even realize they're doing it. Often there's no malicious intent there. It's just the reaction people have when you state big goals. Maybe they're threatened by you and your dreams; maybe by undercutting your goals, they get to justify their own insecurity and self-doubt. Maybe they're just plain cynical, for no reason other than an ingrained habit of being negative. To tell the truth, I don't know what their reasons are, and I don't really *want* to know.

This had been happening for three years now, ever since I'd set my sights on becoming a Navy SEAL. Every now and then someone would say, "Wow, that's great, you'd be awesome at that." But not very often. Usually, when I told anyone my goal, whether teachers, acquaintances, or even friends, what I got back was disbelief and ridicule. Now that I was in the navy, it only got worse. Everyone here knew about the SEALs, or at least knew that it was one of the hardest training programs in the world.

For me this was just fuel for the fire, and the more I heard it the more it kept stoking that fire. I knew the only way I'd be able to prove I was serious about it was to ignore them and do it. That wasn't a hard line to stick to, sitting here in a circle in Orlando. It would get a lot harder in the years to come, and brutally hard once I finally made it to the BUD/S (Basic Underwater Demolition/SEAL) legendary training course, but that wouldn't happen for another four years.

A few weeks into boot camp, the SEAL "motivator" (that is, recruiter) came around. *Finally!* I thought. *It's about time this guy showed up—what the hell was he waiting for?* He showed us a brief video that described the life of a SEAL. We saw guys being tested underwater, shivering in the cold, going through the various trials of BUD/S. It told us about the origin of the SEALs in the 1960s, along with some great footage of guys patrolling the Vietnam jungles in Levi's and black face paint, brandishing some very sizable guns.

I didn't even need to see the video, but I waited patiently till it was over, then went right up to the guy and asked him where I should sign. He shot me a withering look that said, *It's not gonna be that easy.* Understatement of the decade.

There were four other guys who were also interested. The recruiter explained to the five of us that we needed to muster at 4:45 the next morning to begin our physical and mental conditioning. Normally we all got up about 5:45 for a six o'clock reveille. Now we would be getting up an hour earlier. That was one more hour of lost sleep I wasn't looking forward to—but hey, if that was the price of admission, I'd gladly pay it.

The next morning, it was just me and two of the four guys. I guess the other two were excited by the video, but not so much about the reality. Those two were the first of hundreds I would see fall by the wayside on my journey to claim the SEAL Trident.

Throughout the rest of basic training, the three of us would get up an hour earlier than everyone else and head off to a special physical training program to get us in shape for BUD/S. I was fired up about it. This was what I was here for. But man, those PTs kicked my butt.

It was a hundred push-ups just to warm up. Then a thousand flutter kicks: You lie on your back, hands under your butt, and scissor-kick your legs in the air. Murder on the abdominals. Try it. Lie on the floor, on your back, your arms straight down and tucked under your butt, and kick your legs a foot or so in the air in a scissor motion. Then think: *a thousand.*

After that, pull-ups—dozens, then dozens more, and then dozens more. This continued for an hour while all our boot camp buddies were still taking another precious hour of shut-eye. It was brutal, but it got me into shape.

Before long, the three of us shrank to two. Rack up one more body falling by the wayside on the road to the SEALs.

As the weeks went by and we drew closer to graduation, I kept inquiring about my orders to BUD/S. I finally got one of the SEALs' attention, and he looked into the situation for me. I can't say I was happy with the report. A decision I had made almost a year earlier had come back to bite me in the ass.

Back in the summer of 1992, fresh out of my high school senior year, I had gone with my dad to pay a visit to the navy recruiter in Ventura.

A few days after we talked with him, the recruiter drove me the roughly 100 miles down to Bakersfield to the Military Enrollment Processing Station (MEPS).

In Bakersfield they gave me a full physical, followed by a placement test, similar to an SAT, then sat me down at a desk with Petty Officer Rosales. His name wasn't really Rosales; I don't know his real name. In fact, if you had pulled me out of that room and asked me his name right then and there, I couldn't have told you. Petty Officer Rosales was from the Philippines, with an accent so thick I could barely understand a word he said.

I heard him say something that sounded like "Watchaw byuan?" He looked at me expectantly, waiting for my response. It took a minute for the penny to drop—then I got it. He had said, "What job you want?" Okay: This was a placement interview. I knew I had scored pretty high on their placement test, so I pretty much had my pick of tracks.

"I want to be a Navy SEAL."

He looked me up and down, then began scrolling through his computer. It was so ancient I half expected to hear the sound of rusty pipes clunking as it went about its search. After a minute, he nodded and looked up at me.

"I get you into Aircrew Search and Rescue program." His eyes grew big as he spoke these words, like he was telling me I could be in line to be chairman of the Joint Chiefs of Staff. "You be search-and-rescue swimmer!"

Okay—wait. *What?* I wanted to be a SEAL, not an aircrew rescue guy. My face must have registered both confusion and disappointment, because he nodded again and began speaking emphatically.

"This is a great puckin program, men—you get a puckin turd class petty officer outta goddamn program, men."

I looked over at my recruiter. He smiled and nodded. "It's a solid program, Webb, and there aren't many who qualify."

As I would learn, he was speaking the truth. For an enlisted person in the navy, aircrew search-and-rescue (SAR) swimmer is a plum post, one of the four or five top jobs there is.

For a regular navy guy, life on a ship can be hell: twelve hours on, twelve off, in some cases working some pretty nasty jobs. My recruiter was a "hull tech," which is the navy's fancy way of saying ship's plumber. Imagine working on toilets and pulling shitty pipes for six months at a stretch. Whatever your rating (Navy for "job"), if it's your first time on the boat, you're spending three months in the galley: slave labor (the kind Coleman saved me from). Not if you're a SAR, though. As a rescue swimmer, I would be getting up each day and checking out the flight schedule, and if I weren't attached to a flight that day, I'd have ancillary duties, like keeping track of the aircrew logbooks—but I would basically have the day off. The next day, I might have a two-hour flight to drop off an admiral, and that'd be my day. A cherry posting.

I didn't know any of this at that point, and what he was describing sure didn't sound like the track to SEAL training. I looked again at Petty Officer Rosales, still dubious.

"Issa *great puckin job* to get you inna SEALs, men," he insisted.

Here was the problem: Petty Officer Rosales didn't really understand how the path to SEALs worked, and because of that, he didn't have a clear grasp of how to steer me in the right direction. In the years since then they've improved the recruiting process. Today you can go right out of boot camp into the particular training school for your rating and then right into BUD/S. But that's not how it was then. Back when I was joining the navy, they had what they called SEAL source ratings—certain jobs that they routinely sourced for new SEAL candidates—and if you didn't have one of those jobs, you had to go to serve in the regular navy fleet and then enter the long way around. I eventually realized that I could have gone a far more direct route into BUD/S, so in that sense, SAR turned out to be a lengthy detour.

Still, there could have been a hell of a lot worse detours. Petty Officer Rosales was right about one thing: SAR was a great puckin program. It meant I had guaranteed aircrew school and guaranteed Search and Rescue school, after which I could pick my aviation-related job on a plane or helicopter. Also, I would be accelerated from E-1, the entry-level rank for an enlisted sailor, to E-4, a noncommissioned officer (NCO) rank, which would mean a significant boost in both pay and stature. In time, I would be grateful for a number of reasons that I had gotten onto this track—but I had no idea how hard it would be to get out of this program and into BUD/S.

I was put on delayed entry, which meant I wouldn't be showing up for boot camp for a good ten months. I spent that summer, fall, and winter working at Mike Dahan's retail dive shop in Ventura, working and waiting. It was a good time. Mike ran an excellent shop, and I got to be good friends with his shop manager, Keith Dinette, and Keith's high school sweetheart, Nicole. (In fact, we are close friends to this day.) Still, I was impatient to get going and be on the path to becoming a Navy SEAL. Finally, in March, an airline ticket showed up in the mail. A friend drove me to LAX, where I was paired up to room with another guy who was headed for boot camp. The next morning, we were on the plane to Orlando.

And now here I was, just days away from graduating boot camp, trying to figure out how the hell to get myself on the track to BUD/S.

"Sorry, Webb," the SEAL told me. "You have orders to Search and Rescue—and they're undermanned in that program. We can't just yank you out. You'll have to wait until your final duty station and then apply for a transfer."

Talk about taking the wind out of my sails. I pleaded with him to let me switch programs, but he said there was little he could do for me.

"Be patient," he said. "You're showing promise; you've got good traits. Keep at it. Just apply at your next command."

I was not happy about this, but what the hell, I told myself. At least I wasn't headed to a ship to chip paint. Search and Rescue would be a great program, SAR would be a great position—and besides, as soon as I got to my command, I could apply and get fast-tracked to BUD/S.

Hey, how long could it take?

My dad showed up in Orlando for my graduation from boot camp. It was a good feeling, walking out of there knowing I'd accomplished something significant. I could tell he was proud of me.

A year earlier, when he first heard I was serious about going into the navy, my dad had been there for me and cheered me along, even giving me a Ford Ranger to drive, as a combined high-school-graduation/congratulations-for-enlisting-in-the-navy gift. While so many other people were pooh-poohing my aspirations to be a SEAL, my dad had been totally supportive. Given our rocky history together, this had felt especially good to me.

Things had not gone well for my parents' marriage. After returning from that ill-fated boat trip to New Zealand (minus one teenaged son), they had found themselves faced with irreconcilable differences and unable to work things out. Maybe the stress of coming back to reality in the States after their big boat trip exacerbated things. I'm sure finances were no help. Whatever the particulars and reasons of the moment, my dad decided to move out.

My mom was crushed, but in time managed to get past it (if not entirely over it), and eventually she met another guy. Within a few years my dad must have realized what he'd lost, because suddenly he was trying to win her back. It was a one-way bridge he'd driven her over, though, and she wasn't going back.

Every now and then he would come visit me on the *Peace,* Captain Bill's dive boat, and do a little scuba diving. Our relationship continued to be pretty much just as strained as it had been on the deck of the *Agio.* On one of these visits, soon after my seventeenth birthday, we went diving off Gull Island, a little pinnacle rock off the back side of Santa Cruz Island. We anchored up, and he was one of the first guys into the water. A half hour later he headed up toward the surface to see where the boat was—and surfaced right smack into a big patch of kelp. It was a very bad spot, with the surf breaking over an especially rocky coast. He got tangled up in the kelp, panicked, and spit his regulator out.

At the time, I was serving in the role of rescue diver, so I dove in to help him out. I can remember the scene as if it were happening right now: I'm staring out at Jack Webb, this tough-guy hero of mine who is panicking and yelling for help, and I'm the one there to rescue him. It was hard to wrap my head around, but my training kicked in. I dove into the water, swam the 300 or 400 yards in a flash, and pulled his ass out of there. It put us in a weird situation, and we'd never talked about it, but it hovered there, making our already complicated relationship even more awkward.

Right after graduation from boot camp I got my first military paycheck. I couldn't wait to look at it. I ripped open the envelope and stared at the numbers. It was for about $700. Considering I'd been there for two months, that came to a little more than ten dollars a day. I'd been making better money than that working on the dive boat when I was fourteen! I didn't care. It was something—and I was in the navy, on the road to becoming a SEAL.

I had a week before I would be checking into Aircrew Candidate School in Pensacola, so I bought a plane ticket to go see my dad, who was now living in Jackson Hole, right on the Idaho-Wyoming border. I flew into Salt Lake, where he met me, and we drove up to his place, where we had a great time together. We went skiing, drank beer, goofed off. We drove around in my Ford Ranger, which he was keeping for me in Jackson Hole while I was going through my navy training. I had the sense that he was trying to reach out to me, and I appreciated it, even though things still felt a little strained between us.

The week came to an end and it was time for me to get back. I had a few uniforms I wanted to get dry-cleaned. I'd pretty much blown my whole paycheck on the ticket out and my return ticket to Florida, and I had no cash left.

"So Dad," I said, "could you hook me up with a little cash so I can get these uniforms cleaned, pressed, and looking sharp when I go back?"

He looked at me for a moment without a word—and then started giving me a hard time, berating me for hitting him up for money.

What the hell? I stared at him, not believing what I was hearing. After all this time, after all we'd been through, he was going to make me feel guilty about helping me out with a little dry-cleaning? I'd saved his goddam life, for crying out loud, and he couldn't help me make sure I had a clean uniform?

I lost it and started yelling at him—and before either of us knew what was happening I was sitting there behind the wheel of that Ranger, bawling my eyes out in anger and frustration.

Instantly he knew he had screwed up in a big way, and he felt truly terrible about the whole thing—at least so I would learn many years later. At the time, it sure didn't show. A blanket of quiet hostility settled over us. He gave me the money. I vowed to myself that I would never ask him for anything again, ever. I left the Ranger with him and told him it was his now. I didn't want it.

We did not part on good terms. Soon, though hardly soon enough, I was out of there and on a plane back to Florida for the next leg of the journey.

My next stop was Pensacola, way out on the Florida panhandle, where I would check in for two months of training at the Naval Aircrew Candidate School.

Aircrew school was a much more relaxed environment than boot camp had been. While boot camp was all about physical conditioning, aircrew school was mostly about giving us an orientation, as well as screening to make sure none of us had any physiological problems with flying.

We'd get up early, put on our shorts and T-shirts, go do a little PT, eat breakfast, and then hit the classroom. They strapped me into a flight simulator, a big cylindrical chamber outfitted with a seat and handles. Once they shut me in, the thing started moving, spinning at different speeds, now faster, now slower, changing both speed and direction at unpredictable intervals; the whole time a voice was talking to me from some unseen speaker, walking me through the various maneuvers. Clearly the thing was designed to put our inner ears to the test, to push the limits of our capacity to withstand acceleration and extremes of motion without getting vertigo. We called them spin-'n'-pukes.

Some guys washed out right then and there. A few others didn't survive drug testing (I wondered how they'd gotten this far), and one or two had mental health issues that knocked them out of the running.

The PT standards in aircrew school were a bit more severe than we'd had in boot camp. Still, there wasn't much of it. To me, the PT seemed pretty easy, and I could feel myself starting to get *out* of shape. For some of the guys, though, it wasn't easy at all, and a few more washed out because they couldn't meet the physical standards.

Pensacola was a great place to be young and in the navy. We were right on the border of Florida and Alabama, and things were fairly loose. Girls were everywhere, and most places in town didn't check your ID at the bars if you were military. I was in heaven.

Most of our class were headed to work in aircrew jobs or other navy jobs. Only a handful of us were going on to Search and Rescue, and when it came time to graduate we said, "Oh, shit." We were excited but also somewhat terrified. We knew our next step was going to be a good deal harder.

After Aircrew Candidate School I headed down the block for four weeks of Search and Rescue school, and sure enough, here things kicked up a notch. Although it was just down the street, it might as well have been a thousand miles away. Search and Rescue school was a completely different world.

At SAR school they ran a tight ship, and the atmosphere was serious and professional. We showed up early every morning for inspection, and our uniforms had to be perfect. From there we went to PT, followed by a 3-mile conditioning run, followed by some swims, then the classroom, and then we hit the pool for training.

The training environment revolved around a huge indoor pool that simulated sea state, the irregular swell of waves on the open ocean, in a space the size of a large gymnasium. They had huge spray machines to simulated helicopter rotor wash, and parachute-like devices hanging down from cranes, which they used to drag us through the pool. We learned the basics of lifesaving, then moved on to more advanced techniques for rescuing downed airmen.

Imagine you are a pilot and you've had to eject from your craft. It's the middle of the night, and you've parachuted into rough water. You can't see a thing, you're weighed down and badly entangled in a web of parachute shroud lines, and the water is freezing cold. We're the guys who jump out of helicopters into this environment to save your ass.

When people are plunged unexpectedly into the water, they tend to panic, and even though you're the guy swimming out there to save their life, they tend to grab on to you and push you down. It's not conscious, it's out of pure panic. Still, conscious or not, they are doing their level best to drown you. So we did a lot of what they described as drown-proofing.

The objective was to make sure we were ready for whatever conditions might be thrown at us. They taught us how to get the pilot out of his chute and then either clip him into a litter or fit him fast with a rescue strap device that slips under the arms. Then we would have to clip ourselves in and get us both hoisted up and into the waiting helo, all while the victim was panicking and trying to fight us off. There are dozens of different types of harnesses, straps, chutes, and other systems, and we had to know the procedures for every one of them—and we had to know them blind, backward and forward, because we might be dealing with them in the worst of circumstances, with a panicked or incapacitated human being on our hands. We also had to master a range of first-aid techniques, because you never know what kinds of injuries a downed pilot might have sustained.

Near the end of the four weeks, it was final exam time. We all filed into the locker room and sat down on benches to wait while they called us out, one by one, to go to the pool for our turn. When my name was called, I stood up and walked out into the open pool area.

The place was noisy and dimly lit, simulating a nighttime scene. The rotor chop simulator spray was on, the hoist equipment was up and running, and there below me was a downed pilot flailing around in the water, on the edge of drowning.

I leapt off the platform, eyes looking to the horizon as instructed, and felt myself splash down into the tank. I swam directly toward the panicked victim, trying in vain to sense when I was getting close. It was impossible to hear anything over the roar of the machinery and chop of the waves. Suddenly two huge arms wrapped around me like a steel bear trap, and we were both thrashing in the water. I could feel his panic. I knew it was simulated and that he was in reality a skilled instructor posing as a terrified pilot—but he was a good actor, and he was taking me down.

The shroud lines were everywhere. I knew I couldn't let myself get tangled in those goddam ropes, but it was very difficult not to. For an instant I flashed on that picture of my dad, struggling to fight clear of that cloying bed of kelp and spitting out his regulator in panic. I wanted to say, "For Chrissake, calm down—I'll get you out of here!" But I knew that when someone is in a panic, there's no talking to him. Finally I managed to free myself from the guy's grip, wrestle him into the harness system, and get him hoisted up onto the helo.

Once he was laid out on the floor, I saw that he was badly injured. His injuries were simulated, of course, but the special effects were very good—and I had to administer the correct first aid if I wanted to pass the test.

That exam was tough. Fortunately for me, my years of experience on Captain Bill's dive boat had sharpened my water skills to a fine point, and I made it through okay. Not so for some of the others. The drown-proofing was where the most people washed out. In that frantic, darkened, noisy environment, feeling themselves being dragged down by a crazy person, they would lose their grip and panic themselves. A few of our victims "drowned."

Search and Rescue was an excellent training experience. Graduates of this program are an elite bunch. Howard Wasdin, the SEAL who fought in the "Black Hawk Down" battle of Mogadishu and went on to write the book *SEAL Team Six,* started out training as a search-and-rescue swimmer. I was proud when I finished the course, and I'm proud to this day to have belonged to the SAR community.

But I still wanted badly to get to SEAL training.

After SAR school it was time to pick an "A" school where I would receive basic training for whichever specific naval job I elected to do. In the navy, your occupational specialization is referred to as your rating; your rating is earned through "A" school. If you want to be a cook, you go to mess specialist "A" school. If you're a submarine sonar guy, you go to "A" school for sonar.

Search-and-rescue swimmers were deployed on helicopters, and as far as I could see, the only job on an aircraft that didn't involve turning wrenches was antisubmarine warfare operator, or AW. This was the early nineties, when we hadn't yet shifted from Cold War thinking and were still largely oriented toward a big Soviet submarine threat that no longer existed. Today the same rating is called aviation warfare systems operator. By whatever name, it boils down to being the guy who works the sonar in the back of the helicopter—and that sounded damn exciting to me. I put AW at the top of my wish list.

The navy is usually pretty fair in awarding top finishers their choice of orders. Since I had been at the top of my class at both Aircrew Candidate School and SAR school, I got my pick, and soon I was headed for Millington, Tennessee, for four months of antisubmarine warfare/sonar operator training.

They taught us some fascinating skills in Millington, including how to read a sonar gram (not the same thing as sonogram). We would drop sonar buoys out the back of a helicopter, then read the signals they emitted on a screen or, more typically, burned onto a printout. We learned how to see harmonic frequencies in the readout, and from these pick out the blade rate and discern how many blades were on that particular prop. There would be a whoosh-whoosh-*whoosh*—that last being a top rotation where it would cavitate (create an air pocket that then implodes), and by counting the number of whooshes between cavitations we could tell it was, for example, a four-bladed prop. Other clues from the sonar frequencies would tell us how many cylinders the engine had. It was amazing: From this little screen or printout we could say, "Okay, we've got a one-cylinder engine, four-blade prop—so that's a type 209 class Soviet sub." We memorized a ton of different submarine traits and characteristics so that, in a clinch, we could classify any one of them immediately without even thinking about it.

Toward the end of my time at "A" school I again inquired about orders to BUD/S. It turned out, the rules had just changed. In the past, it had been possible to go right from "A" school to BUD/S. In fact, one guy had just done that a few months earlier, but he was the last to go through that door before it slammed shut. They had since restricted anyone from leaving "A" school with orders to BUD/S. Once again, I was told I'd need to wait and take up my request after arriving at my final duty station. This would be when I deployed as part of an active helo squadron—which would not be for close to a year.

Graduation day came, and we all sat huddled in the classroom waiting for our orders. We'd heard that half of us would go to the West Coast and half to the East Coast. Wherever we each ended up was where we would spend the next three or four years of our lives.

We knew they used class rankings to pick our assignments for our next duty station, so everyone with mediocre grades was horse-trading—a thousand dollars cash, sex with their sister, *anything* not to be sent east, or sent west, depending on the person's particular aversion. There were guys from the Midwest who were terrified they would have to go hang out with those fruitcakes in California. In my case, the destination was helicopter training, then duty station with a helo squadron, which meant orders either to San Diego or Jacksonville, Virginia. I did *not* want to end up in Virginia. BUD/S was based in San Diego, and I knew I'd have a better chance of making it into SEAL training if I was already stationed right down the street.

I've never been a great student, but I've always been able to pull out A's and B's when I absolutely had to, and I was graduating near the top of the class. Still, I feared I would end up being sent to an East Coast squadron.

It turned out I was worried for nothing: The orders were *all* for the West Coast.

I was going home.

After nearly a year out east, I returned to California in January of 1994 with orders to report to HS-10, the helicopter training squadron in San

Diego where I would learn the ropes before finally deploying as part of an operational squadron. However there were a few more hurdles to clear first before joining HS-10, and the toughest of these was what came next. Before you can become a pilot or rescue swimmer, or take any other job where there is significant risk of capture, you need two things. You have to have secret clearance, and you have to go to survival school.

The term "boot camp" was first used by the marines back in World War II, "boot" being slang for "recruit." Those of us who showed up for Survival, Evasion, Resistance, and Escape (SERE) training that January might have already been through many months of training, but we were clearly still green, still *boots*—and survival school was boot camp on steroids.

Based on the experiences of U.S. and allied soldiers as prisoners of war, the program's aim is to equip its trainees with both the skills and the grit to survive with dignity in the most hostile conditions of captivity. It was far and away the most intense training I'd encountered so far.

We mustered at the SERE school building at Naval Air Station North Island, on the northern end of the Coronado peninsula, where we were scheduled for a week of classroom training, followed by a week of field-work. We spent that first week covering history and background, including lessons learned from World War II and Vietnam. We learned such things as how to tell a captor just enough to stay alive—but not enough to give away secrets. The week went by fast, which suited us fine. We were looking forward to getting into the field.

That day came soon enough. We were all lined up and checked head to toe for smuggled food items before heading out. We had been warned not to try to sneak any food into our clothes or boots, but as I would learn again and again during my time in the navy, there's always one in every bunch. Sure enough, a few guys got caught with a variety of ridiculous food items stashed on their person. I had to give it to them for trying.

After inspection, we drove about ninety minutes to the northeast, heading into the mountains of Warner Springs, California, where we were broken into groups of six and then into two-man evasion teams. I was paired up with a big Recon marine. These are Special Ops guys, similar in many ways to SEALs, including some who specialize in deep reconnaissance and others, called black ops, who focus more on direct action missions. I didn't know if this guy was black ops or not, but regardless, as survival and evasion partners go I figured I could do a lot worse.

Then we were set loose in the wild with nothing but the clothes on our backs, simulating the experience of being on the move behind enemy lines. We spent the next three days learning basic survival and evasion skills, including trapping, tracking, and land navigation. We ate everything we could get our hands on, which wasn't much. Survival school classes had been going out to this same spot for years, and practically everything that qualified as edible plant or animal had long ago been snatched up and eaten. Soon we were wolfing anything that wasn't tied down, including bugs, some scruffy plants, and one lucky rabbit. By day 2, we were starving.

The nights were rough. Our first day out my partner and I built a shelter in preparation for the cold mountain night, but we way overbuilt. Being manly men, we wanted a nice roomy setup so we would each have our space and wouldn't have to sleep so close that we would touch each other. Having since experienced that kind of cold a number of times, both in training in the States and thousands of feet above sea level in the wilds of northern Afghanistan, let me tell you: All that manly bullshit goes right out the window and you are more than happy to be nut to butt with anyone who has a pulse and warm blood coursing through his veins. After waking up the fourth time, chilled to the core and teeth chattering, my marine buddy and I grunted a few words of manliness and then nestled up to each other like a scene right out of *Brokeback Mountain*.

After three days of this, we were ready to get on with the evasion-and-captivity portion of training, which included an evasion exercise lasting about twenty-four hours, leading directly into the simulated POW camp portion of the training, which would be three days long. During the evasion exercise, which simulated the circumstances of a downed aviator, we would be out in the woods attempting to evade capture by the enemy, who would actively hunt us down. The rules of this exercise were pretty simple: Don't get caught. If we did, we would win a prize: extra POW time.

When the time was up, they would sound a loud siren, at which point those of us who had made it to the time threshold without being caught would walk to the nearest road and turn ourselves in. The "turn yourself in" part sounded crazy to me, but what the hell. It was their rules.

My marine buddy and I did very well at the evasion exercise—so well, in fact, that by the time they sounded the siren the next afternoon, we had cleared way to the south and were completely out of earshot. We eventually realized we had gone way out of bounds and the time limit must have expired by now, so we found a road and started walking north toward the exercise boundary. Soon we were picked up by a truck full of foreign-looking men who looked quite pissed off. Hoods were yanked over our heads, and we were smacked around for a while. Good times. Later we learned that these guys had been out looking for us for almost four hours and were none too happy about it.

Once we reached camp, our hoods were removed and we were marched into a processing area, where we were each given our own war criminal number. I remember my number to this day: I was no longer Brandon Webb, I was now War Criminal 53.

There were two rules here, and we learned them pretty fast. "Grab your rags!" was the first. The second was "Eyes to ground, whore dog!" *Grab your rags*: That was intended to remind us to grab the sides of our pants (which did indeed resemble rags at this point) so the guards could see our hands at all times. *Eyes to ground*: That one was to ensure that none of us war criminals would look around and gain any increased awareness of our surroundings—awareness that we might be able to use later to our advantage.

I decided to test out this second rule. Quietly, carefully, without moving my head or neck, I rolled my eyes just a few degrees to steal a glance around. *Whack!* My head rocked back from a swift backhand to my face. I could feel my jaw crack. I was a fast learner, or at least not the slowest: I tried it once more, and after the second numbing smack across the face figured they were enforcing the rules pretty well. From that point on I grabbed my rags and kept my eyes to ground. I did not look around. (Okay, I did—but I was a lot more careful about not getting caught doing it.)

Once we were given our new rags and number, we were all asked very nicely what we preferred for dinner.

"War Criminal 53! You want the chicken or the fish?"

Both sounded damn good to me—but I suspected it was a trick question and that what they really wanted was our signatures. We had to sign for our choice of dinner in the ledger, and they had instructed us to use our real names. I'd heard enough stories to realize that they could use this against us in any sort of future propaganda campaign. I might have been a prisoner in their camp, but I wasn't about to roll over. I wrote my choice in the ledger (I chose fish) and signed it without using my name, writing simply, "Fuck you—sincerely."

After signing up for dinner we were gathered in a room where we could talk to each other. There were some pretty nervous guys in there. Strange though it sounds, I felt pretty relaxed. I'm not sure if this comes from early experiences being on my own or if it's just my temperament, but I've never been one to lose my cool in a high-stress situation. This would prove to work to my advantage more than once, both now and especially later on, once I was finally in training as a SEAL.

After a few minutes, the camp guard came in and asked for a show of hands from anyone who was U.S. Spec Ops. I couldn't believe it. Did he really think we were going to fall for that?

"Come and answer us, you American whore dogs! Who is U.S. Spec Ops and pilots? We know your U.S. spy planes and Spec Op soldiers are on the ground in our country! Turn yourselves in now and save yourself pain and suffering. We will give you hot meal!"

The accent was Russian and sounded quite authentic, but the request was so funny and so obviously full of shit that it took an effort to suppress laughter. In the next instant my amusement turned to shock and dismay when I saw several of my comrades' hands fly up. What the hell were they thinking? Those unfortunates were asked to sign a confession and then immediately separated from the rest of us. I don't know where they were taken or exactly what their special treatment was, but I can promise you two things: first, it hurt, and second, it was *not* a "hot meal."

Next I was assigned to a small concrete box, about three feet tall, though somewhat larger in width and depth (thank heavens), which I was expected to enter. Not much alternative here. I crawled in and did my best to find a comfortable position. Hunching down a bit, I could just manage to sit cross-legged, sort of. I am not a tall man, and in that moment I was grateful for this fact.

In the box I noticed a Folgers coffee can. I was told its purpose. "It is for you to piss and crap in." Ahh, all the amenities. There was a little canvas flap one could pull down for a little privacy when it came time to use the can, that phrase having now taken on its literal meaning.

This would be my home for the next few days.

I wondered what would happen next. It wasn't that terrible being crammed into this ridiculous box, but I wanted them to haul me out and start interrogating me. *Let's get this damn thing over with,* I thought.

Nobody came.

As the hours crawled by, a sort of routine began to establish itself.

People were randomly selected (at least it seemed that way to me) to be pulled out of their boxes and taken away into the night. A short while later, we would hear screams. Then the music would start: bad songs, the worst, over and over. Other times it would be a recording of a little girl pleading for her daddy to come home. Whatever it was they played on the loudspeakers, it would go on for hours. When daybreak came this routine continued. Screaming, complaining, whining, beatings, and bad music.

My most vivid memory of time in the camp was being crammed into another tiny box, this one of wood and no more than 3 feet in all dimensions. This wonderful location would be my accommodations for the next few hours while they subjected me to the interrogation portion. (Be careful what you wish for.) I've never had a problem with small spaces, but when I was stuffed into that box (yes, stuffed), my left leg started to cramp. This was the kind of cramp you can quickly relieve simply by straightening out your leg, but in that damned box, there was no straightening anything out. That leg cramp—and even more, my complete and utter inability to do anything about it—drove me near to insanity. It took everything I had to keep it together in the box.

On day 2 they gathered us all together and gave us a speech.

"Nobody cares about you worthless turds. Nobody on the outside is thinking about you. You're ours, and no one gives a shit. So we've made a decision. We were supposed to keep you here for three days and then let you go, but that was the old plan. That was before we had a chance to find out just how weak and pitiful you are. We decided we're gonna keep you pieces of shit here and keep punishing you for a lot longer. Maybe five days. Maybe ten. We haven't decided yet."

Now, this sounded pretty far-fetched. We all *knew* that the POW portion would last only three days. At this point, though, it was weirdly believable. When you haven't had a decent meal in four days, you haven't slept much, and you've gone through a full twenty-four hours of that POW environment, I don't care who you are or how tough you are, it starts to mess with your head.

After this bizarre announcement we were returned to our concrete homes. Shortly thereafter, my neighbor in the next hole over, War Criminal 51, asked to see the camp commandant about his swollen feet. He was ignored and soon asked again, this time louder—and again, and then again. He kept repeating his request, over and over, and was ignored every time. After more than a dozen repetitions, his demands moved from pleading to urgency to hysteria, and still he kept at it.

Finally he started screaming.

He was *done* putting up with this *bullshit,* and everyone could *stop* playing games now, *right now.* "My orders end tomorrow, man! I'm not playing this fucking game anymore! Get me the fuck out of here, man!" He sounded like Private Hudson, the Bill Paxton character in *Aliens.* ("That's *it,* man, game *over,* man, game *over*! What the fuck are we gonna do now? . . . We're all gonna *die,* man!") He had completely lost it.

After about an hour of this, I had to pull down my little canvas flap so the camp guards wouldn't see me laughing. I know that sounds sick, but I couldn't help it. There were only two ways to see it: Either it was terrifying or it was funny as hell. I went with funny as hell.

Suddenly I heard the scuttling of running feet. I jerked open my canvas flap just in time to see War Criminal 51 making a run for it! I could hardly believe my eyes. Did he really think he could get out? Who knows. My neighbor (I never did learn his name) had cracked.

I don't think anyone had ever tried to run right out the main gate before, and he actually took the guards by surprise for a moment—but only for a moment. They grabbed him up pretty quick. I never saw him again.

Not that he was the only one who thought about escaping. But it is an established rule in the U.S. military that even in a prisoner-of-war situation you still use a strict chain of command. For example, if you want to make an attempt to escape the camp, you have to run your request chit (fill out the form) and ask permission from the senior person. This was difficult for me to accomplish because of the location of my concrete box and my lack of proximity to our senior person. I made two attempts to run escape chits, but none of the people I passed them to were successful in getting a chit all the way up the chain of command.

In the middle of the second night there, we were told to strip naked. We stayed that way while they hosed us down with freezing cold water. Time for your bath. What else could you ask for?

During the course of these few days we learned a lesson that had been learned the hard way by real POWs before us, mostly from people imprisoned in the Hanoi Hilton in North Vietnam: *In any prisoner-of-war situation, the goal is to survive with honor.* If you act like a jackass, if you are arrogant and refuse (or appear to refuse) to cooperate, you will be quickly executed. Don't be a smart-ass. That is not the way you play the game. As much as is humanly possible, you stick to name, rank, and service number.

A few guys took the opposite tack and acted out, being as obnoxious and uncooperative as they could. Their reward: They got waterboarded. After the course was over, these guys started bragging about being waterboarded for bad behavior, as if it were a badge of honor. They were quickly disabused of this notion. In our debrief after SERE, it was made crystal clear that if you got waterboarded, this showed that you were not putting into practice what you'd been taught about surviving in a prisoner-of-war situation. In short, you were a fuckup.

A few guys pushed it even further, and their punishment went beyond waterboarding: They were executed. (Simulated, of course, but still
not fun.) More than a few people failed out for getting "executed" or completely losing their cool. Three days doesn't sound like a very long time,
and under normal, everyday circumstances, it's not—but under POW camp
conditions, it doesn't take long to wear down a man's sanity.

After day 3 we were liberated from the camp and soon found ourselves back at North Island getting debriefed on our POW experience.
Our guards had seemed callous and brutal, like they neither knew nor
cared who we were and didn't even notice us except to punish us. It was
a ruse. In fact, they had watched us all quite carefully and taken thorough
notes on each individual prisoner the entire time. I was happy to find out
that I did pretty well.

I asked about War Criminal 51, the guy in the hole next to mine
who'd made a run for it.

"He lost it, completely and totally," I was told.

Would he be able to go on with his training, I asked, or was he out of
the navy?

"Don't know," they said. "We're still evaluating him. Either way,
though, he will not be continuing on in his current high-risk assignment."

They gave us advice on how to make a solid transition from our exhausting training back to normal, real-world living. "Remember," they
told us, "you guys have not eaten in almost a week. Take it easy, and definitely refrain from having any alcohol for a while, because it can induce
hallucinations."

I think they told us this last piece at least three times, but they could
have said it thirty times and it probably still would not have mattered.
Try telling a nineteen-year-old who has just been liberated from a simulated POW camp that he should "take it easy" and "refrain from alcohol," and
see what happens. I went out that night with all my friends and classmates

to the Surf Club on base, and we got absolutely trashed. I don't remember much about that night, but I vividly remember waking up Sunday morning with a massive headache, peeing bright yellow from dehydration. I didn't care. Boot camp—all of it—was over.

Now all I had to do was figure out how to get to BUD/S.

THREE

OBSTACLE COURSE

At the end of January I got about a week to recover from survival school, then classed up in an advanced program called "C" school, where I spent the next three months learning the advanced sonar concepts that were the theoretical foundation of the "antisubmarine warfare" sonar operator's trade before I could go on to join HS-10.

During these three months I began to get a taste of just how much complex knowledge and technical know-how I would be absorbing over my years in the military. For weeks at a stretch, we pored over material in courses with names like Electronic Warfare, Oceanography, Advanced Acoustic Analysis, and Aural Listening. Just two years earlier I'd been a teenager struggling through high school math. Now I was absorbing all kinds of advanced concepts and academic material and, oddly enough, doing so without breaking a sweat.

The simple truth was, it was fascinating. It had to do with tracking things underwater—something I had no trouble relating to.

In "A" school we had learned the basics of reading submarine acoustic signatures. Now we really dove into the subject, pouring hours into studying the harmonic frequencies emitted by bodies in the water.

As you descend, the water changes temperature; however, it does not do so gradually, along a smooth continuum, but in discrete chunks, something like a layer cake. I knew this from experience, because you can feel these temperature breaks as you dive. As I now learned, these distinct temperature layers are called thermoclines. The interesting thing about these layers is that they trap sound, and consequently the way sound waves travel is dictated to some degree by the layout of thermoclines: As a sound wave hits the bottom of a thermocline (or, depending on how you're looking at it, the top of the one below it), it spreads outward, trapped within that layer of depth.

Because of this, if you have a submarine hiding down at, say, 50 feet, you're not necessarily going to hear it if you (or your sonar buoy) are at 30 feet. In other words, submarines can literally hide within thermoclines. If the vessel makes enough noise, it may create sufficient energy to bleed through into the next layer—but a modern submarine is so stealthy that you have to be *in* that thermocline to hear it. I filed this information away; a few years later I would use it to my advantage in a most unexpected circumstance.

I made it through "C" school uneventfully—with one exception.

Since I would be spending at least the next few years of my life here in San Diego, I wanted to make sure I could keep up with two of my favorite pastimes, surfing and spearfishing. While in "C" school, we had ample time off for extracurricular activities, so I went up to my mom's place in Ventura, got a surfboard and one of my spearguns out of storage, and brought them back down with me to Coronado.

One day, coming back from class to my barracks room, I found a note saying that my room had been inspected and I needed to come to the military police HQ to pick up my speargun. Thinking nothing of it, I grabbed a jacket and headed off.

When I arrived at HQ, I was promptly arrested. The charge: possession of a deadly weapon on base. They put me in a holding cell.

I could not believe what was happening. Possession of a deadly weapon? I was a diver, for heaven's sake. Spearfishing was what I *did*. Besides, I obviously wasn't trying to *hide* the speargun. I couldn't have even if I'd wanted to: It was too big to fit in my locker. I'd had it lying out in the open. Were they serious?

They were. The MPs acted like jackasses, doing their best to intimidate me and impress upon me that I had screwed up big-time, that my navy career was over.

Yeah, yeah. Bite me.

They called one of the chiefs who happened to be on duty at my school and told him what was going on. To my great relief, as soon as he showed up they remanded me into his custody. My relief soon turned to surprise: The moment the chief and I were alone together, he started laying into me. I knew enough to keep my mouth shut and just take his shit, but it seemed strange and a little silly that they were making such a big deal out of it.

The rest of the instructor staff at "C" school thought the whole thing was pretty funny, and they gave me quite a lot of crap about it, as did all my classmates. When it came time to graduate, they all got together and created a special Jacques Cousteau Award for the poor slob who got arrested for possession of a speargun. I still have that award. I never got my speargun back.

The day after graduation one of the other chiefs called me into his office. He told me he didn't agree with the way the first chief had handled the situation. "You're a diver and a spearfisherman, Webb," he said. "I respect that, and I'm sorry the navy confiscated your speargun."

"Yes, Chief" was all I said, but it felt good to have someone in a leadership position say what he did. I could understand their need to enforce the rules, but I was still angry about it. They had destroyed a perfectly good speargun.

It wasn't the last time I'd see what seemed to me examples of good leadership and poor leadership side by side. It also wasn't the last time I'd find myself in trouble.

In April, fresh out of "C" school, I was finally assigned to HS-10, the helicopter training squadron where I would spend the next six months learning how to function as an aircrew member and operate the systems in the back of assorted types of H-60 helicopter.

The H-60 is a broad class of U.S. military helicopters that includes the Sea Hawk, the Ocean Hawk, the famous Black Hawk, and a handful of others. At HS-10 they put us into several different kinds of simulators representing the various helicopter platforms we would soon be flying. One had a heavy sonar package; another, which we called a truck, was completely gutted out and used mainly for combat and search-and-rescue exercises.

After learning all the technology on the simulators, it was time to go out on live trainings. They put one instructor in front with the pilot and another instructor in back with the aircrewmen. Here they taught us how to operate the hoist, how to use the proper terminology to talk from the front to the back, radio etiquette, and all the different systems on the aircraft.

In mid-October, after six months at the helo training squadron, I got orders to Helicopter Anti-Submarine Squadron Six. HS-6, also known as the Indians, was my first deployment. Yes, I was still in training—but I was now part of an actual, operational helicopter command. I was in the navy fleet now.

And a helluva command it was. The squadron had an illustrious history stretching back nearly forty years. The Indians had rescued more than a dozen downed pilots in Vietnam and helped underwater demolition teams (the predecessors of SEALs) pluck moon-walking Apollo astronauts out of the ocean on splashdown, had earned a long succession of trophies and awards, and would years later go on to serve the efforts in Afghanistan and Iraq. I was excited about becoming part of HS-6. It was a damn good squadron—and I was out to make a name for myself.

Back in April, when I had first arrived at HS-10 for training, I had made another strong push to get orders to SEAL training. Once again, I'd been told I would have to wait until I got to my final duty station. Well, here I was at my final duty station, and I was determined to do a kick-ass job so I could apply for BUD/S and get the hell out of there as fast as I could.

Which turned out not to be very fast at all. In fact, I would continue serving as part of the Indians from October 1994 through the summer of 1997, encountering obstacle after obstacle in my quest, before finally getting my orders to SEAL training nearly three full years later.

In the spring of 1995, about six months after becoming part of the Indians, I went on a six-month deployment on the aircraft carrier USS *Abraham Lincoln* in the western Pacific, called a WESTPAC. An aircraft carrier normally sports a full-time crew of several thousand. When it leaves port for a WESTPAC, though, all its associated helicopter squadrons populate it and disembark with it, which brings the total onboard population up to around five thousand, and it becomes like a small city unto itself.

We had gone out before for shorter trips of up to a month. The WESTPAC was different. Now we headed out west clear across the Pacific, stopping in Hawaii, Hong Kong, Thailand, and Australia, and then on to the Persian Gulf, where we spent the next four or five months as the U.S. aircraft carrier presence there. This was something like being a cop on the beat. We weren't necessarily engaging anyone or seeing any action, but we were the show of force, ready to be tapped for whatever need might arise.

For those of us still in training, the WESTPAC gave us the opportunity to learn everything we could ever want to know about all the systems on the different helo platforms we were using at the time. For me, though, it meant one thing: earning as many qualifications as possible so I could get to BUD/S. As great as life was in the squadron, I wanted nothing more than to get the hell out of there, the sooner the better.

At the center of BUD/S training is a monstrosity I'd heard about called the O-course, a brutally difficult setup aimed at developing superhuman endurance while inflicting maximum punishment. Later on, when I finally got the chance to face the actual O-course, it would nearly beat me. Meanwhile, I decided that if I kept facing obstacles in my path, I would treat them as my own private O-course and use them to make me stronger.

The problem with letting people know I wanted to go into SEAL training was that everyone knew about the absurd attrition rate at BUD/S, where typically some 80 percent wash out. To make matters worse, the aircrew community has a terrible reputation for sending in guys who wash out more than 90 percent of the time. This made my life pretty rough at HS-6. By this time, though, I'd figured out that when people tell you that you can't do something, you can use it to your advantage, and every time someone else told me I was crazy and would never make it to BUD/S (let alone *through* BUD/S), I was determined to use it as more motivational fuel. My operational philosophy was "I'm just going to do the best job I can and get all the quals, and then they'll let me go."

And right now, that meant getting my tactical sensor operator (TSO) qual.

Over the course of our deployment on the USS *Lincoln*, I completed all the requirements I needed in order to take my TSO test. The TSO ran the show and was the senior guy in the back of the aircraft. In essence, this would mean getting my qualification for crew chief. One September day, toward the end of that WESTPAC, the time finally came for my first check ride. Pass this, and I would have that crew chief qual I needed. I was ready to go and totally psyched.

"Check ride" means exactly that: From the moment we lifted off the flight deck and flew out over the Gulf, they checked every move I made, testing me on *everything*—language and terminology, correct procedures and sequences, how I operated every system I touched. If you're tracking a submarine, for example, then you're managing the sonar and making decisions in the back. If you're on a rescue operation to pull a downed pilot out of the drink, then the level of control intensifies. As sonar operator, once you're in search-and-rescue mode on the scene of a recovery operation, the pilot toggles hover control over to you and you are running the show. In a sense, I had to demonstrate that I could function as a pilot, too.

The entire check ride lasted about two hours. We touched down on the flight deck, and I turned to my instructors to get their feedback.

"You did pretty well," they said, "but you need more experience."

I stared at them, stunned. They were *flunking* me.

Technically speaking, I actually *had* passed the minimum requirements of the check ride, and I knew it as well as they did. The instructors are given some latitude in the scoring process, though, and there were a few senior guys in the squadron who were not exactly looking out for me. In the course of our deployment, I had knocked out all the requirements so fast that it kind of freaked a few of them out, and they wanted to see me cut down to size.

I didn't argue, but I was annoyed as hell. Now I had a negative mark on my record. In retrospect I realize that I shoulder some of the blame here: I had probably pushed too hard to take the test before being fully ready for it. Then again, if they'd already decided I wasn't ready, why did they let me take the test?

•   •   •

A few days later an event occurred that gave me one of the most vivid experiences in my life of great leadership and terrible leadership, side by side.

We were out on nighttime maneuvers over the Persian Gulf. Our pilot that night, Lieutenant Burkitt, was the sort of officer you can't help disliking: a slimy guy who alienated officers and enlisted men alike. Lieutenant Burkitt's copilot, Kennedy, was a good guy and quite smart, though a little on the geeky side. Rich Fries and I both served as crewmen; Rich was senior to me. In terms of rank and experience, I was the low man on this totem pole.

It had been a long night, and in order to make it all the way back to the *Lincoln,* we had to stop and refuel on a nearby destroyer. The night was pretty calm, but visibility was against us, as there was absolutely no moon out, and it was damn close to pitch black out there.

A destroyer's deck is pretty tight to land on, especially as compared to an aircraft carrier like the USS *Lincoln,* and even more so at night with such low visibility. Because of this it was common operating procedure to slow the helo down to 90 knots (just over 100 mph), then open the cabin door and have one of the crewman spot the deck, that is, assist the pilot with verbal commands. On this occasion, the crewman doing the spotting was me.

As the helo slowed down to under 90 knots, I passed a message over the ICS (internal communications system) that the door was coming open. The door cracked open, and I looked out to get a visual on the destroyer's lights. For some reason, I couldn't make anything out. I kept straining to see something and finally caught a glimpse of light—but it was at eye level, which I thought was strange. I looked down and realized that we were not where we were supposed to be. We were not slowly descending and approaching the deck. Our pilot had put us down at water level.

We were about to crash into the ocean.

"Altitude! Altitude!" I yelled. All hell broke loose. Rich immediately realized what was happening and joined in with me. I will never, in all my life, forget what happened next. Suddenly we heard Lieutenant Burkitt's voice shrilly piercing through our yells. "What's happening?" he screamed. "I don't know what's happening! Oh God, oh God!"

He kept repeating that: *Oh God, oh God.*

For a split second Rich and I gaped at each other in disbelief. This was our pilot. This was our aircraft *commander*, screaming like a frightened schoolgirl.

We were done for. I held tight onto the cabin door. By now there was a foot of seawater in the main cabin, and any second we would be swamped and overrun with ocean: the point of no return. In my mind's eye, I could see the rotor blades sabering into the water and splintering into a thousand pieces, the helo flipping upside down and sinking into the Gulf. Everything slowed way down and a stream of contrasting thoughts tore through my mind:

So this *is why we go through the helo dunker training blindfolded.*

Is this is really how it's going to end?

No—I am not *going to let this jackass Burkitt kill me!*

Then something happened that turned it all around in an instant. Kennedy, our copilot, somehow torqued his shit together and hauled us and that damned helo up and out of the water. It was inches short of miraculous. Hell, maybe it *was* miraculous.

The crew on the destroyer thought we had crashed and were goners for sure, and they were shocked and thrilled to see us suddenly popping back up on radar.

Rich immediately replaced me on the door, exactly as he should have (he was senior to me and had thousands of hours in the H-60 under his belt), and he rapidly talked Kennedy down onto the deck after a few missed approaches. Burkitt was an utter disaster the entire time, mumbling to himself like a street person with a drug habit.

Despite our reports, nobody on the destroyer believed that we had actually put the bird into the drink. Not, that is, until the maintenance chief tore the tail section apart—and seawater started pouring out. A short investigation followed, but it went nowhere. The CO of HS-6 didn't want his career to end over this incident, and he kept things tightly under wraps.

I don't know how he did it, but Kennedy saved all our lives that night, and he deserved a medal for it. However, that wasn't what happened. Instead, *both* Burkitt and Kennedy had their helicopter aircraft commander (HAC) papers suspended. Kennedy, the guy who had saved us all with his heroism and remarkable calm under pressure, got punished right along with Burkitt, the guy who cracked apart like an eggshell and nearly guaranteed our watery demise.

I came away with from that near-disaster with a resolve never to judge a person based on appearance. Kennedy had always seemed like a smart and very competent guy, but not one I would have figured for a hero. You never know what people are capable of until you get to work with them, side by side.

I hope I get the chance to shake his hand again one day.

In the long run, my fast-track-to-BUD/S strategy backfired on me. I had thought that if I gave everything my best, I would prove to my superiors that I was a hard worker and they would approve my assignment to BUD/S. In fact, the opposite happened. The better I did, the more valuable I was to my superiors—and the more reluctant they were to let me go.

And when I say "they," who I'm really talking about is Chief Bruce Clarin.

Chief Clarin was an East Coast guy who hated being out on the West Coast and among what he described as "the fruit loops." When he looked at me and some of my buddies, all he saw was guys who spent their whole lives surfing: We were all slackers. A few guys in the shop sucked up to him. Nobody else could stand him. To this day, I am amazed that this guy made chief and was put in charge of an aircrew shop. Clarin was a walking, talking textbook illustration of how *not* to lead. He played favorites and rewarded people he liked, based not on any accomplishments but purely on the fact that he happened to like them. The guys he happened to like the most were also those who did the least amount of work and continually dragged down the rest of us.

In March 1996, about five months after returning from the USS *Lincoln* WESTPAC, I submitted my first BUD/S package, that is, my application along with all the necessary supporting documentation. It was quickly denied.

Instinctively, I knew that Clarin had screwed me. It was only months later that I would learn in full detail what had actually happened.

In order for me to get out of my AW job and get orders to BUD/S, permission needed to come from the appropriate rating detailer, the person who controls where people transfer to or work next in the navy. As it happened, our rating detailer was a man with the mind-blowingly unfortunate name of Petty Officer A. W. Dickover. (Someone, somewhere, must have seen the humor in this and assigned him the job based on his name alone.) Chief Clarin had put in a call to Petty Officer Dickover and asked him *not* to approve my request for orders to SEAL training.

You are probably wondering how I learned what had happened. I learned it because Clarin himself actually admitted to me what he'd done.

The truth was, I was the only third-class petty officer in the squadron who was NATOPS-qualified (Naval Air Training and Operating Procedures Standardization), which meant I could do things like give annual qualification tests or test someone who wanted to become a crew chief. After failing that first check ride, it hadn't taken me long to test again— and pass. Now my rapid advancement came back to bite me.

"You have all these quals," Clarin said. "Sorry, Webb, but I need you for this deployment."

The son of a bitch. Now I would have to stay with the squadron for at least another year and do a whole other six-month WESTPAC deployment.

A few months later, in July, I applied to attend a one-week pre-SEAL selection course, held at the navy's boot camp facility in Illinois, called Naval Station Great Lakes (or, unofficially, Great Mistakes). This is not a pass/fail kind of course, and going through it wouldn't give me any technical qualification. Still, depending on how I did, I could come out of it with a recommendation to the real BUD/S—or without one. In a sense, it would be an informal entrance exam. If I flew through pre-BUD/S, it would boost my chances of getting orders to the real deal. And if I couldn't make it through the week at Great Mistakes, I could forget about surviving the seven months of the genuine article.

Calling pre-BUD/S a condensed version of the real thing would be a stretch. It is designed to give you a glimpse of what the actual BUD/S training experience would be like, but only a glimpse. I knew that. Still, it was one way to demonstrate that I was serious, and hopefully I would come out of it with an endorsement.

There was a mix of guys in the program, some straight out of boot camp, some who were already regular navy, like me. One guy there cut an especially intimidating figure: a six-foot-tall, blond, Nordic-looking dude named Lars. Lars had thighs like tree trunks and could do push-ups from sunup to sunrise. He just crushed everything they threw at him. I met up with Lars again a year later when I finally made it to BUD/S and will have more to say about him at that point in the story.

I passed the program with flying colors, and they recommended me for BUD/S—but my obstacle course wasn't over yet.

After he admitted to his duplicity in tanking my first BUD/S package, Chief Clarin and I had for the most part stayed out of each other's way. Our mutual animosity came to a head, though, during my second WEST-

PAC deployment, which started in October of 1996. I had now been part of HS-6 for exactly two years, and I was determined to make it to BUD/S before another full year went by. I submitted a second BUD/S package and was pretty confident that it would go through. After all, I had done the pre-BUD/S course and come out with a strong recommendation.

However, I also knew that if I wanted to pass the entrance qualifications for BUD/S when I got back stateside, I needed to get into shape. On the aircraft carrier, it was hard to keep up high fitness standards: I couldn't swim, I couldn't really run (running on a steel deck is not exactly great for the joints), and getting in a full workout routine was difficult. *Six months* in those conditions would really set me back.

I went to Chief Clarin and told him my situation.

"Don't worry," he said, "I'll send you back on early detachment [that is, guys who were flown back early to prepare the home command for the rest of the group's return]. In fact, I'll send you back a month early, so you can train and get in shape before you have to qualify."

I was a little surprised and quite grateful that he would go out of his way to do this. As it turned out, he was lying through his teeth. He never had any intention of sending me back home early. He didn't want me to go to BUD/S and was determined to prevent it, whatever that took.

A few weeks later, a friend in our squadron admin took me aside and told me I was getting railroaded (navyspeak for "screwed over") by Chief Clarin on my upcoming evaluation.

Evaluations go a long way in making rank in the navy; they're put into the mix with your rating test to yield a final multiple that determines whether or not you are promoted. Normally you would not have a chance to see how your peers break out during an evaluation period unless you exchange notes. Through my friend, I learned that I was being rated as low as the brand-new check-ins.

I was not about to take that lying down. If I had deserved a low eval, that would be one thing, but that was clearly not the case. I had busted my ass to get every qual I possibly could and volunteered for every shit detail to prove to my peers and superiors that I deserved a shot at BUD/S.

Here's how the process works: After receiving your written eval and having a one-on-one debrief with whoever wrote it, you sign your name at the bottom. There is a tiny box there by the signature line that you check if you intend to submit a statement along with your eval. Hardly anyone ever marks a check in that box. I still remember the look of utter horror on Chief Clarin's face when he saw me check the box. He knew that *I* knew what he was up to. He knew he had fucked up.

At the time I was taking a few college classes on the ship (they even had professors on board; as I said, an aircraft carrier is like a small city) and had just finished English 1302. I thought this would be a prime opportunity to put my writing skills to use. I prepared a formal statement, which I took great care in writing. It contained not a single whine or complaint, nothing but the facts, line item by line item.

Apparently, my statement created quite a stir. After it landed on my department head's desk, he ran it up to the commanding officer (CO). Pretty soon I got word that Chief Clarin and I were both wanted in Commander Rosa's office.

When I arrived, Clarin was already there. I nodded at him without a word. It was obvious that he was not too happy with the situation. Chiefs run the navy, and in the navy culture it is extremely rare for anyone to go against a chief or question his judgment or leadership, but I would be damned if I was going to roll over and take this. Maybe this came from my time on the dive boat, when I often felt I had to prove myself to all the older guys. Maybe it was an echo of the times I stood up to my dad—or maybe I got it *from* my dad, and it reflects the times he stood up to *his* father. Whatever its source, there is a stubborn streak in me that refuses to knuckle under to what seems to me a poor decision or unfair judgment.

We were both ushered into Commander Rosa's office, where we stood for a moment while the commander continued looking down at his desk at the eval and written statement spread out in front of him. He looked up at me, then at Chief Clarin, then back at me. "Look," he said to me, "what's the deal here?"

"Sir," I said, "in block 1, Professional Knowledge, I should be rated a 3.0. I'm the only guy in my shop who has these quals."

The rating system went from 1.0, "Below standards," to 4.0, "Greatly exceeds standards." I had been qualified as a NATOPS instructor, and at the time I was the only third-class petty officer in the squad who had done so. It's hard enough for a senior guy to get this qual, let alone a junior guy. I wasn't even asking for a 4.0, just a 3.0, "Above standards." Clarin had rated me with a 2.0, "Progressing."

Commander Rosa looked at each of us again in turn, saying nothing, his face reddening. The chief looked like an idiot. It was clear that he had given me this poor rating purely because he didn't like me.

The CO turned back to me and said, "Petty Officer Webb, if the chief can't figure this out, you write your own eval." He paused, then said, "That's all."

We were both free to go.

I did not leave the WESTPAC early but was kept on for the full six months. Not long after this encounter, Chief Clarin transferred out of HS-6. We did not stay in touch.

My experience on those two WESTPAC tours taught me another powerful lesson about leadership great and lousy.

When I had first deployed on the USS *Lincoln,* back in May of 1995, it didn't take long to realize that morale on the ship was generally horrible. "This ship stinks," I heard people say, and it was true. It was unkempt and funky. Everyone hated being there.

The strangest thing happened on the *Lincoln*. For a few weeks, there was a pervert running around. This guy, whoever he was, would come quietly up to the door of a female crew's room, slip one hand inside the door, hit the lights, then run in, cop a quick feel, and run out again. It freaked us all out. This was the kind of thing you might expect on a college campus, and even there it would be creepy—but on a Navy fighting vessel?

Here is the most bizarre thing about it: They never caught him. Nobody ever knew who it was. In a way it was ridiculous, almost absurd, but it was also unnerving, not only for the women, who never knew when the guy would show up, but for the rest of us, too. In a weird way, the episode underlined that pervasive queasy sense that the place was never under tight command.

The following year, when my second WESTPAC deployment came around, I dreaded it. This time we would be stationed on the USS *Kitty Hawk*. This old boat was not a spanking new nuclear vessel like the *Lincoln*; it was a conventionally powered ship that had been around since Vietnam. When our squadron deployed onto its deck, my heart sank. I figured if the brand-new ship was such a shitty experience, then this one was going to be downright awful.

But it wasn't. In fact, it was the opposite. The moment I was on board the *Kitty Hawk* I could feel the difference. It was clean. The crew was happy. Everything hummed along. This place was wired tight.

It didn't take long to understand why. That first night I was surprised to hear the captain of the *Kitty Hawk* come over the PA loudspeaker, welcoming us and giving us a brief rundown of what was happening that day.

This *never* happened on the *Lincoln*. The captain of that vessel hardly ever talked to his crew. Never said a goddam word. It was weeks, months, before we ever heard his voice over that PA system, and that happened maybe twice during the entire six-month stretch.

Not on the *Kitty Hawk*, though. It wasn't just the first day that the captain addressed us. He did it again the next day, and the next—and every one of the roughly 180 days we were aboard his ship.

"Good afternoon, shipmates, this is your captain," the familiar voice would say. "This is what we're doing, here's where we're going, these are the decisions we're making." He never revealed any details or specific plans that he shouldn't have, but he made sure that everyone felt included in what we were doing.

The difference this made was amazing. It may have been a much older vessel, but it was spotless. Morale was consistently high.

The two experiences were like night and day, and the difference came down to a single factor: Captain Steven John Tomaszeski and the leadership he brought to the ship's crew. That crew loved their captain because he took care of them, and they knew it. I would have ridden that boat to the gates of hell with Captain Tomaszeski, and I'm pretty sure every single person on that boat felt the same way.

This was a lesson I would see played out again and again, and it's one I have striven to embody every day, whether it was running a covert op in Afghanistan or Iraq, reorganizing the SEAL sniper course in the States, or in business since getting out of the service. People need to be talked to and kept in the loop.

Years later I often found myself reflecting on the lesson of the two captains: the importance of talking to your people, sharing the plan with them so they know where you're headed and the purpose behind it. It's not rocket science. Engage your crew. Have a dialogue; let them know that you know they exist and that they're part of what you're all up to. Leaving people in a vacuum is no way to lead, yet it's a mistake I've seen made way too many times.

When I got back from that second WESTPAC in April of 1997, there were orders waiting for me at North Island. I was elated. It had been more than four years since I first set foot in Orlando for boot camp, and after a seem-ingly endless stream of obstacles, I was finally on my way to BUD/S.

I went to the squadron office to pick up my orders and found Lieutenant Commander John Vertel there, subbing for our usual position officer. John was an excellent pilot and a great guy. We called him "Admi-ral." It was great to see him.

However, it was not so great once I saw what he handed me. There were my orders to BUD/S, all right, along with another eval. I glanced through it and felt my face pale. Normally, when you transfer out to another station you're going to get a decent eval. On this eval, they'd given me a low rating in the Professionalism category.

"Sir," I said, "excuse me, but what is this? I'm being dinged for lack of professionalism?"

"Here's the thing, Brandon," he said. "You're excellent at everything you do, but sometimes you're too hard on some of the pilots. Everyone kind of noticed it."

I had to stop for a second and think about that.

Was I sometimes hard on my pilots? Yes, if I was going to be brutally honest with myself. I'm somewhat aggressive by nature, and I knew I needed to learn how to tone it down a bit at times. If you're too aggressive in the back of the helo, that can transfer to the ready room. There's an expression in the military, "Shit rolls downhill," and if you dump on some-one, the chances are good he'll turn around and dump on someone else.

At the same time, the pilots I was hard on deserved it; hell, they *needed* it. There were some solid pilots in the squad whom I respected, and I *never* gave them a hard time. John was one of those; another was Jim Cluxton, who ended up being the training officer of a helo squadron. It was an honor to serve with both of them. But there were also guys who were more mar-ginal on the stick, and I did *not* respect them. After all, one of them had almost gotten us killed in the Persian Gulf.

Still, justified or not, I could see that my leadership style could stand some refining.

Okay, they had a point—but no one had said anything about this to me before. Wasn't that why we had reviews, before the formal evals came out, so they could tell us where we were strong and where we needed improving?

I took a deep breath.

"Sir," I said, "that's great, and I acknowledge it and take it for what it is. The problem is, this is the first time I'm hearing about it, in this formal eval situation. Prior to this I was never given the opportunity to correct the deficiency. To be honest, sir, I'm happy to get the fuck out of here. I've worked my butt off to get these orders, and I appreciate it. I just want to get that point across."

He nodded and sent me off with my orders. The next day he called me back into his office.

"Webb," he said, "you're absolutely right. Here—" and he showed me my eval. Under Professionalism, where it had read 2.0, it now read 4.0.

He nodded. "Best of luck."

Even though I already had my orders to go to BUD/S, I still had to demonstrate that I could pass the Physical Screening Test, or PST, before I could check into the program. Here is a quick overview of the minimum requirements applicants are required to exceed:

- a 500-yard (460-meter) swim, breaststroke or sidestroke, in 12.5 minutes or less (9 minutes or less is better, if you want to be seen as competitive)
- at least 42 push-ups in 2 minutes (shooting for at least 100 to be competitive)
- at least 50 sit-ups in 2 minutes (again, preferably 100 or more)

- at least 6 pull-ups from a dead hang (no time limit, but you want to shoot for a dozen or more)
- a 1.5-mile (2.4-kilometer) run in boots and pants, in under 11.5 minutes (better yet, under 9 minutes).

That Friday, I went down to the pool where the test was being held and found myself grouped up with a bunch of guys who were all going through the PST. We got down there in the pool and did our swims, then got out and hiked across the street, where we did our sequence of push-ups, sit-ups, and pull-ups. After that, they took us outside for our 1.5-mile run, with boots.

We waited around for a few minutes while they tallied up all our times, then got our results. I almost crapped in my pants. My run time was twelve minutes—thirty seconds past the absolute maximum. *Thirty seconds.* Not only was I not competitive, but I had actually failed the test. And not by a sliver of a margin: I had failed it badly. The memory of the devastation I felt has stayed with me ever since. I had run smack into the last and toughest obstacle in my four-year quest: *myself.*

It's easy to remember the times you excelled, the tests you passed, the achievements you scored. It's not as much fun to remember those times when you failed—even worse, those times you failed miserably—but often it's those failures, and not the wins, that end up securing your future.

I told myself that the important thing was not to feel sorry for myself, to get my shit together. I practiced that test over and over until I knew beyond any shadow of a doubt that I had it nailed, and then I took it again. This time I passed, and it felt great. But I was still badly overestimating what kind of shape I was in.

I would find out soon enough.

FOUR
NEMESIS

On Friday morning, June 14, 1997, two days after my twenty-third birthday, I arrived in my dress whites on the main quarterdeck of the pretraining office in Coronado to check in for Basic Underwater Demolition/SEAL training. It had taken me more than four years to get this far, and I was aware that the odds of making it through the course were somewhere between one and three out of ten. I was nervous as hell.

The grunt on duty handed me a check-in sheet with a list of signatures to collect that would grant me admission, signatures for such items as Medical, Dental, Admin, and Physical Training Rehabilitation and Remediation, or PTRR. As I scanned the page, I heard a roar like the crash of a gigantic surf coming from outside. The sound practically shook the building.

"FORTY-NINE! FIFTY! FIFTY-ONE!"

It was a BUD/S class doing their PT on the grinder, the

legendary concrete-and-asphalt courtyard just outside the quarterdeck doors where BUD/S calisthenics take place. I can still feel the shivers that ran up my spine as I stood there in the sweltering June heat hearing the thunder those guys produced.

Walking outside, I saw about thirty hard-looking guys in brown shirts and tan UDT shorts doing PT in the courtyard with a chiseled blond instructor leading them through the exercises. The students were lined up on the black concrete, their feet positioned atop staggered rows of small white frog-feet outlines painted onto the grinder's surface. Just off the edge of the concrete hung a shiny brass ship's bell with a well-worn braided rope trailing down from the ringer. At the foot of the bell, more than a hundred green helmets lined the ground in a neat, mournful row, each helmet inscribed with the name and rank of one more would-be SEAL who would never go on to graduate training.

"SIXTY-ONE! SIXTY-TWO! SIXTY-THREE!"

This was the infamous brass bell, one of the most dreaded symbols of SEAL lore. If you reached the point where you decided you just couldn't take it, I'd heard, where the training was just too brutal to go on, you would signify that you were stepping out by leaving the grinder and ringing the brass bell three times. You would leave your class helmet behind. The brass bell was a one-way street out of BUD/S.

It was good to finally see that thing, sitting there silently suspended in the air as if it were taunting me. *Go on, sit there and wait,* I almost murmured out loud. *I'll be damned if I'll ever touch you.*

I walked to the PTRR check-in office to get my processing started. The door was closed, and I had to knock quite loudly to be heard over the roar of the class as they counted out their push-ups.

"EIGHTY-FIVE! EIGHTY-SIX! EIGHTY-SEVEN!"

"Have a seat," said a guy about my age, sitting on a bench outside the door. "They'll be right with us." I sat down next to him and asked him what duty station he was from. He told me he'd come here right out of boot camp. He nodded at the guys we were both watching.

"They just finished Hell Week," he said. "That's why they look so hard and fired up." We both sat and watched the thirty guys pounding out their PTs. "That's why they're wearing those brown shirts," he added. "They give you those when you survive Hell Week. *If* you survive Hell Week."

Everyone in the navy knew about Hell Week, which comes near the end of First Phase, typically starting on a Sunday evening and ending the following Friday. Hell Week is where you are pushed hard for five and a half days straight, with scarcely more than an hour's sleep per day, right up to the limits of physical and especially mental fortitude.

I was sitting there gazing at these guys who were in a place I envied, chatting with my new buddy, swapping bits and pieces we'd heard about Hell Week, when I was suddenly snapped to attention by a voice that sliced the air like a steel blade.

"What the fuck do you think you're doing?" The blond instructor had focused his attention on the two of us. *"What are you looking at?"* Clearly this was a rhetorical question, and I didn't even try to answer.

"You are not fit to breathe the same air as this class!" he yelled at us. "If you know what's best, you will *turn the fuck around* and *shut the fuck up,* or I will personally ensure that you are on the first boat leaving San Diego Bay for the western Pacific Ocean *this week!"*

Jesus. I hadn't even started checking in, and here I was already being faced with the threat of going back to the fleet. I quickly turned the fuck around and shut the fuck up, and my benchmate followed suit. A few minutes later we were let into the PTRR office and given our room assignments. We would be starting the following week.

BUD/S Class 215 consisted of 220 men, at least at the outset. That number wouldn't hold for long. BUD/S training is broken into three phases, preceded by a five-week indoctrination phase, called indoc. The six weeks of First Phase focus on physical conditioning and include the infamous Hell Week. Second Phase consists of eight weeks of diving and water skills, and Third Phase, nine weeks of land warfare. The whole thing adds up to more than seven months, the whole purpose of which really boils down to one of two things: to prepare you for the real training, which comes after you graduate—or to spit you out.

It started spitting us out right away.

That first week of indoc we all did the initial BUD/S PT test over again, and not all of us passed. Just during indoc, we lost twenty guys. Boom. Ten percent of the class gone, and we hadn't even started First Phase yet.

There were two guys in my BUD/S class whom I already knew from that pre-BUD/S course we'd taken in Great Lakes a year earlier: Rob "Disco" Stella and Lars, the blond überdude with the tree-trunk thighs. Stella was quite the comedian and became a good friend. Lars I never had the chance to know well; in our first week of First Phase, he quit.

Our first week. This completely flipped me out. Seeing guys like Lars quit, especially so early on, was a revelation. This was not about who could do the most push-ups or the shortest run times. This was about persevering, about not quitting. These guys might be able to knock out twice as many pull-ups as I could, but that didn't necessarily mean they could handle the mental stress—being constantly yelled at, ripped apart, and put down, at the same time that we were being put through physically punishing environments.

Over the coming months, I saw guys who looked like Conan the Barbarian, accomplished athletes who had been at the top of their game in professional sports, who had qualified for Olympic trials, seriously tough, mean-looking dudes, cry like babies as they walked across the grinder to go ring that brass bell. And I saw guys who weighed barely 100 pounds take the most brutal physical and psychological punishment and keep on trucking without complaint.

However, there was little time or cause to feel smug about any of this. Frankly, I was relieved to have made the first cut. I knew that the first six weeks was a weeding-out process—and that I was already a pretty good candidate for being one of the early weeds. As I had feared would happen, my long months on the USS *Kitty Hawk* had made me soft. Before checking in to BUD/S I had taken a thirty-day leave, and I spent a lot of those thirty days trying like hell to get back into some kind of condition. By the time I got to BUD/S, I thought I was in pretty decent shape. I quickly learned that I was wrong.

In fact, I learned it on the first Monday morning of First Phase.

Our PTRR instructor in charge said a few words and turned us over to the First Phase instructor staff. Everyone in the class knew that we were about to enter a world of hurt, and the moment we were handed over to the First Phase staff on that warm mid-July morning, we did. All two hundred of us had lined up on those staggered white frog feet painted on the black grinder, and we now faced someone we would quickly recognize as our worst enemy.

The men who gravitate to become First Phase instructors are among the most physically fit people on the planet. They see themselves as guardians of the gate, and they are there to punish and bring the pain. They are the most feared, meanest, ugliest, most physically conditioned guys you'll ever meet. We had eight instructors for First Phase, but four of them comprised the A-list, the ones who would be a constant abrasive presence in our lives until we either made it on to Second Phase or rang that damned brass bell.

Instructor Kowalski was a monster of a guy, 6'4", pushing 300 pounds and all of it muscle and bone.

Instructor O'Reilly, a menacing Irishman with strawberry blond hair, 6'3" and completely ripped, looked like he was carved out of a freaking piece of granite.

Instructor Buchanan was slightly younger and smaller, with a more average build, but he had a cocky swagger and the excellent conditioning to back it up. He was a tremendous athlete and mean as hell.

Finally, there was Instructor Shoulin.

In Greek mythology Nemesis was the spirit of divine retribution against those who offended the gods. Nemesis was a goddess without remorse, a deity whose sole motivating force was exacting vengeance. In modern usage, the word has come to mean "archenemy." Sherlock Holmes had his Moriarty; Superman had his Lex Luthor.

In BUD/S, I had Instructor Shoulin.

I never knew Instructor Shoulin's first name. He was a small guy, Norwegian, with ice blue eyes and an ice cold heart. He was all business. Of the four he had perhaps the least imposing appearance, at least superficially—and appearances most definitely are deceiving. All our instructors were incredibly tough on us, but if they were demons from hell, as far as I was concerned, Instructor Shoulin was Satan himself.

I would learn about Instructor Shoulin in time. Today it was Instructor Buchanan who gave us our initiation. Shirtless, cut like a jungle tiger, he stood on his four-foot podium looking down at us, ready to stomp us all, his vantage point ensuring that any weakness would be immediately identified and dealt with accordingly.

Then it started. First evolution, as they call it, was grinder PT, and he truly brought the pain: two hours of grueling punishment.

"Push-ups! Are you ready?"

"Hooyah!"

"ONE! TWO! THREE! FOUR!"

After we passed a hundred I started to shake. I couldn't support my own body weight; my arms were on fire and giving out.

"On your feet . . . On your back . . . Push-ups! Ready? Begin! ONE! TWO! . . . Flutter kicks, are you ready? ONE! TWO! THREE! . . . ONE HUNDRED FIVE! ONE HUNDRED SIX . . . !"

I immediately stood out as a weak link. I kept falling behind in the cadence. All eight of our First Phase instructors were there to welcome us, and within minutes I had arrived at the very top of all their shit lists. It wasn't just my physical condition. A lot of my classmates had come right from boot camp. Coming in as a fleet guy, I had a bit of seniority—and they really don't like guys with a regular-navy mentality. It's culture clash, and they give fleet guys a little bit of extra business.

Between my fleet background and my subpar physical shape, I was the one out of two hundred who stood out like a turd in a punchbowl. With our last names neatly stenciled on our white shirts, they knew exactly who we all were, and all I kept hearing was our instructors shouting my name in conjunction with obscenities.

"Webb, you fucking piece of stinking dog shit! How the fuck did you make it through the door? If you look up weakness in the dictionary, they have a picture of you next to the text!"

Soon I couldn't even tell what evolution I was supposed to be on.

I remember hearing "Hit the surf zone!" multiple times. Hitting the surf zone involved running about 500 yards out of the compound and down onto the beach, getting completely wet and sandy (and if the instructors found a dry spot, you were back down there immediately to do the job right), and then sprinting back to the grinder for more punishment. The ice-cold Pacific ocean was actually a welcome break—but soon I was shivering uncontrollably and had sand in places I never thought possible.

Off to the side of the grinder there was a podium that held a roster book in which we signed up for remedial PT training sessions if we were so instructed. At the end of that first session, I was so instructed. I limped over to the podium and wrote my name in the book. Each morning I would now have to finish wolfing my breakfast earlier than everyone else and run back to start in on the remedial fitness training session and *then* join in on the regular evolutions with everyone else.

Our day started at 5:00 A.M. on the beach with grueling PT and from there on was a never-ending endurance contest of both flesh and will. By the second week my hands were shredded. I developed two calluses on my left hand and three on my right, all five of them soon ripped off with a half-inch of flesh exposed from doing those wet and sandy push-ups on the beach. When the class corpsman applied tincture benzoate to seal the wounds and prevent infection, it felt like he was sticking a hot iron into each wound. I could barely stand up in the morning. My arms were aching. My body was in complete breakdown.

It didn't matter: They would still single me out. I was marked. They have a saying in BUD/S training, "Don't be *that guy.*" *That guy* is one the instructors pick on, the one who's always on the receiving end of the worst punishment. Whatever you do, you do not want to be *that guy.*

I was *that guy.*

The following four weeks were utter misery. Everyone in the class quickly came to know me by name, because it was the name our instructors typically called out to do an extra hundred push-ups before dismissing the class and allowing us to run across to the other side of the base for chow. It was humiliating, degrading, and painful. I would get up to FORTY-TWO! and suddenly hear, "Webb, you piece of shit! Start over!" While this was going on, the rest of the class was forced to remain in the lean and rest (that is, push-up) position and participate in my wretchedness. I can still hear the plaintive sounds of Class 215 pleading with me, "Webb, for Chrissakes, do a hundred good ones so we can get the hell out of here!"

It was terrible to see those guys suffer because I was so out of shape. I quickly learned that as a team you are capable of great feats—but ultimately you are only as strong as your weakest link. Unfortunately, the weakest link in this case was me.

To the standard PT routines we'd done in our entrance physical (two thousand push-ups, one thousand flutter kicks, et al.), our instructors now added new punishments: a 1-mile base swim in under seventy minutes, then another 1-mile base swim in under fifty minutes, then a 1.5-mile ocean swim in under seventy-five minutes, working up to a 2-mile ocean swim, which was the standard for the rest of BUD/S. A 50-meter underwater swim. A 4-mile timed run, in boots and pants on soft sand, in thirty-two minutes or less.

Those 4-mile conditioning runs just about killed me. Since we were running 5 miles to and from breakfast, 5 more for lunch, and 5 more for dinner, we were now running a total of 19 miles a day. On the 4-mile I kept ending up in the back of the pack, a.k.a. the Goon Squad. Being in the Goon Squad meant that while everyone else was stretching, drinking water, and having a brief recoup, we few unfortunate dregs were getting destroyed doing bear crawls up and down the beach and push-ups in the surf. Day after day, I got Goon-Squaded every time. Soon I learned to push myself so hard in that damn conditioning run that I would throw up as I ran. Eventually I began just making the cutoff to keep myself out of the Goon Squad.

Then, of course, there was the dreaded O-course, in fifteen minutes or less.

As I mentioned earlier, the BUD/S O-course was built for pain and suffering. It is one of the best-constructed obstacle courses in the world. In start-to-finish order, the course consists of the following:

- *Parallel bars.* You shimmy along a set of steel tubes canted at an upward angle for 12 feet.
- *Tires.* Multiple tires spread out that you have to step through rapidly.
- *Low wall.* An 8-foot plywood wall you jump up and swing over.
- *High wall.* This one is about double the height of the low wall; you use a thick rope to climb up and over.

- *Low barbed-wire crawl.* Exactly what it sounds like: Stay low or hook skin.
- *100-foot-high cargo net.* Climb up and over.
- *Balance logs.* You run along a series of rolling logs while keeping your balance (or trying to).
- *Hooyah logs.* "Hooyah" is the ultimate SEAL catchall word, meaning everything from "Yes, Instructor!" to "Oh, fuck!" to "Fuck you!" This is a pile of 3-foot logs that you step up and over while holding your hands up over your head.
- *Rope transfer.* Climb up one rope, transfer to another, then slide down.
- *Dirty Name.* Aptly named (yes, we actually called it Dirty Name), a double set of log beams: You jump up, grab the first log beam, and pull yourself up, then get to your feet and jump up and onto the higher log beam, swing around and over, and drop down to the sand. This station is a rib-breaker, which is how it got its name.
- *Weaver.* Metal bars spaced about 3 feet apart and shaped like a shallow triangle. Weave over and under, all the way up, then down, and you're out.
- *Burma bridge.* Climb a 15-foot rope, then transition to an unstable rope bridge, cross the bridge, and slide down a second 15-foot rope on the other side.
- *Hooyah logs* again.
- *Slide for Life.* A four-story set of platforms with an angled rope that slopes down about 100 feet to the bottom. Climb up all platforms to the top, then mount the rope from the bottom with your legs wrapped around, hang with your arms, and worm your way down. Next, transition to an assault style on top position (much quicker). Disrespect this one and

you have broken bones, which happened constantly. Fall off
and you have a good chance of getting medically disqualified
from BUD/S.

- *Rope swing.* Grab the rope on the run and swing up, then
  let go at just the right moment to hop up and onto a high balance log beam.
- *Tires* again.
- *Incline wall.* Scoot up, slide over and down.
- *Spider wall.* A high plywood-and-log wall you climb up and
  shimmy along sideways. Similar to rock climbing, it's all
  about finger and toe strength.
- *Vaults.* A series of logs set at intervals. Jump up and over
  each one on your way to a sprint finish.

For the first few obstacles, I had no problem. Parallel bars, tires, low
wall, high wall, barbed-wire crawl—I was doing great, or at least keeping
up. The first obstacle that gave me trouble was the Weaver. It slowed me
down, and by the time I got to the top of the Slide for Life I was whipped.
Soon I found myself hanging on for dear life by my legs, four stories up and
upside down. All my grip strength was gone, and my hands were burning
from the torn calluses. We've had guys drop off that rope and break arms
and legs. In a last-ditch effort not to fall, I hooked both elbows over the
top of the rope and attempted to recover some grip strength.

Within a few seconds Instructor Kowalski was screaming at me.
"Webb, you big piece of shit!" (This was Instructor Kowalski's habitual
form of address for me.) "You have two seconds to let the fuck go of that
rope with your fucking elbows, and you already used them up!" He ordered
me to let go *now* and shimmy the hell down.

I unhooked my elbows and continued to hang upside down by my
legs, delaying the inevitable four-story fall. *Oh, shit,* I thought, *this is going*

to hurt. A memory flashed through my mind of a hapkido class I'd taken when I was a kid, when we'd been taught the importance of knowing how to survive a fall. That memory, together with some dumb luck, saved me from getting too badly hurt. I let go, and a terrifying moment later I hit the ground like a sack of ready-mix concrete.

I lay there in pain for a few seconds.

Instructor Kowalski walked over, kicked me in the stomach, and said, "Hey, you alright?"

"Hooyah, Instructor Kowalski," I managed to get out.

"Well then *get your ass up* and get going!" he yelled.

I got my ass up and got going.

When I had finished, one of the guys in the class said, "God, man, we all saw you fall from that thing, and we thought you were finished!" I wasn't, at least not yet.

Our water skills training in First Phase were modeled on the experiences of the underwater demolition team (UDT) guys in World War II, who were the SEALs' direct predecessors. These guys would swim ashore secretly, ahead of a troop landing, with nothing beyond their mask, fins, and snorkel but a demo knife and explosives, to scout out and blow up any obstacles that the enemy might have planted to prevent our flat-bottomed landing craft from coming ashore. In Second Phase we would get into more intensive water training, but for now they walked us through the basic skills of underwater demolition: breath hold (no tanks), long underwater swims, underwater knot tying, and the like. The point was to get used to the water, push our limits, and realize that we could go a lot further than we thought we could go.

I'd done drown-proofing in Search and Rescue school; now I got it again, but ratcheted up a notch. Hands tied behind my back, feet tied together, tossed into a 20-foot dive tank, I had to survive for an hour doing various exercises like diving down and picking up objects on the bottom of the pool with my mouth.

They had us do hydrographic surveys, another old-school remnant from World War II days when the UDT guys would swim in close to shore, gather as much data as they could, and put it into a hand-drawn map for the landing crews (or use it to blow things up). They lined up ten of us on the beach, spaced about 2 yards apart, and sent us walking out into the surf with small boards to write on. We jotted down data until we couldn't touch bottom, and at that point we swam out with a lead line that we dropped down to take soundings as we kept heading farther offshore, 12 feet, 15 feet, 20 feet, and on. Eventually we started diving down for obstacles in our lane, mapping out everything we could find, before returning to shore and putting all the data we'd collected into a hydrographic chart.

If it sounds exacting and tedious, it was—only it came at the end of an incredibly long, brutally hard day when we were exhausted, ready to hit barracks and collapse. We had to get each detailed chart exactly right, *perfectly* right, or the instructor would rip it up and send us back out into the night surf to do it over again.

The water tests in First Phase were tough. We did an underwater breath-hold 50-meter swim, which went like this: We jumped into the pool feet first (we weren't allowed to push off the wall), did a somersault, then went 50 meters down and back, holding our breath the whole way. Guys were popping up to the surface like goldfish corpses. Not that they had quit intentionally—they had just passed out.

Another water test was the underwater knot-tying trial. You submerge, tie your first knot, then wait for your instructor to inspect and approve it. Once your work is okayed, you go up to surface for a moment, catch a breath, then go down to tie the next knot, and on through a series of five knots in all.

Typically the instructor takes his time inspecting your knot, looking it over very slowly and methodically. Not because he needs to, but just to bust your balls. What he's really doing is trying his best to force you to run out of air. This is exactly what happened to me—only with a twist.

Instructor Shoulin really had it in for me, so it should have come as no surprise when he came over to "support" the underwater knot-tie exercise and singled me out. "You're in my lane, Webb," he said. What he really meant was *You're mine now, I own you, you piece of shit.*

There was something about me that Instructor Shoulin didn't know: I practically grew up underwater. I may have been a wreck physically and at the bottom of the heap in basic PT, but when it came to water skills, I felt I could do anything they threw at me. That attitude would get me in trouble later, but for the moment it served me pretty well.

We dove down under, Instructor Shoulin on my tail like a shark tracking a baby seal. I tied my first knot. He started looking it over, real slow. He couldn't find anything wrong with it, and I knew it, and he knew that I knew it—but that didn't make any difference. He took forever, knowing there was nothing I could do but sit there and take it.

Finally he looked over and gave me the thumbs-up: *This one's okay, you can surface now.* Only I didn't head up to the surface. Instead, I methodically moved on and started tying my second knot. I didn't dare look in his direction, but I sure wish I had. I'd love to know what the expression on his face looked like.

After I finished the second knot and he had inspected it (more quickly this time) and approved it, I ignored his *Okay, you can surface now* gestures once again and went on, starting in on my third knot.

That was it. Instructor Shoulin couldn't hold out any longer—he went up to the surface to gasp for air. He was so pissed off. I had embarrassed him. I was pretty sure I'd pay for it, too.

By the fifth week of First Phase, I was a wreck: exhausted, humiliated, just about beaten into a corner. Then one afternoon, just a few days before Hell Week was to begin, it all came to a head.

Every afternoon we formed up in seven-man boat crews, grabbed our heavy rubber boats, threw them up on top of our heads, and ran with them to the beach to get tortured for a while. On this particular afternoon we were on our way out to the beach when Instructor Shoulin called over to my team. "Webb, get over here."

Michaelson, my boat crew leader, said, "Hey, what's up, Instructor Shoulin? Where is he going?"

"Don't worry about Webb," he replied. "Just go get your fucking boat ready." I looked over and realized that O'Reilly, Buchanan, and Kowalski were all with him. *Uh-oh.* I peeled away from my boat crew and headed with them out to a section of beach where it was just us, alone: me and the four alpha instructors.

"Drop, Webb," said one of them. "Eight-counts, begin." This was one of their favorite forms of punishment. The eight-count bodybuilder goes like this:

1. Start from a standing position.
2. Drop to a squat, hands on ground.
3. Push legs back to basic push-up position.
4. Execute a push-up.
5. Scissor-kick your legs apart.
6. Legs back together in push-up position.
7. Pull your legs up to your chest.
8. Jump back up to standing position.

They had me do a hundred of these babies, then took me through push-ups, flutter kicks, the whole works, and all the while they were shoveling sand in my face and yelling at me, all four of them, at the top of their lungs.

"You are a worthless piece of shit, Webb! Do you even know what a piece of shit you are? You are the biggest piece of shit we've ever seen! You're weighing your whole class down. You are a one-man walking disaster. You are fucking it up for everyone else. You don't belong here, you fleet piece of shit. Do you even know how badly you're fucking this up, how much everyone wants you gone? You're a disgrace, Webb. You're garbage. You need to quit. Nobody wants you in Hell Week."

On and on for the next hour. It was beyond brutal. I could feel how intensely they all wanted me to get up, limp away, and go ring that goddam brass bell.

The worst of it was, I knew they were right. There was a reason they were singling me out. I *was* physically out of shape, and that *had* been affecting the entire class, and that bothered me. In fact, this is something I've continued to be conscious of and careful about to this day: If you show up late, if you don't have your gear together, or your facts together, or whatever shit it is you need to have together, then you are affecting the whole team. They were right, and it was a lesson I would never forget.

If I was not physically as tough as I needed to be, I had one thing going for me. I was very tough mentally.

There is a common misperception that to make it through SEAL training you have to be a superathlete. Not so. In its purely physical requirements, the course is designed for the average athletic male to be able to make it through. What SEAL training really tests is your mental mettle. It is designed to push you mentally to the brink, over and over again, until you are hardened and able to take on any task with confidence, regardless of the odds—or until you break.

I was not about to break.

My body at this point was nowhere near as conditioned as it would become in the months and years ahead, but mentally, I was ready for anything. That was the only reason I survived that hour on the beach. That was the only reason I made it through BUD/S.

People have asked if I ever thought about quitting during the SEAL training, if I ever had one of those dark-night-of-the-soul moments you hear about, those moments of piercing doubt and anguished uncertainty. The answer is *Never—not once*. Lying there facedown in the sand with these four hardcase psychopaths doing their level best to break me, something else happened instead: I got what we call a fire in the gut.

Of the four, it was Instructor Buchanan who was the most in my face. So I looked up at him, nailed him with the coldest stare I could muster, and said, "Fuck you, Instructor Buchanan—*fuck* you. The only way you're getting me out of here is in a body bag."

He glared back at me, gauging me, weighing my intent. I meant every word, and he knew it. He took one step back and jerked his head, gesturing up the beach toward where my boat crew was prepped and waiting. "Get back to your crew" was what he said, but the way he said it made it sound like "The hell with you."

From that point on, my experience in BUD/S completely turned the corner. Those instructors left me alone. When Hell Week started a few days later, it felt almost anticlimactic. *Welcome to my world*, I felt like saying to the other guys. I'd been playing these games throughout First Phase.

There is a saying in BUD/S: Ideally you want to become the gray man. In other words, you become invisible, nobody notices you, because you do everything so perfectly that you never stand out.

I had gone from *that guy* to gray man.

Which is not to say that Hell Week was easy. It was as brutal as all the legends say, and then some. From the morning it began, my classmates started winking out like cheap lightbulbs.

The first night, they disoriented us. We were up all night, and that was only the beginning, because we were going to be up for five days and nights straight. Sunday, Monday, Tuesday, and Wednesday were the worst. If you were hanging in there by Tuesday night you didn't have a lot of company, because most of the guys had already quit. They really brought on the cold and the punishment those first three days.

They had us do something they called steel pier. At two in the morning, they walked us into the ocean and threw us on a steel barge, where we lay half naked, our body temperature dropping to hypothermia levels. Then, just as I didn't think we could hang on to consciousness any longer, they had us get up, jump in the water—and then climb out and get back on the pier. This went on for four hours. It was pure misery. That first night we heard the air broken by the doleful sound of that brass bell ringing through the dark, again and again.

One way they kept us busy during Hell Week was having us do log runs. Seven of us would lift a huge log—essentially a telephone pole—and heft it up onto our shoulders, carrying it while being force-marched at a steady trot, sloshing through the surf, instructors right behind us yelling at us. After 6 miles through the surf line, we put down our telephone pole, drank a little water, then picked the log back up, turned around, and headed back the way we'd come, back 6 miles—then dropped the log, grabbed our rubber boat and swung it up onto our heads, and headed the other way again. Another 6 miles, up and back, and so on, for about eight hours. There was one especially huge log, dubbed Ole Misery by past BUD/S students, that had the words MISERY LOVES COMPANY carved into its side. This thing was an evil creature worthy of Stephen King's pen. One class stole it and tried to torch it, but it refused to burn. It's probably still there today, torturing each new class of BUD/S students.

As hard as this all sounds, the physical punishment wasn't the worst of it. It was the psychological torture that broke so many of us and kept that brass bell ringing. We never knew what they were going to pitch at us next. The whole five days was designed to throw us off balance and *keep* us off balance, and it worked.

On day 3 they put us in a tent to get some sleep. We laid our weary bones down on thin, uncomfortable cots, but to us, it felt like heaven. We drifted off—until about fifty minutes later, when my sleep was interrupted by the most unwelcome sound I've ever heard. I don't know if I had been dreaming or was just immersed in the heaven of inky blackness, but all of a sudden lights were going on and I was hearing a voice shouting at me.

"Up, Webb, time to go hit the surf!"

We had just slipped into REM sleep when they woke us back up to start in on us all over again.

I'll tell you what it's like when you have just gone through three solid days of physical punishment, around the clock, and then you finally have the chance to get to sleep, only to be yanked out of it again less than an hour later: It's torture, and that is no figure of speech. In fact, this is one of the most common techniques used in the actual torture of prisoners of war.

I opened my eyes. Guys around me were completely disoriented, jerking upright and staring around desperately, literally not knowing where they were or what the hell was going on. Next thing we knew we were all running out to go lie on the freezing cold beach, right down in the surf, faces toward the ocean so the waves could wash sand and saltwater into our eyes and noses and mouths. I've never had much problem with the cold, but that waking episode was hard.

The worst, though, was the chow runs. In the same way that they gave us just enough sleep to survive, they pared the experience of eating down to the bare minimum.

We not only ran for miles on the beach with those big rubber boats on our heads, we carried them *everywhere*. Some of the guys got cuts, scars, or bald spots from carrying those damned boats. We even had to carry them to chow. When it was time to eat, they raced us to the mess hall, where they had us run around a small building, carrying our boats, while they let a few crews at a time in to eat. I remember the feeling of my neck being jackhammered, my head in pain. Finally it would come our crew's turn to eat. We would quickly put our boat down, run inside, shovel down our food, then run out again.

Sometimes when we got back outside, we realized we were a few people short. *What happened?* we wondered. Those guys never showed up again. They were out. The instructors reshuffled the crew to compensate, according to our height, and off we went again.

Thursday night we did an exercise they called Round the World. Each boat crew paddled its boat out some 20 miles to a checkpoint and then back. It took about eight hours and was all done, of course, at night.

We ran out into the surf, carrying that damned boat on our heads, then heaved it into the water, clambered in, and started paddling like crazy. Hours later, we were still paddling. I looked around and realized that everyone was falling asleep. I whacked a few guys with my paddle and hissed, "Hey! You guys! Stay awake!"

By the time we finished it was deep in the middle of the night. We were the first boat to reach shore, and from out of the gloom came a voice. "Hey! Get over here!" It was Instructor Shoulin. He stepped into our boat like an evil George Washington crossing some Delaware in hell and told us to paddle him out to meet up with the rest of the guys, who were still coming in.

Suddenly I heard Instructor O'Reilly's voice floating in from the direction of the shore. "Webb," it growled, "if you dump boat right now I'll secure you from Hell Week."

What he was saying was, if I would dump Instructor Shoulin into the icy cold water right then and there, fully clothed, then he would give me an immediate free pass out of the rest of Hell Week.

Instructor Shoulin's head swiveled and he stared at me. I didn't say a word, but my face said it all: *Let's dump this fucker!* Instructor Shoulin said in a terrifyingly quiet voice, "Webb, you sonofabitch, if you dump me, you will pay."

I grinned. Looking straight at him, I muttered, "Let's do it!" loud enough for the whole team to hear it. The team was too afraid of him, so it didn't happen—but Instructor Shoulin saw it in my eyes. I was ready to dunk him. I wonder what would have happened if we had.

Friday they put us in a fenced-off area on the beach they had filled with seawater. They called this seawater swamp the demo pit, but it was nothing more than a muddy bog strung with rope bridges. We stood there, exhausted, caked head to toe with mud, barely able to stay on our feet— and they started firing grenade simulators at us.

At this point we were zombies. I don't know how fast I moved, or even if I moved at all. I know some guys just dropped into the bog and lay there.

Then they ran us up to the compound and lined us up on the grinder, and someone said, "Class 215, secured from Hell Week."

Secured. *Secured?*

It was unreal. We had been suffering so badly it felt like time had slowed down and stretched out until the punishment was a raw experience of eternity. It was like the ancient Greeks' concept of hell, Sisyphus pushing a heavy stone up a hill till it was near the top, when it would roll down again and he would have to start over from the bottom, continuing the process forever. Suddenly it was over and we were being handed our brown shirts.

Secured.

I'll never forget the feeling of putting on that dry, warm, clean T-shirt. I ate an entire pizza, drank a quart of Gatorade, called my parents to tell them I'd made it through Hell Week, and crashed into deep sleep. At some point I came to long enough to pee in the empty Gatorade bottle before falling back asleep again. I woke up two days later.

Of our original 220, we were now down to 70.

They gave us two weeks to recover, during which we did some lighter stuff, writing hydrographic charts and such, while we got ourselves ready for what came next: the seven weeks of Second Phase.

The dive phase of BUD/S is in a way the core of the whole course. BUD/S is, after all, fundamentally a course in underwater demolition, so the focus is on water skills. Because I was already a strong diver, I thought this phase would be a breeze.

As it turned out, dive phase was no joke. Yes, they now focused our time more on teaching us specific skills than on raking us over the coals and sifting out the early quitters. Now that we were wearing brown T-shirts, they treated us with a little more respect, but it was still brutal.

Our new instructors were just as intent as our First Phase instructors on letting us know they were not messing around. Right away, they had us on the ground doing push-ups, yelling and screaming in our faces. Whatever else we were doing—our classroom work, dive training, instruction in scuba, how to use a rebreather, and other key dive skills—the basic physical training kept going in the background, every single day, and it got harder and harder, the bar higher and higher, the times shorter and shorter. Our conditioning runs went from 4 miles to 6 miles to 8 miles. All our minimum times started dropping. The 2-mile ocean swim dropped from eighty minutes to seventy; the 4-mile soft-sand run (in boots) went from thirty-two minutes to under twenty-nine; the O-course time dropped from fifteen to eleven minutes.

While we were in the classroom most of the day, it was not what you would think of as a normal classroom. For example, they kept buckets of ice water (which we had to keep filling) placed above us on racks over our heads. If someone started nodding off in class, the instructor could tug on a string—and ice water would pour down over the entire table. This was not community college. This was BUD/S.

About halfway through the dive phase we had a test called pool comp (short for "pool competence") that was Second Phase's version of Hell Week.

I jumped in with my gear, a set of double aluminum 80s and an aqualung rig, and sank down about 15 or 20 feet deep into the combat training tank. Suddenly three instructors were on top of me—they call this a surf hit—and without warning they ripped my mask from my face and yanked off my fins, leaving me with nothing but a set of tanks and a regulator in my mouth.

Then they started in on me, one of them ripping the regulator hose out of my mouth and quickly tying it in knots.

I hadn't known exactly what to expect, but I knew it would be something like this, and I was as ready for it as I could be. That's the drill in pool comp. They put you through five or six really bad situations underwater, and you have to get out of them. If you come up to the surface, you fail.

I also knew that right at the end of the ordeal we would be hit with a truly messed-up situation, something so difficult that it's essentially impossible to get out of. This is called the whammy. You deal with it as best you can, then signal that you're okay and head up to surface. You're not expected to get out of the whammy, just to stick it out as long as you can.

I reached the point where I was sucking air directly out of the tank valve, because I absolutely could not undo the knot that bastard had put in my hose. I'd been down there for maybe fifteen minutes, getting worked over by several instructors, and it had seemed like an eternity. Now I was sucking in whatever air I could get out of that tank, trying to breathe in the little air bubbles that were leaking off my regulator. Finally I figured there was no way out of this whammy, so I signaled and headed up.

As I broke the surface, my instructor said, "Webb, that wasn't the whammy."

"What?" I gasped. That *had* to be the whammy. There was no way anyone could get that hose untied. The pisser of it was, I could have stayed down there longer, but I was positive that my test was over. Well, it wasn't.

I practically felt nauseous. I had failed pool comp on my first try—and we only got two tries. Occasionally they would hold a review board and decide to give someone a third shot at it, but that was the exception, not the rule, and I had no illusion that this would happen for me. No, I had just one shot left.

This was a Friday, so I would have to wait until Monday to retest. That weekend was torture.

Monday finally came. I went back down in the tank, and no matter what they threw at me, I stayed down there. I don't even remember what the whammy was like, because I was so focused on the fact that I was not going to surface, no matter what. I'd stay down there until that tank ran out of air—and then stay down there some more.

Finally an instructor swam down and started shaking me, yanking me up by the hair and making urgent *Come up!* gestures. At that point, I figured it must be okay. It was. My whammy was over.

I was relieved that I passed, but it still blew my mind that it had taken me two tries. I was supposed to excel in anything water related. There was that lesson again, which I would strive to remember always and in all situations: Don't be cocky. Don't make assumptions going into a challenge—ever. No matter what you know, or think you know, put your ego in check, and keep your eyes open to what you can learn.

By the time pool comp was finished, we had lost another twenty guys, one of them being our class officer in charge (OIC), Kim Terrance.

Every BUD/S class has a senior OIC, typically the highest-ranking student in the class. Terrance was a gifted athlete who swam for Stanford and was probably the best swimmer in our class (along with his swim buddy, Travers, about whom I'll say more later). About halfway through Second Phase he ended up being rolled for medical reasons, and we got a new OIC named Rob Byford. Rob was a mustang officer, meaning he had started out as an enlisted man. Having Rob take over as our class OIC was a gift: He was a standout leader who always stood up for his guys, and everyone looked up to him. I keep in touch with him to this day.

Toward the end of Second Phase we had one more test, an open-ocean swim that covered a course of 5.5 nautical miles (a little over 6 statute miles). This evolution had no time limit; we just had to complete it.

When the day came for our swim, the weather had turned bad. In fact, it turned out that we had the worst conditions our instructors had ever seen for this evolution. A persistent south wind had risen up that morning, making the waves choppy. We were going to be swimming due south, the wind and chop in our faces. That wind never let up, not for a moment.

They stood us on the Coronado beach for inspection. We wore nothing but our UDT shorts and a wet-suit top with a beavertail; equipment consisted of a dive knife (which had to be kept sharp as hell), canteen, and signaling flare, along with a mask, pair of Scubapro fins, and UDT life vest with CO_2 cartridge inflator. There would be a safety boat hovering in the vicinity, but that was only for dire emergencies. We would be swimming in pairs, on our own out on the open ocean.

We swam out until we were about a quarter mile from shore, then turned left and headed due south, bound for the Mexican border. That nagging south wind blew in our faces the whole time, making the ocean rough and choppy and dashing cold saltwater in our mouths. It made the swim take forever. That far offshore, and with that constant wind and chop, even keeping our sense of direction was a challenge. Fortunately for me, I had learned how to do this as a kid and was able to pick out landmarks from the mountains onshore, keep my bearings, and swim pretty much a straight line. Looking up every once in a while, I saw other guys (including some who were much faster swimmers than I was) tacking back and forth as they went, swimming in a long series of S-patterns.

After a few miles, my swim buddy, Disco Stella, was having problems keeping up, and he started tapping me periodically so I would slow down. We stopped every so often to tread water and drink from our canteens, but never for more than a few seconds. In an exhausting situation like that, you don't want to lose your momentum, because once you do you might not get it back. Eventually Stella got so tired he went belly up, a dead stop in the middle of the ocean. We had about a mile left to go.

"I need a break, man," he said. "We need to stop."

"No, we have to keep swimming," I said.

"I need some water!"

Both our canteens were empty by now, and Stella was starting to hallucinate.

"Dude," I said, "the only water around here is saltwater. We *can't* stop."

"No, I gotta stop now," he said.

"Look," I pleaded, "just keep going for another mile. We have to make it to the finish line—there'll be plenty of water there."

It did no good. He wouldn't budge. Finally I grabbed him by the belt and started swimming. I swam the whole last damn mile dragging him along with me. I thought that mile would never end. When we finally reached the finish line and I pulled him in to shore, I felt ready to die.

On the bus back to base that night, nobody said a word. Instead of the usual joking and giving each other shit, the bus was filled with a weird, solemn silence.

Third Phase was nine weeks of the basic soldiering skills of land warfare, SEAL-style: explosives and demolition, marksmanship, land navigation and reconnaissance. It didn't get any easier. Our O-course time dropped from eleven minutes to ten and a half, the 4-mile timed run went from twenty-nine minutes to twenty-eight, and they added a 13-mile run, in boots.

As Third Phase began we were issued new equipment. Now, instead of the BUD/S greens we'd been wearing, we got camouflage outfits and web gear, which we call second-line gear. (First-line gear would be the clothes you're wearing, your pants, your belt, and so forth. Second-line or web gear, also called H-gear, is your chest harness, which carries all your magazines for your bullets, your compass, and your other kit. Third-line gear is your backpack.)

We started out doing basic firearms training, both rifle and pistol, first with classroom study and then on to practical application in labs, taking apart the weapons and putting them back together. We also did some shooting, although nothing like what I would be doing later on, in advanced SEAL training. The bulk of this part of Third Phase was a big land navigation course up in the Laguna Mountains east of San Diego. We packed up our gear and a load of MREs (Meals, Ready-to-Eat) and headed up there. It was December 1997, just before Christmas.

After a few days of orientation, we spent a week of classes doing map and compass work. The whole thing culminated in an individual land nav exercise, almost like a race. It was freezing, snow on the ground. We didn't get much sleep. The instructors were sitting around a raging bonfire in the middle of their camp, drinking beer. Not us. In the earlier phases we'd been organized in boat crews; now we were organized into squads of seven guys each, all the squads sprinkled around this big camp. None of us had fires, and they took away our MRE heaters, so we were eating cold food. We were in our tactical layout, boots on, standing watch and rotating every couple of hours.

After a while the instructors started giving radio calls to make sure we were up and paying attention. God help you if you missed a radio call, because if you did, it would be a long night. Luckily in our squad we had our stuff wired tight. When we got called, we answered, and the instructors didn't mess with us. We could hear other guys getting rousted in the middle of the night, and the next morning we could tell they hadn't slept.

The instructors had them running back and forth between their camp and the instructors' camp, doing push-ups in the snow, making their lives just miserable. They were cold and wet all night long. In many ways, it was not so different from what we would be doing a few years later in the mountains of Afghanistan, although there, the stakes would be higher.

We walked away from that land nav exercise knowing how to navigate even without a map or compass.

The land nav portion concluded with a test that dissolved the squads. Now it was every man for himself. The air started crackling with tension. We all knew that if we didn't pass, we didn't graduate.

For the land nav test the instructors had planted a series of navigation points out among the mountains. At each point there was an ammo box with a unique code inside, and when we reached that point we would open the box, radio in that number along with our coordinates, so they'd know we were on the right mountain, and then move on to the next. We had to hit all the points and hit them in the right sequence.

I ran into another one of the guys out there and said, "Hey, how's it going?" He just stared at me, frantic. "I think I just missed my last point!" he blurted, then pointed off into the distance. "I'm supposed to be on that mountain way over there!" He went trundling off frantically through the forest. Poor bastard.

I was lucky: For some reason I did not have much difficulty with the navigation. Here again, I think my background helped. Growing up on the sailboat, being around charts and maps and compasses, I'd learned how to find my way around without street signs, storefronts, and all the usual landmarks most of us learn as kids. As a result, I finished my test a few hours early. I didn't want to go back to camp; they would just find something else for me to do. So I slipped back near to camp, tucked in under a bush, and lay down to catch a few hours of shut-eye.

Next thing I knew I was getting kicked and hearing a familiar voice.

"Webb, what the fuck are you doing?" I opened my eyes and looked up. Was I awake, or was this some cruel nightmare?

It was Instructor Shoulin.

I thought I'd left him behind in First Phase. No such luck. He had dropped in on our Third Phrase land nav test to help out. Of course, he had found me.

"What. The fuck. Are you doing?" he repeated slowly as if speaking to a child.

I didn't really have an answer, and I was just coming out of REM sleep after a long time of no sleep at all, so I wasn't all that coherent. Besides, the question was rhetorical: He knew damn well what I was doing. He checked my coordinates and could plainly see I had finished the course. "You sonofabitch," he growled, and he cracked a slight, evil smile. *Oh, shit.*

For the next thirty minutes, he had me bear-crawling up and down this mountain, on all fours, in the snow. That was my reward for trying to sneak some time off. After torturing me for a while, he finally sent me back to camp. He had made me pay for that little bit of stolen sleep. Although I had to admit, it was worth it.

That day something happened that shook us all.

We had an officer in the class named Travers who had been Kim Terrance's swim buddy. Travers was another outstanding athlete, an absolute physical specimen, and up to that point he had been a gray man, performing smoothly and quietly blending in. During the land nav portion of Third Phase, Travers's squad started screwing up right and left—falling asleep on radio watch, messing up their patrols, just not getting the hang of things and consistently being called out and punished for it. Suddenly, because of the poor performance of his squad, Travers was *that guy.* He couldn't take it—and he threw in the towel. He quit.

I was absolutely stunned. We all were. Travers was not only an accomplished athlete, he was a frigging U.S. Naval Academy *officer.* The standards for these guys are so high and they have been so thoroughly vetted by the time they've reached this point that for one to quit BUD/S was unheard of. He had quit in our sixth month—just five weeks before graduation.

Of all the things that happened throughout BUD/S, Travers's quitting was one of the most sobering. People often assume that Hell Week is the big thing, that once you get past Hell Week you're over the worst of it and it's all downhill from there, but I would have rather done Hell Week twice than have gone through Third Phase. They just kept cranking up the pressure, pushing us to our limits, adding on layers of physical and mental stress, sleep deprivation, and increased responsibility (like working with demolition and live fire while exhausted), and it never let up for a moment.

The next day, Friday, we packed up our site, loaded the trucks, and were just about to pull out when the last few guys who had failed their tests and spent all night doing it over ran into camp wild-eyed and caught our convoy just in time. They were so exhausted they couldn't say a word, but they'd made it.

And just when I thought we'd *all* made it, I found out that for me, at least, it wasn't over yet. Sitting on that bus, as we relaxed and headed back to civilization, my left quad suddenly seized up, just above the knee. It was excruciating—and crippling. I don't know if it was all the adrenaline coursing through my system from the land nav, or the sheer cold, or what caused it, but when I woke up the next morning in Coronado I could barely put any weight on my left leg.

I was now in deep shit. Third Phase wasn't over yet. To meet the criteria for Third Phase we needed to pass at least two out of four timed runs. I still needed one more run—and I could barely walk. I spent that weekend worrying.

The following Monday I went into BUD/S Medical and told the guy I had a bad quad. He pulled my file, glanced at it, and said, "Holy shit."

"What?" I asked.

He looked up at me. "You've never been in here before!"

A few of the guys (we called them Sick Call Commandos) were constantly going in to Medical, complaining about this or that. Almost everyone had been in at least once or twice. Not me. In six months, I had never once come in to Medical.

The guy took care of me, hooked me up, got me on crutches—and I lucked out. It happened that we were just then hitting Christmas break. For the next two weeks all we had to do was show up for one PT a day, and they didn't count toward our passing. That gave me two weeks to heal. I went in every day, and while everyone else did PT I sat and read magazines.

When January came, there was no more putting it off. I had to get out there and finish that 4-mile run, and do it in less than thirty minutes. Strange to say, the instructors were quite encouraging. They knew I was dealing with an honest injury and wasn't sandbagging it. They could see I was in pain.

Four miles is about 6,436 meters, and a meter is about my stride, which means that during that run, my left leg came down hard 3,218 times, and each time was agony. It took everything I had, but I finished the run.

After Christmas we shipped out to San Clemente Island, about 80 miles off the coast of San Diego. This island is completely dedicated to navy activities, and the SEALs have the northwest end to themselves with a BUD/S camp out there we call the Rock.

Once we all got out there, our instructors said, "Hey, fellas, no one can hear you scream out here. You're pretty far away from the flagpole," meaning base command on the coast. There was not a lot of oversight here, no commanding officers strolling by at lunch to see how things were going. These instructors had us out here to themselves, and they made sure we knew it. This was our final four weeks before graduating—or not graduating, as the case might be. They would make sure we each earned it.

There was some sort of physical evolution before each meal, and how well we did determined what our meal experience was going to be. Every meal, we had to earn the right to eat dry.

For breakfast we all lined up outside the compound, separated out by squad. On their signal, they told us, one squad would sprint over to Frog Hill, a big hill nearby, and climb to the top as fast as possible. The first four to reach the top would come down and go eat breakfast. The three stragglers (there were seven men to a squad) would come down off the hill, go jump into the freezing cold ocean, and *then* take breakfast outside, covered with sand and soaking wet.

On the signal we lit out at a dead sprint—seven guys clawing their way up this hill. My lungs were burning. I am not a great runner, and I could still feel that pulled quad. Every morning I found myself smack in the middle of the pack, worried I would fall behind the cutoff point and end up with sand up my ass while I wolfed cold eggs. Somehow I managed to make it into the top four every day.

That was breakfast. For lunch, we had to bang out a minimum of a hundred push-ups with all our gear on: a canteen full of water, magazines full of ammo, and all the rest of our H-gear kit. If we didn't get all our push-ups in on time, we ate lunch wet.

For dinner we had to do an 80-foot rope climb and then a minimum of twenty pull-ups with full kit. Do it, or we were getting wet.

Every morning I woke up with the same thought: *I hope I don't have to eat wet today.*

By this point there were about 40 of us. Of those 40, 17 had been medically rolled in from a previous BUD/S class, which meant that of the 220 when we started six months earlier, there were now 23 of us left. One of those who had rolled in was a guy named Eric Davis.

Eric is a charismatic redhead who looks out for everyone and is impossible not to like. He fit in right away, and we clicked immediately. He's one of the funniest people I know—and one of the most creative. In fact, the way he got himself into BUD/S in the first place involved considerable creativity on his part. When he first applied, he was crushed to learn that his color-blindness disqualified him from even trying out. That defeated him—for about five minutes, which was how long it took him to come up with an elaborate plan for faking his way through the color-blind test. No easy task, but somehow he did it and, sure enough, made his way through BUD/S. He guards his secret strategy to this day.

Call it karma or historic irony, but this came back to bite him many years later, when Eric decided he'd had enough and was ready to get out. I asked him how he planned to do that, since he had just signed up for a lengthy reenlistment. He assured me of his foolproof plan: At his next physical he was finally going to come out to the doctor about his color-blindness. He fully expected that this would give him an early out from his contract—but the doctor refused to believe him, would not even administer the test, and blew Eric off with a clean bill of health. I still give Eric a hard time about this whenever I see him.

Our schedule at the Rock was so intense it felt like we weren't getting any sleep at all. By Third Phase standards, a good night's sleep was three to four hours. Our first week there, Eric said, "Hey, they can't keep this up forever. I mean, we're handling explosives, right? Next week, they've *got* to let us sleep more." As the days wore on he kept assuring us (and no doubt assuring himself at the same time) that it would get better, that they would *have* to let us get a little more sleep.

They didn't: not the next week, or the week after that, or ever.

One night they just about broke us. We had screwed up some exercise or other, and our instructors had us in the water in the northwest harbor for fours hours or so, torturing us. We were just miserable. I heard guys muttering, "Jesus, when is this going to end?"

We had been through treatment like this many times in the past few months, but somehow, this was worse. Whether it was the accumulated weight of the past months' experience or simply the bitter cold that February night, at some point everyone just stopped talking. An eerie silence fell over us as we continued hammering out our PTs, the sounds of legs and arms thrashing in the cold surf punctuated only by the instructors' periodic barked commands.

It's one thing when guys bitch and moan, but when everyone *stops* bitching and moaning, when it all goes silent, that's when you know things are truly serious. We were pushing up against the absolute limits of our physical and mental capacities.

"Out!"

Mercifully, right at that point they called us out of the surf and onto the beach, where they ran us up and down the sand hills for a few minutes to get our circulation going. I have no doubt that as we ran, every one of us was thinking the same identical thought: *Thank God that's over.*

"Hit the surf!"

Were they serious? They were. Just as we started feelings our limbs, they put us back down in that ice-cold surf again, flutter-kicking, arms linked in one long chain of human suffering.

The guy next to me, Chris Osman, started muttering under his breath. *"Fuck* this . . . *fuck* this . . ."

Osman was a former marine who had rolled into our class and was on my squad, and I did not like him. I had to admit, the guy was amazing: he could recall every bit of military minutiae, every detail—the effective range and fire rate of any rifle, which weapons were used in which conflicts, the blasting capacity and recommended application of every conceivable kind of explosive, all kinds of random crap. I thought he must have grown up reading military manuals instead of comic books like the rest of us. The dude was hardcore. I could not get along with him, though. I thought he was a loudmouth. We had almost come to blows a few times. Now it looked like maybe he was starting to crack.

I glanced over Osman's head and caught Eric's eye. Eric happened to be on Osman's other side. Eric and Osman were good friends. Eric and I were good friends. Osman and I hated each other. It was a complicated sandwich.

Suddenly Osman stopped muttering and said out loud at full volume, "Okay, *fuck* this. I am *out* of here! I am *not* doing this anymore!"

"Chris!" Eric hissed. "C'mon, keep it together!"

Good riddance, I told myself, but I didn't think he was serious. He was. He shook himself and broke free of both our grips, shucking off the inviolable circuit of locked arms, ready to walk out of the surf and head on up to the beach. Eric and I both gaped at him, stunned. He was on the verge of quitting the exercise, quitting BUD/S, quitting the SEALs. We were only days away from the end of our course, so close to the finish line—and he was *quitting*.

Except it was so dark out there that no one but the two of us had seen what Osman was doing. We heard a whistle go off, and a crisp voice. *"Okay, move it! Out!"*

The instructors were calling us out of the surf and back onto the beach. There was a dark clatter of splashes as we all scrambled to our feet to make the mad dash up the hill, but by the time we got there Osman was already surrounded by the instructors, not fully grasping what was happening. One instructor grabbed his arm, jerked it up into the air, and yelled at the rest of us.

"You see this? That's what I'm talkin' about! Osman here is the only one out of all you fuckers who's really putting out!"

Suddenly Osman was a hero. The instructors handed him a mug of hot chocolate and told us again what losers we all were, that we hadn't gotten there nearly as fast as Osman did. No one but Eric and I ever knew that the only reason he got there first was that he had had enough and was ready to get the fuck out of there when they blew the whistle.

And here's the amazing thing: Osman and I eventually became friends. In fact, we ended up serving together as SEAL snipers in Afghanistan. We're good friends to this day.

I still give him shit about that night on the beach.

As part of our final training exercise, we went through a major nighttime op on a Zodiac, a large inflatable boat. The surf was big that night, and at one point we abruptly got a signal to come in. Our lane grader, the SEAL instructor who was evaluating our whole operation, was worried because the water was getting rough. I knew this particular section of beach: We were dangerously close to a seriously rocky shoreline. Beaching a rubber boat on a shoreline filled with sharp rocks is not something you want to take lightly. It can kill you.

Rich Honza, our boat crew leader, said, "Okay, they're signaling us, we've got to go in right away."

"Guys," I said, "I think we have to wait and time it so we don't get wrecked on the shore."

No, said Rich, we had to go right in, right then and there.

"Look," I said, "I surf, I know this area. The waves come in sets. The only way we're not going to get pummeled on those rocks is if we wait for the big set to come, and then haul ass right after that."

He insisted, though, and he was the crew leader, so there was nothing I could do about it. We were going right then, immediately. *Oh, man,* I thought, *this is not going to be good.* We started paddling like crazy, heading slowly for the shore. There was no way we would make it in time. I could feel the swell coming. Sure enough, we started rising, then lowering, and then the next rise was bigger—and then I knew we were about to get hit.

"Guys," I yelled out over the roar of the surf, "get ready, the big one's coming!"

A moment later a monster wave broke right on top of us. The next thing I knew I was the only one left in the boat, and I was hurtling toward shore. If I didn't want to get sliced to ribbons on that treacherous shoreline, I was going to have to manage the entire damned Zodiac myself. This was bad. In fact, there was no way this situation could get any worse.

Then it got worse.

Darting a look backward, I caught a glimpse of something at the stern of the Zodiac. I looked closer—it was someone's fingers. One of the guys had managed to hold on. Then a head bobbed into view, and I groaned. It was Mike Ritland.

Mike was an Iowa farmboy who had never seen the ocean live until the day he showed up for SEAL training. He swam in pools at school and was a decent swimmer, but the ocean was totally foreign to him, and his entire time out on the Rock had been a struggle. Now here I was, alone in our runaway Zodiac with everyone else back there somewhere in the ocean, with Mike hanging on to the stern for dear life—and the two of us were about to hit the rocks.

I had one thing going for me: I still had seconds' worth of the lull that follows after a big set breaks—but only seconds. Somehow I got control of the Zodiac and managed to surf the damn thing safely up over the rocks and close enough in that I could touch bottom. I glanced back for a split second. No more fingers on the stern. I didn't know what had happened to Mike and had no idea where anyone else was, but I couldn't let myself think about it. I jumped out and scrabbled for a foothold in the rocks, then grabbed the Zodiac and started hauling it in, timing the moves so I was pulling it a little farther each time a wave came in. As I approached the shoreline I hopped back into the boat to make sure everything was strapped down—and felt something strange at my feet. What the hell? There was something underneath the boat, something pushing up.

No, not some*thing*. It was some*one*.

"Holy shit!" I yelled as I threw myself out again, grabbed the Zodiac with both hands, and heaved with all my might to free it from the pull of the water, pushing it up, up, and finally flipping it over to the side. A figure came gasping up out of the surf like a creature in a horror movie.

It was Mike. He'd been trapped under the Zodiac for more than two minutes, wedged in the pitch blackness.

"I was—I was—" He tried to talk at the same time he was wheezing and gasping for air. When he finally got enough breath in him, he finished the thought. "I was . . . gonna die. I was . . . sure I . . . was gonna die."

No doubt he was absolutely right. Mike had the look of someone who had stared death in the face and known it had beaten him. "Fuck this," he mumbled as I pulled him up onshore. "I shoulda been an Army Ranger . . . fuck this . . . this water stuff is not for me . . . you can have it."

As Mike and I stood there on the shore, him leaning on me while he caught his breath, one of the instructors came running up to us. I figured he would be anxious to know if Mike was alive. I was about to shout out, "It's okay! He's okay!" but I was cut off by a string of obscenities followed by these words in a familiar voice:

"Webb! Get me a count of those fucking weapons!"

It was Instructor Shoulin.

It was like the guy had been put on this earth to find me and torture me. Just as with our land nav exercises up in the Laguna Mountains, here was my nemesis, helping out in Third Phase—and busting my balls.

Fortunately for all of us, we'd had our guns clipped in tight on the Zodiac. These were real weapons, and if any of us had lost one we would have been in seriously deep shit. Losing a gun is a career-ender for a full-fledged SEAL, let alone a BUD/S student. If we had lost any of those weapons while we were out there, we would all likely have been kicked out, and it would have been a problem for our instructors, too.

We didn't lose any firearms, and we didn't lose any people, either. Within another half minute everyone else was coming in to shore. Honza, our crew leader, came up to me and said, "Man, we should have waited for that set." I didn't reply.

Poor Mike had recovered his breath, but not his composure. He was beaten and he'd made his decision. He was going to go find that brass bell and ring it hard.

He didn't, though, not that night and not the morning after, either. For the next few days he kept talking about it, and I kept talking him through it. "It was a freak thing, man," I said. "Don't worry about it. It could have happened to anyone. You're fine." I couldn't tell if he was hearing any of it. It didn't look like he was. Those two minutes had really rattled him. He'd been sure he was a dead man, and he was quitting.

Except he didn't quit. Ritland stuck it out and saw the thing through. In fact, we ended up together later in our first platoon deployment as part of SEAL Team Three, and Mike went on to become a solid operator and have a strong career as a SEAL. The brass bell never got him.

By the time we all got off that island, we were a pack of uncaged animals. Stepping off the plane back in San Diego, we felt like we could conquer anything. Nothing I've ever experienced quite compares with how it felt to know that we had made it all the way through BUD/S.

Of our original two-hundred-plus, just over twenty of us had made it to the end.

The night before graduation, it's tradition for all the graduating students to take the instructors out for a night of drinking. We went with them to a pub on Coronado Island called Danny's that was strictly off-limits to students. The instructors started buying me shots, and then the night devolved into an endless series of beers. At some point I turned and looked at who it was that had shoved the latest beer in front of me.

It was Instructor Shoulin.

It was the weirdest thing. Here was this maniac who had done everything in his power to get me to quit, this guy that I hated, this guy who was my nemesis—and we were having a guys' night out, drinking beers together.

"You know, Webb, I hated you," he said. *Hey, don't hold back,* I thought but didn't say. *Tell me what you really think.* He took a slow sip of beer, then continued talking in that soft, icy killer's voice. He was looking straight ahead, speaking almost as if I weren't there.

"I did *not* want you to make it through. I did *not* want you to be a SEAL. We all thought you were going to quit. We thought we could *make* you quit."

He stopped talking again. Maybe he expected me to say something. Maybe not. In any case, I kept my mouth shut and waited to see if he had anything else to say. He did.

"But you shoved it in our faces. You stepped up. I watched you turn a corner—and I was impressed." He took another long pull on his beer, then quietly added, "You earned our respect."

Those few minutes were worth all the shit I'd been through.

We drank until the sun came up. I overslept the next day and almost missed my own graduation. One by one, they called us up to receive our certificates. My parents were there, along with my grandparents, down from Canada. It was an unbelievably great feeling. I had made it through BUD/S. I was finally on the threshold of becoming a Navy SEAL.

I was still completely hungover from the night before.

FIVE

GETTING DIRTY

Nineteen ninety-eight. It was a strange time to be part of an elite military corps. This was the waning phase of the Clinton years, and there was a sense in the military that we and the current administration did not have the best of relationships. Frankly, there also wasn't much conflict happening in the world, or at least no major clashes in which our forces were directly involved. Some guys were wondering just exactly what we were doing here and would grumble that we weren't really being employed. We all felt a kind of tense anxiousness, as if we were dogs on the leash just itching to be let loose. We wanted to *do* something.

Instead, we *trained*.

In a way, the BUD/S training is not really training at all, but one seven-month-long entrance exam, winnowing out all but those who refuse to quit. Now the training started—and we trained, and trained, and trained. This is something about the SEAL experience: The training never stops.

When it came time to be assigned to a specific SEAL team, they had us list our top three picks in order of priority. I figured if anything important was going to happen it would be in the Middle East. At the time, each team was responsible for a particular area of operations (AO), and the Middle East was Team Three's AO. I wanted to be wherever the action was. What's more, Team Three had a really good reputation. For my top three picks I listed Team Three, Team Five, and Team One (all West Coast teams), in that order. I was elated when the assignments came down: I had gotten my first choice.

When I arrived at Team Three I did exactly the same thing I'd done back as a new guy in HS-6: put my head down, kept my mouth shut, and made sure I did a good job at everything they threw at me. In the SEALs, a new guy is someone who has not yet gone on an overseas deployment with a SEAL team, and I learned very quickly that new guys are better seen and not fucking heard. We hadn't yet earned our SEAL Tridents; we were still on a six-month probation, and they never let us forget it for a moment. Once we proved ourselves on a deployment, we would be treated with more respect. Until then, I was back on the bottom of the totem pole again.

The next big step after being assigned to a SEAL team as a new guy was to class up to SEAL Tactical Training (STT), a three-month intensive program of advanced training. (Today this is called SEAL Qualification Training, or SQT, and is part of advanced BUD/S, but it's much the same thing.) STT was where we would really start getting into close-quarters battle tactics, room-to-room, where we would shoot thousands of rounds on the range, and go through more challenging land navigations and extended dives. It was where we would prove ourselves—where we would actually start *becoming* SEALs.

It was time to get down and dirty.

And this brought me face-to-face with my first major challenge as a SEAL new guy: I needed to demonstrate that I could perform up to par when it came to shooting a weapon.

Some of the guys I was training with had already served in the Marine Corps; many of them had shot guns since they were kids. Most knew their way around guns, for one reason or another. Not me. There'd been a little bit of shooting in boot camp, and we'd had a little time on the range as part of SAR training and again as part of BUD/S, but only a taste. When it came to firearms, I was green as the grass. Would I be able to measure up?

I would have a chance to find out soon enough in SST.

Right off the bat we spent a week at the Naval Training Center (NTC) range, where we shot a variety of firearms, including the M-4 semiautomatic assault rifle, SIG SAUER P-226 semiautomatic 9 mm pistol, the Heckler & Koch USP .45 semiautomatic pistol (USP stands for "universal self-loading pistol"), and the H&K MP-5 9 mm submachine gun. The designation "submachine" means it fires subsonic rounds. Bullets that travel faster than the speed of sound create an audible *snap!* like a miniature sonic boom. It sounds like someone clapping his hands together sharply. That's how you know you're being shot at: In addition to the *crack!* of the round's actual discharge, you hear these tiny *cracks* around your head.

This was all new to me, and I found myself seriously behind the curve. Almost from day 1 I had instructors climbing all over my ass, saying, "Hey, Webb, what's your problem?" It was like being back at the beginning of BUD/S all over again: Suddenly I was *that guy.* I had to get my shit together and do it fast, because we were about to take it up a notch.

After a week at the NTC we went out to the La Posta Mountain training facility, about an hour's drive east of San Diego. An old satellite observatory, La Posta covers about 1,000 square miles perched 3,500 feet up on a mountaintop—not exactly Denver altitude, but higher up than what we were used to, and beautiful. It would become especially valuable as a training site within a few years because the terrain there so closely resembles parts of Iraq and Afghanistan.

At La Posta we conducted some patrol and land nav exercises, similar to what we'd done in BUD/S only tougher. Still, to me these didn't seem that difficult. Then it came time to get into serious training on the shooting range. A few weeks in, they started running us through combat drills they call stress courses. Stress courses is right: For me, this was the moment of truth. I would either step up my game or show up as lame.

It wasn't that I was worried about flunking out. This was about *reputation*. As I was coming to learn, reputation is like a house that, once you burn it down, is almost impossible to build again. This is true in business, in communities, in the world at large—but in the SEAL community it's true times ten. There's nothing more precious to a SEAL than his reputation. In the stress course drills, mine would be at stake.

The drills took place on a course that was set up with barricades every 10 to 20 feet. The idea was to spring through the course, taking cover at each barricade and shooting different kinds of targets, hitting as many as you could within a given time. I knew how it worked. It's not rocket science. Run fast, stay hidden, shoot the bad guys. What I didn't know was whether I could do it.

When my turn came, I checked my M-4 assault rifle, cleared my head, and felt my breath coming steady. I knew the next few minutes would stay with me in the team's eyes, for better or for worse, for months to come.

The instructor yelled *"Go!"* I tore off on a 20-foot sprint to take cover behind the first barricade. I peered around the right edge, down low, and engaged the target. *Crack! Ping!* These were steel knockdown targets: You hit one and it flips down backward. *Crack! Ping! Crack! Ping!* Shooting steel was satisfying, because each shot gave off that instantaneous report, much better feedback than shooting paper targets. After firing off a few quick rounds, I was sprinting to the next barricade, where I repeated the process, and then to the next. At the third station there were half a dozen head poppers, targets that suddenly popped up with just their heads showing. The goal was to take out all six in rapid succession. I fired off six rounds, *ping! ping! ping! ping! ping! ping!* and then took off for the next station.

A few stations later, with plenty of targets still left to shoot, I ran out of ammo. They had designed it this way on purpose. They wanted to see how we did when our primary weapon went dry. I swept my rifle to the side, letting it swing on its sling by its own weight, immediately drew my pistol and fired off several more rounds at the remaining targets, then holstered the sidearm, grabbed my rifle, and brought it back up as I sprinted to take cover and reload. *Cover, not concealment.* We'd been drilled on the difference. *Cover* is when you hide behind something that can actually provide you with physical protection. *Concealment* means you're hiding behind something that shields you visually, like a bush, but the other guy can shoot through the bush and hit you. I took cover, dropped my depleted M-4 mag, slammed in a fresh magazine, loaded a fresh mag in my pistol, too, in case I needed it, then sprinted off to engage the next series of targets.

The whole thing was a whirlwind—there was no sense of stopping and starting, taking this step and then that step, just one unbroken stream of actions and reactions. It was over before I even had time to think.

Our instructor did a double take that was almost comical. "*Damn,* Webb," he said. "Where the fuck did *that* come from?"

I looked around and realized the other guys were all staring at me. I hadn't missed a single shot. I had smoked the whole course.

In all my previous experiences shooting at paper targets, I'd always struggled, always felt stressed out, never felt like any of it came naturally, and I'd never been nearly as good a shot as the rest of the guys. But now, when I hit that first steel target and heard that *ping!* something just clicked into place.

I puzzled about this for some time, and later came to some conclusions about it. I'd had no firearms experience or training whatsoever before joining the navy—but I had done an awful lot of undersea hunting. There's something instinctive about spearfishing. That speargun doesn't feel like a tool—it's more like an extension of your arm: You just point your arm and fire. Target shooting had never felt like that to me, at least not up to that point. Once we were out on this more realistic drill scenario, though, that instinctive sense kicked in. It wasn't like I was shooting *with* a rifle. I was just pointing my arm and shooting.

Rob Byford, my OIC from BUD/S days, was there on the range that day. He'd seen the misery I went through in First Phase, seen me when I was *that guy* and must have looked for all the world like I'd never make it through BUD/S.

"Goddam," he muttered loud enough for all to hear. "I'll take Webb in my platoon any day. The fuckin' guy never quits!"

Thank God, I thought. I'd redeemed myself.

From La Posta we headed out west into the desert to a godforsaken place called Niland, by the Salton Sea, where we spent the next six weeks in one of the strangest environments I've ever seen. This was our desert warfare phase, and I can't imagine a more perfect location. The Salton Sea is essentially man-made, the result of an accident early in the twentieth century when some engineers were trying to redirect the Colorado River and lost control of the project. Now it's one of the most brackish bodies of water on the planet, saltier than ocean water and filled with agricultural runoff.

On the northeast end of the lake is the funky town of Niland, occupied largely by meth labs and trailer parks. It reminded me of the post-apocalyptic landscape in *The Road Warrior.* There are guys out there called scrappers who collect anything and everything. We'd be out on the range, doing contact drills, laying down thousands of rounds; we'd walk a hundred yards away to get a water break, drink, reload, and go back out—and all the brass shell casings we'd just left behind would be gone, the ground picked clean. Off to the side we'd see a guy with wild hair dragging along a sack and wearing his road-warrior goggles. It's an odd bunch.

I'd been out to Niland about six weeks earlier, just before starting STT, with one of my buddies from Team Three, John Zinn. John and I were both surfers who'd grown up in California. He looked like your average skinny surf bum, but he was an excellent waterman and a great athlete. When I arrived at Team Three we hit it off right away.

As new guys, John and I were sent out there for a week to help support one of the SEAL platoons doing some training. One day we'd been sent out on some sort of resupply mission in a bare-frame, stripped-down Humvee. We'd completed the work and were done for the day. We were out in the desert, and no one else was around. We said, "Hey, let's see what this bad boy can do." We took off, taking turns driving, busting around the desert mountains and launching that Humvee over rises in the barren desert terrain like the Dukes of Hazzard.

As we were tearing ass down a long desert stretch, I saw a dip up ahead and started slowing a little to navigate it. John said, "C'mon, man, punch it!" and I stepped on it. Suddenly there was a gap in front of us. I accelerated, doing my best to jump it. All at once we were airborne. Everything slowed to a crawl. John and I turned and looked at each other, eyes wide, in slow motion: a Thelma and Louise moment. It couldn't have been more than a second and a half that we were airborne, but it felt like a full minute. Then we landed. We had managed to clear the gap, but we came down so hard on the other side that it blew out the left front tire and bent the rim. We had no spare. How the hell were we going to explain this?

We radioed in. The guys at the base said they didn't have anyone free to come out and get us, so we should hang tight for the night. We weren't sure exactly where we were, but we knew we were somewhere in the vicinity of an area designated for ordnance exercises. In plain English: a live bombing range.

We slept out there that night in the Humvee and woke up early the next morning to the sound of F-18 jets screaming overhead and ordnance dropping in the distance. Were they getting closer? We weren't sure.

We got on the radio and said, "Um, hey, guys, can you get us out of here?" We passed them rough coordinates and asked them to hurry. They came out and brought us a spare; we changed the tire and drove back to camp. Now we had to explain what had happened.

At the time the camp was run by a SEAL named Steve Heinz. This guy was like something out of a cartoon. Take whatever overdrawn, exaggerated picture you can form of a ridiculously tough Navy SEAL and exaggerate that by a factor of three. That's Steve: an ogre of a man, chewing scrap metal and swallowing it. He ran that camp with an iron fist. Nobody screwed around there—nobody. So here we were, a couple of new guys who'd just busted one of his vehicles. We had been afraid of those F-18s. We were *terrified* of Steve.

First we went to see the mechanic and explained that there had been some rough terrain out there, and we blew a tire. He looked at the bent rim, then back at us. "How do you explain *that*?"

"The terrain was rough," said John.

"Very rough," I echoed.

He looked at us. "What the hell were you guys doing?"

John looked right back at him and said, "It was very, very rough terrain."

The next few hours were not fun, waiting for the hammer to drop. Finally we were called into Heinz's office. He lit into us. *"What the hell were you doing out there? You want to tell me you guys weren't out there hotdogging and fucking off in my vehicle?"*

"No, sir," John managed to get out. "We were just driving."

"It was really rough terrain," I added helpfully.

Heinz glared at us, then dismissed us with a growl. "Get the fuck out of my office." That was the end of it.

John went on to BRAVO platoon and did four years there. He met a food chemist named Jackie, fell head over heels in love with her, got out of the service, and married her. When 9/11 happened, John was one of the first guys doing private security for companies like DynCorp and Blackwater as an independent contractor. The pay was outrageous, especially once we went into Iraq. He did that for a few years, then took a pile of earnings and formed an armored car company called Indigen Armor with an army buddy from their experience driving around being shot at over there. I like to think that our crazy outing at Niland helped plant a seed for his later success.

A few years later John and his buddy sold their majority interest, and he and Jackie had a child. Then in 2010 he was killed in Jordan in a freak accident. John was a good guy, one of the best. His dad, Michael, is a great lawyer, and he and I became good friends after John's death. We are friends to this day. John was as solid as they come, and I miss him.

When John and I were first out there it had been spring, which is no picnic in Niland. Now it was summer and hotter than hell, hitting 115°F most days. It sometimes got so hot out there that we couldn't put blasting caps in the ground in our demolition exercises, because the heat of the ground would set them off.

They put us through our paces in land nav and land warfare exercises, simulated drills where we'd come up against enemy contact and have to fight our way out of it. We also did some advanced demolition work there as part of an assault package: we'd go into a mock village, stage a prisoner snatch, shoot up the place, then set our C-4 charges everywhere and pull smoke on those charges—and we'd have fifteen minutes to get out of there before it all blew.

At Niland we were introduced to some of the heavier machine guns, the .50 caliber and .60 caliber, and we also got some practice on the Carl Gustav, an 84 mm recoilless rifle handheld rocket launcher, and got to fire some LAW (light antitank weapon) rockets. Although we mostly used live fire, for some exercises we used a laser setup called Multiple Integrated Laser Engagement System (MILES), which fires blanks, a little like playing paintball. We used this system when we went up against each other in teams in OppFor (Oppositional Force) exercises. The focus, though, was not on that kind of force-on-force situation. Going in en masse and taking down a known force, like charging a machine-gun nest, is not a typical SEAL mission. We're not the marines. Our preferred methodology is to insert ourselves in the middle of the night when no one's looking, hit them, and get out. We're not really there to fight; we're there to tip the scales. At Niland, our focus was on demolition—and on getting a taste of what it takes to survive in the most god-awful, inhumanly hot conditions imaginable.

Near the end of our time at Niland, they took us out in the desert a little before noon for a six-hour land nav course. It was miserable out, August in the Niland desert. We spent the day roaming about that burned-Mars landscape like postapocalyptic scavengers, following the preset course and racking up points, finally arriving back at camp exhausted and dehydrated.

"Drink some water, guys," the instructors told us, "and get some rest. In a few hours, we're doing a little run."

Turned out it wasn't just a "little run." It was a 12-mile timed run with weapons and full rucksack loaded with 50 pounds of gear. We started in after dinner, about eight in the evening, running along an aqueduct road. Running, not walking. The time we had to beat was no joke, and in Niland in August, eight o'clock is still damned hot.

Some of the guys were really good runners, and they were out in front right away. I'm a middling runner, not the best and not the worst; I was more or less in the middle of the pack. We got to mile 3, then mile 4, and I expected we would soon start seeing our fastest guys coming back the other way after hitting the 6-mile turnaround point. But we saw nobody. We hit mile 5. Still no one coming the other way.

Then finally we saw one, and then a few more—but only a few. *Something's wrong,* I thought. *There should be more guys coming back.*

We soon found out what was wrong: Our guys were dropping in their tracks right on the road, and the medics were pulling them off to the side (where we wouldn't see them) and getting IV bags into them. On torture runs like this, I had learned, you need to drink water nonstop. I was pounding the stuff down. I was *not* going to get dehydrated.

I reached the turnaround point, and there was Disco Stella, my BUD/S classmate and Team Three teammate. He looked bad, and I could tell he was hurting. Stella was a faster runner than me, but right now he was slowing down. We set off on the return leg, running together.

"I'm hurting, man," he panted. I start to worry about whether he was going to make it. Normally he would be way out ahead of me, but he was clearly dehydrated and not doing well. Almost immediately, he started drifting back. He never caught up again.

After a few miles, I stopped at a water station to grab more water— and the moment I stopped moving, both my legs seized up. I started falling backward. There was nothing I could do about it. I grabbed my gun and just fell out, right on the ground. A guy I'd just met recently, Glen Doherty, was there as part of the support staff, manning the water station. Glen saw me drop to the ground and ran over to me. "Hey," he said, "you okay?"

"Yeah," I managed. "I'll be fine," hoping that maybe saying it would make it true. I spent the next few minutes massaging and hitting my legs, putting everything I had into it, trying to get the muscles to let go just enough so I could stand up. Finally I managed to get back onto my feet. Guys were starting to trickle into the station, telling us about who had dropped out. Glen and I were both flabbergasted. There were some real studs in the group who weren't running anymore. That did it for me. I finished my water and got back on the road.

I was not going fast, but I was near the top of the pack. As I got to the 10-mile mark, 2 miles short of the finish, a Humvee pulled up beside me with a medic and another guy. I couldn't believe my eyes when I saw who it was. Dan Oldwell was not only a true stud, he was Honor Man in our BUD/S class. Honor Man is something like the class valedictorian, the guy who never quits, the most outstanding guy in the class, the one whose example inspires everyone else. Now here was our Honor Man—riding in a Humvee. He had quit.

"Hey, Webb," said Oldwell, "we're just letting you know, the instructors sent us out to tell everyone. People are dropping from massive heat exhaustion. They're calling it. Hop in."

It was twilight, and I could see the lights of our base camp on the horizon. I did *not* run 11 miles and put myself through all that misery to quit a mile from the gate. I looked up at Oldwell. "Thanks," I said, "but no thanks. You're not putting me in that car. No fucking way."

I turned back and kept going.

A few minutes later I reached the camp gate. I stood there panting, feeling the pain coursing through my legs, feeling like a wreck, but it was a good feeling. "Good job, Webb," I heard someone say.

Just then an instructor walked up to me and said, "Hey, why is your weapon dirty?"

I looked down at my weapon. The guy had a point. Some dirt had gotten on my gun when I fell over at the water station. It's a code they had pounded into us: You take care of the team's gear first, *then* you help your buddy, and once all that's done, *then* you take care of yourself. You *always* make sure all your team's shit is squared away before you go hop in the shower. It's a code I believe in. I think it's a great value to have.

I looked up at the guy and didn't say a word, just gave him a look that said, *Fuck you*. He nodded and walked away.

It felt really good to finish that run. Out of a class of some eighty guys, some of them truly elite athletes, only Chris Osman and I and four others had done it. My stock was going up, and these things get back to the teams. It's a little like an NFL draft: The teams are always looking for new guys, and they keep their ears to the ground. Every community is by definition a small community, and the SEALs are no exception. Tests, points, grades, certification—they all matter, but nothing counts like reputation.

The brutal heat of Niland was followed by a few weeks at Camp Pendleton in a block of extensive land nav training, followed by four weeks of combat swimmer training off the San Diego pier at the Thirty-second Street Naval Station, doing four- and five-hour dives to plant explosives on gigantic destroyers.

An Arleigh Burke–class destroyer is nearly a tenth of a mile long and has a displacement (total mass) of 9,200 tons. Imagine diving underneath one of these babies. Visibility is poor, and it's easy to lose track of what's up and what's down. Normally you can orient yourself deep underwater by watching the upward trail of bubbles from your exhale, but with the Dräger rebreather system we were using, we weren't emitting any bubbles, so there was nothing to follow. We learned to follow the seams of the welds on a ship's hull to track our way to the surface. To make things worse, those ship's generators are incredibly loud—and sound carries like crazy underwater. So there you are, deep down in the darkness, somewhere underneath a 9,200-ton vessel and surrounded by this intense *RRRrrrRRRRRrrrrRRRRRrrrrRRRRR* and no sense of up or down. It's pretty easy to start thinking, *Oh my God, am I even on the right boat?*

These ships have huge bilge pumps that suck in seawater with tremendous force. The specific ships we targeted were supposed to shut down their bilge pumps for our exercise—but if you're stumbling around down there and get too close to the wrong ship, it's not hard to get sucked right in. Guys have died that way.

The first time I got down underneath one of those monsters, I couldn't help thinking about Mikey Ritland trapped under that Zodiac off San Clemente Island. This sucker was a lot bigger than a Zodiac.

Fortunately we made it through the dive work in one piece. I graduated from SEAL Tactical Training on August 14, 1998, and headed back to the team to get back to work—and start preparing for my Trident board.

The SEAL Trident is the only badge in the navy that has no rank. When you wear that Trident, anywhere you go in the military, people get out of your way, no matter what rank they are, because they know what it means to earn that thing. I've seen commanding officers approaching in ship passageways step aside and let us through when they see that Trident. In that moment they aren't seeing rank or seniority—they are just seeing that big budweiser on your chest.

In order to get my Trident, I first had to go collect signatures on my Personal Qualification Standard (PQS). I went to the dive locker and got signed off by the master diver there, to the air locker and did the same, then the first lieutenant of the boats rack, and on through all the individual people who had mentored us in each particular field. One by one, they signed off, and once I had the whole form completed I put in a formal request to go before my Trident board.

The day finally came, a Wednesday in late 1998, six of us standing in the hallway in our starched, pressed desert cammies (the standard uniform, made of camouflage material). We waited together out in the hall on the top floor of the Team Three area. One by one, they called us in. Each guy was in there probably no more than thirty minutes, but it seemed like hours. When my turn came, I went in and sat down in the center of a horseshoe of instructors, who immediately started in on me, firing away with their questions, starting with weapons specs.

"What's the max effective range of the M-60 machine gun?"

"What's the max effective range of the M-4?"

"What's the muzzle velocity of the MP-5 submachine gun?"

"How many movements does it take to clear-and-safe a SIG SAUER 226 pistol?"

A comms guy asked questions about communications—shortwave and long-wave radio signals, different antenna setups, all the types of radios we use. Then a corpsman asked all kinds of first-aid questions. Then it went to the boats guy, the diving guy, the air guy. Everyone was firing crazy questions at me. I had to have the answers all down pat, and I had to answer *fast*. It was incredibly intimidating. I had studied my ass off for this, and I was pretty sure I was doing well. Still, they held my future in their hands.

Then one of them asked, "Why do you want to be a SEAL?"

I don't know how anyone else answered that question, but it made me stop and think for a moment. Why *did* I want to be a SEAL?

I had always wanted to be a part of something special, something that not many people can accomplish. Honestly, that was my real driving force, the chance to be part of an incredibly elite group.

I had struggled some in high school, and while I'd managed to graduate, it was hardly with flying colors. There was no way I would have qualified for an ROTC scholarship or the Naval Academy. I had always wanted to be a pilot, but I hadn't done well enough academically to get onto that track, either. In a way, I had something to prove to myself: that I could be part of something special, that I could set a high bar and make it.

I didn't go into all of this with these guys. I just said, "Look, I love the water, grew up in the water, and feel I'm well suited to it. I want to be a part of this special community, and I know that not many people can achieve this."

I walked out not knowing whether I'd made it. In fact, there were a few guys who didn't, who screwed up some questions and would have to go back and retest later. I wasn't one of them. When my turn came, the board of instructors brought me back into the room, messed with my head a little bit, then told me I'd passed.

When that Friday came, I showed up in my cammies at SEAL command, down by the beach, for quarters. "Quarters" is the naval term for the daily assembly. All the platoons would muster up in their groups at 7:30 in the morning, the CO would come out and talk about what was happening that day or that week, and then we would change out to go do PT and get on with the rest of the day. On Fridays, anyone who was getting an award would be recognized during quarters.

That Friday morning the CO came out and talked for a few minutes. Then I heard my name called and went up front. An instructor pinned a Trident to my uniform. I was no longer a search-and-rescue swimmer, a navy regular, a BUD/S student, a Team Three member on probation, an STT student.

I was a Navy SEAL.

The next instant, a throng of guys started running toward me—and I took off as fast as I could. There is a SEAL tradition: Once you have your Trident, you get thrown in the ocean, fully clothed. I did my best to outrun them and throw myself in, but no dice. They grabbed me and tossed me in the Pacific. Then they hauled me out again, soaking wet, took me back onshore, and started pounding my Trident.

This is another navy tradition. A normal pin has a little metal or plastic backing that secures it on, like a tie tack, and keeps the pin from sticking into your skin, but there was no backing on my Trident. Used to be, when you'd earn your flight wings in the navy, they would call them your "blood wings," because the guys would literally pound the pin into you, beat it into your chest. That's old school, and the regular navy doesn't do that anymore—but the SEAL teams do. SEAL teams are hardcore.

So they pounded in my Trident, right over my heart. It felt good. Other than the three days that each of my kids was born, and one other moment that we'll get to later, this was the proudest moment of my life.

A few days before receiving my Trident, I found out that I was being placed into GOLF platoon, one of the A-list platoons. I would spend the next two years with these guys.

GOLF platoon was an odd assortment of characters, a strange but solid mix of personalities. Having the skills and the objective qualifications is one thing, but there's something you can't quite measure in tests that has to be there, too. For us, the chemistry was great. With SEALs in general, you're dealing with a group of people who are pretty extreme, every single one an alpha male, like a wolf pack or group of Viking warriors. Each guy is constantly putting the others in check, but while they may beat each other up, when it comes down to it, it's all for one.

From the start, we were a very tight group:

JAMES McNARY, our OIC, was a classic navy officer: straight shooter, not a hair out of place. When Lieutenant McNary got out of the service in 2000, he went to Harvard Business School and went on to become principal security engineer at Raytheon.

DAN, our chief, was a big guy and a California surfer like me. Chief Dan had gone through BUD/S at the age of seventeen and had pretty much been brought up in the teams. He ran that platoon; he was one of the smartest SEALs I've ever known, and McNary pretty much let him have free rein.

TOM, our LPO (leading petty officer). Next in seniority after Chief Dan, Tom was a big monster of a guy, quiet and soft-spoken. For me he exemplified everything it means to be a good leader, constantly showing us the ropes and making sure we knew exactly what we were doing at every turn. Tom and Chief Dan shaped who we were as SEALs and taught us what it meant to be solid team guys and sharp operators. As I would later discover to my chagrin and detriment, not everyone in the teams had that caliber of training and leadership.

ERIC FRANSSENS was a brute of a guy; Franny and I had gone through STT together, and he would shortly introduce me to my wife.

GLEN DOHERTY, whom I'd first met at Niland when he was part of the support team when I went through STT. Glen went through STT himself right after I did and then joined us in Team Three. Glen would in time become one of the most important people in my life.

MIKE RITLAND, my classmate from BUD/S, the Iowa farm boy who got trapped under the Zodiac and lived to tell the tale. We called him Mikey "Big Balls" Ritland.

RANDY was a short, skinny guy we called "the Rat." I've never seen a guy be so intelligent and so distracted at the same time. He could ace any academic advancement test you'd give him, and completely forget where he was supposed to be five minutes from now. The Rat was a Columbia graduate and Wall Street stockbroker before he became a SEAL.

TOM KRUEGER. We all had nicknames, but Krueger came up with his own: Bad Ass. Chief Dan had to take him aside and tell him you don't get to choose your own nickname—especially not one like that. We called him all sorts of names (including Jackass, though only behind his back), but none that ever stuck. We could tell Krueger had had a rough time when he was a new guy because he took obvious pleasure in any opportunity to haze new guys—as I would soon discover to my considerable dismay. Krueger ended up going into DEVGRU, the antiterrorist group that used to be called SEAL Team Six, and was shot and killed in Afghanistan in 2002.

SHANE HYATT, whom we called "the Diplomat." Shane marched to the beat of a different drum. With a shaved head and pierced tongue, the Diplomat had absolutely no inner monologue; he would just say whatever was on his mind, anytime, anywhere. You did *not* want Shane around anyone important, because he would offend people at will. Three months shy of graduating from an ROTC program at the University of Arizona and getting his officer's commission, Shane told off his ROTC commander, got kicked out of the program, and had to pay back some $60,000 in tuition.

CHUCK LANDRY was one of our youngest guys, just twenty when he joined the team, a big kid, 6'2" and sharp, but he had quite a mouth on him. We called him a liberty risk: When you went out on liberty with Landry, you never knew what would happen. One night he walked onto base drunk and started hassling the security guard. They handcuffed his hands behind him, but he managed to slip his hands under his feet and out in front again, whereupon they freaked out and drew their weapons to hold him in place. He ended up on double probation and couldn't leave the team area for a month.

BOB HARWARD served as team CO for my first month there before moving on to another command. Bob was a serious hard case; he had graduated BUD/S as Honor Man of Class 128 and had a reputation for being frighteningly smart and just as tenacious. He has pissed a lot of people off in his career just because he is fearless and uncompromising. The dude has a scar running from his chin right up to his forehead, and you take one look at him and say, *Okay, I am* not *fucking with that guy.* Bob was incredibly competitive, and I learned a dirty trick from him one day when we were doing a run-swim-run: First you do the run, then you throw your shoes in the team truck, jump into the water and swim 2 miles, then you get out of the water and rendezvous with the truck on shore, grab your shoes, and run the rest of the race. I was out of the water right behind Bob and saw him grab his shoes and yell at the driver, "You're in the wrong spot! You need to drive another half mile down the beach!" Son of a bitch if he didn't put a half mile between himself and the rest of the pack so he could win the race. That was Bob. Classic. Today Harward is a three-star admiral. When I later served in Afghanistan supporting Task Force K-Bar, Bob Harward was my commander.

There were others, too: "Foxy," "Cooter," "Data," Dave Scott, "Grogey," "Mongo," "Uncle Jesse." Last but not least, there was me.

I'm not sure exactly where my nickname came from, or why. I think at first it had to do with a few guys seeing me as someone who didn't bathe often (which is strange, because I'm actually a pretty clean person), but soon it expanded to embrace a decidedly sexual connotation. We all had our stories of sexual conquest, but mine tended to be on the outrageous side, and for a while there I was pretty busily slaying the young women of San Diego. The other guys frequently shook their heads over my exploits, saying, "Webb, you dirty bastard," and the name stuck.

Dirty Webb.

There was one more person who came into my life around this time and would be a key figure in the years to come.

It started with Franny; we were always trying to set him up with a date. Johnny Sotello, one of the guys, had a girlfriend from Norway named Monica, and one day he told us that Monica had a friend named Gabriele who would be perfect for Franny. Johnny set up a date so that Franny and Gabriele could meet at a local bar.

I was at that bar the night of the blind date, and I couldn't believe what I saw: Franny showed up *with another girl*. "Dude," I said, "uh, what the hell are you doing?"

"Don't worry about it," Franny said. "It'll be fine."

Wait a second, I thought. He was bringing a girl to the bar where he was supposed to be meeting another girl for a date? How exactly was that supposed to be *fine*? But there wasn't much I could do but sit back and watch.

A few minutes later Monica showed up with an absolutely beautiful blonde. I could tell immediately that she was a foreigner—German, was my best guess. She was gorgeous.

Franny went over to her with this other girl trailing along with him, got introduced to her, and proceeded to try to explain the situation. I wasn't close enough to hear what either of them said, but it wasn't hard to read their body language and see how the conversation was going. Franny was explaining to Gabriele and Monica how, yes, he was here with this other girl, but it was really nice to meet Gabriele, and he was wondering, could he still get her number?

Gabriele swiftly made it clear, with the aid of an emphatic hand gesture that involved her third digit, that she wanted nothing to do with this idiot. It was pretty funny watching the whole thing go down.

Eric walked back over to the other end of the bar where I was sitting.

"Hey, Franny," I said. "Didn't go so well, did it?"

"No," he said glumly. "You were right."

I took a pull on my beer, set it down, stepped away from the bar, and started walking back in the direction Franny had just come from. Here was this beautiful girl who'd come in expecting a date, and my troglodytic roommate had fucked it up. So I made my move. Walked up, leaned against the bar, nodded to her, very friendly.

"Do. You. Speak. English?" I asked, speaking very clearly and slowly. Very considerate, very thoughtful. Suave.

"Uh, yeah," she replied. "I'm from Thousand Oaks. You know? California?"

Now *I* felt like an idiot. Why I had decided she was foreign, I have no idea. Maybe it was because I knew her name was Gabriele, or because Monica was from Norway. Maybe it was because she looked exotic to me.

We kept talking. I got her number, and we started dating. She had me hooked, right from the start. I immediately and completely gave up all the sexual escapades and wild living that was our normal navy way of life, and Gabriele and I took it relatively slow. I courted her for two solid months. What finally did it, I think, was an air show I took her to see.

I had volunteered to participate in this show up in Ventura, my hometown. My mom was there for it. It was cool. We did a thing called spy rigging: You clip into a helicopter through a harness on your back and they lower you on a rope so that you hang there, 100 or 150 feet down, while it goes through all sorts of maneuvers with you flying through the air at 3,000 feet. We put on a big demonstration with all kinds of complex maneuvers. I think it impressed her. That night our relationship went to a deeper level, and within months we were engaged. Just like that, two young kids in love.

Looking back, it's not hard to see that we were too young and really hadn't spent enough time together. And we never would. Gabriele was in school full-time, and I was always going off somewhere, whether it was to all the different training programs or, later on, to deployments in other parts of the world. Being a SEAL and being a family man are two very different realities that are extremely tough to reconcile.

Our marriage would last for years, long enough to have three incredible children. In the long run, though, the marriage itself never really had a fighting chance.

The training continued. We spent the next eighteen months in a lengthy workup, a seemingly endless procession of training blocks that took me all over the country and through some of the finest programs in the world. We would spend three or four weeks with the platoon, stationed in Coronado, then go off to a specialized school somewhere in the country for a training block, then rotate back home and repeat the cycle.

The truth is, SEALs never *stop* training. When we aren't actually deployed we're always learning new skills, continuing to hone our existing skills, and keeping ourselves in peak physical condition.

Rigger School

Four weeks of parachute training at an army school in Fort Lee, Virginia, learning to pack, repair, and jump with different kinds of chutes. We learned how to jump with a "stacked duck": you take two Zodiacs, wrap them up with their engines and equipment, stick on two chutes, toss the whole thing out the back of a C-130, and jump with it. We were mixed in with army guys right out of boot camp, to their instructors' great distress, because we were a totally corrupting influence. We drank hard and chased women every night, then showed up barely sober for class every morning. It was pretty rowdy.

Marine Operations (MAROPS)

We would take fully loaded Zodiacs 50 to 100 miles out onto the open ocean. Nothing like navigating on the choppy Pacific surface in a 15-foot rubber boat 100 miles from shore.

Over-the-Beach Training

About a month, part at Coronado Beach and part on San Clemente Island. We went through drills where we had to get our team extracted *off* a hot beach (that is, while being fired at), and others where we had to get our team *onto* a hot beach—all with live fire.

Land Nav

A few weeks at Team Three base in Coronado, followed by four weeks in the Laguna Mountains, much like what we'd done in Third Phase of BUD/S but a good deal more intense.

Desert Warfare

Niland again for four weeks. This was one of the most important training blocks, and I'll say more about it in a moment.

Dive Phase

Four weeks off the San Diego docks—will say more about this one, too.

Close-Quarters Battle (CQB)

At John Shaw's famous shooting range in Mississippi; more on this shortly also.

Gas and Oil Platforms Training (GOPLATS)

In the event that terrorists ever took over an oil platform out on the ocean, we needed to be ready on a moment's notice to go out there and take it back. This involved nighttime dives 50 to 100 miles off the coast of Los Angeles. We would swim underwater for miles using a Dräger rebreather, then come up out of nowhere, hook a titanium caving ladder up onto the rig, snake up the ladder, and ambush whoever was up there. Sometimes there were bands of terrorists (simulated) we would have to capture and subdue. Because of my diving experience, they often made me point man on these ops, which meant the whole platoon relied on me to put them on the target. (It was quite an honor, especially being a new guy.)

Visit, Board, Search, and Seizure (VBSS)

This is a critical part of training, essentially the Navy SEALs version of piracy on the high seas; it is similar to GOPLATS, only in this case we were going out on fast boats and taking over ships on the open ocean. Less than two years later, in my capacity as a sniper, I would be point man on an operation just like this with a genuine terrorist ship in the Persian Gulf—and in that one we definitely *would* be loaded with live fire.

Air Support

Working with an A-10 squadron outside Las Vegas, calling in live fire at night. The A-10 Thunderbolt (Warthog) was the first U.S.

Air Force plane designed specifically for close-quarters support and saw its first serious combat use during the Gulf War. It's amazing how much ordnance those A-10s can deliver. Those air force guys are excellent pilots, and I loved working with them. It was my first experience getting on the radio and calling in ordnance—something that would save my life, and the lives of quite a few other guys, a few years later in the mountains of Afghanistan.

Inter-Operations (INTEROPS) Training

A week in northern Virginia with some intelligence people from the Defense Intelligence Agency (DIA), the Department of Defense's version of the CIA. We did things like inserting a guy on the beach and then linking up with another agent and transporting him to a safe house. It was fascinating to be exposed to that world and see how intelligence agents work in hostile territory. It was also something I would learn a great deal more about many years later on the mean streets of Iraq.

One of our biggest and most important training blocks was the land warfare training, which took place, once again, out at Niland. A lot of the combat training we'd had up to that point, even in STT, consisted of basic contact drills, and a lot of the tactics taught there had been developed in the first years of the SEALs' existence, which happened to be the Vietnam years of the sixties and early seventies. As a result, the entire approach to direct engagement was primarily oriented around the conditions of jungle warfare: You come into enemy contact, lay down a ton of fire, and quickly disappear into the jungle canopy. The whole point of guerrilla warfare is to avoid open, direct contact. When U.S. troops first encountered that style of warfare in the jungles of Southeast Asia it completely threw them, but that was the style of combat SEALs cut their teeth on.

In the desert, though, it's a completely different scenario. You're in the open, and there are not a whole lot of areas you can disappear into. How do you successfully survive an enemy contact out in the open desert? It's a context that's going to last much longer than the five or ten minutes of the typical enemy contact in a jungle-warfare scenario.

This was Team Three's specialty: As a team we were responsible for Southwest Asia and the Middle East. Back then Team Three owned the training philosophy around open desert contact with the enemy. Just a year or two before, a SEAL named Forrest Walker had taken a few guys from his training cell all over the world to visit with various Special Ops units to learn from their experiences with desert warfare, especially the British and Australian SAS, and they had built a solid desert warfare program. Team Three was fortunate to be the beneficiaries of Forrest's excellent work. (I would later serve in Afghanistan in the same platoon with Forrest.) We practiced in contact drills that would last up to an hour: sixteen guys moving constantly, using the desert terrain, conserving our ammunition, and at the same time putting down a continued rate of firepower. It takes some skill to conserve ammo so that nobody runs out, at the same time maintaining a steady rate of return fire, and all the while staying in constant motion and using the difficult desert terrain to your advantage.

It also takes a massive amount of coordination. We would suddenly have contact, which always brought with it an element of surprise; even though we were expecting it, we never knew exactly when it would come or from what direction. The lane graders (instructors) who had set this whole scenario up ahead of time would constantly shift the elements of the scenario, challenging us throughout the process. To simulate incoming fire, they would throw grenade simulators into our midst. Often these exercises took place at night, and they would have rigged chem lights on the targets that they could trigger, simulating muzzle flashes. They also had remote detonation devices so that, depending on how our response was unfolding, they could instantly change up the scenario by blowing up something off to our left, or our right, or behind us, big fireballs going on all around us through the course of the hour. We would instantly have to figure out which direction that initial contact was coming from, respond immediately with a blistering volley of overwhelming fire, and at the same time identify an out—exactly which direction do we go to extract ourselves from this contact unscathed? Whoever found the out first had to communicate it instantly and effectively to the rest of the squad.

In a firefight, you can't afford the luxury of coming up with a great plan. You don't have five minutes to think about it. A decent plan executed right now is a lot better than a great plan executed five minutes from now—when you're dead.

Typically the squad would split up into two elements. One guy would peel off and say, "Hey, I've got an out over here!" and while half the squad was laying down fire, the other half would stop firing, get up, run back, get down, and start laying down fire—at which point the first half, having heard the lull and then the renewed fire, would start shifting in turn. It had to work like a perfectly choreographed routine, all unfolding on the fly, taking into account the terrain and conditions as well as the fact that the source of enemy contact might be on the move, too.

What's more, all of this was happening with live rounds. This is something that sets SEAL training apart from most other military training: Everything we do, we do with high-speed live fire, real bullets—hundreds of thousands of rounds. You have to be incredibly careful. We were.

We also had four heavy M-60 machine guns in the platoon. An M-60 is gas operated, air cooled, and belt fed and weighs 23 pounds. It can deal out a sustained rate of about 100 rounds per minute, or in bursts of 200 rounds per minute (9 rounds per second), with a muzzle velocity of 2,750 feet per second. We'd typically fire it off in bursts of three, four, or five rounds; three is ideal because that gets the job done but also conserves ammo. I was one of the M-60 gunners and carried 1,000 of those 7.62 mm rounds on me. My roommate Franny had one of the other big guns, and we would sig off each other: I'd go *dat-dat-dat, dat-dat-dat, dat-dat-dat,* then I'd pause and move as I heard Franny pick it up, *dat-dat-dat, dat-dat-dat, dat-dat-dat.* We'd keep switching back and forth, conserving each other's ammo, playing off each other as if we were musicians in a band, catching each other's rhythm and riffing off one another, keeping that tuneful fire going. This would last for an hour or more.

We did one big final exercise where they combined everything we'd learned and ran us through a few hours of contact. They went out of their way to make it realistic and threw everything in there—bombs going off, live helicopters coming in to extract some of us, jets dropping ordnance, everything. Most people in the military never see training like this. The realism was remarkable.

During our workup's four-week dive phase, I had a new and unique underwater combat experience: going up against dolphins.

In their arsenal of defensive strategies, the EOD (Explosive Ordnance Disposal) guys sometimes use sea lions and/or dolphins as a front line of harbor defense. They train these animals to track down enemy divers, outfitting them with a device strapped onto the head that contains a compressed gas needle. Once the dolphin has tracked you down, it butts you; the needle shoots out and pokes you, creating an embolism. Within moments, you're dead.

Obviously they didn't use the actual device on us, but they had training devices that looked and behaved just like the real thing. When a dolphin succeeded in nailing you, a little foam float would pop up to the surface, indicating that you'd been "killed." The dolphin would then swim to the surface and be rewarded with a sardine. You, on the other hand, would be rewarded with a low score—or with having to do it all over again. Those suckers really packed a wallop. I heard that when you got nailed, you'd be sore for days.

Chief Dan was my partner on this exercise. We could tell when those little bastards were approaching because we could hear their sonar clicking—but that didn't make it any easier to escape them, because they swim *fast,* way too fast for us or any other human being to outrun them.

As a rescue swimmer, though, I'd worked with sonar, and I was pretty sure I understood how the dolphins' sonar sense worked.

"If we stay shallow enough," I told Chief Dan, "and stay close enough to that big rock breakwall, it will mess with their sonar. They won't be able to get a good return signal."

That was our strategy close to shore. Farther out, where there was no way to screw up their sonar, we decided to try using thermoclines to our advantage, going deep and taking care to keep a solid temperature break in between us and the dolphins.

We didn't get hit once.

Our next block was *close-quarters battle* training. CQB is the term for situations where you have to enter a hostile building and comb it, room to room, clearing rooms, taking out bad guys, rescuing hostages, or whatever the mission entails. This is a critically important block of training for a SEAL platoon, because a lot of what we do involves being able to move quickly and fluidly through a complicated environment—whether that means taking over an oil platform, clearing a multistory house, or clearing an entire village—and moving like lightning through close quarters without shooting any hostages or other friendlies, including each other.

This training would prove crucial both in Afghanistan and in Iraq, and it was our training here in STT that made those later live operations work as effectively as they did.

This kind of operation requires an incredible degree of on-the-fly fluidity, flexibility, and adaptiveness. You have to be able to respond, re-act, adjust, and invent on split-second timing, all while avoiding being killed or killing someone else you didn't mean to kill. Typically, the number one man in will go left automatically—but maybe in this case he can't go left because there's an immediate wall there, or the left-hand passageway is blocked off for some other reason. We always had a planned choreography, but plans and reality are usually two different things. These exercises simulated reality as much as possible, in all its unpredictable and messy glory—and it was all with live fire.

For CQB we went to John Shaw's famous shooting-range ranch in Mississippi, the Mid-South Institute of Self-Defense Shooting. They gave us our choice of sidearm: We could use the SIG 226 9 mm pistol, or the H&K SOCOM, which is a big .45 built to SOCOM (Special Operations Command) specs especially for SEALs and other Special Operations forces. I took the Heckler & Koch.

In the past months, as I had gotten to know the various firearms, I had become a big fan of Heckler & Koch. This is the same company that makes the MP-5 9 mm submachine gun (which we also used in these exercises), and its weapons are just so damn reliable. I also like the .45 round. The SIG is a good weapon, but the magazines for the SIGs at the time were not the same quality. (I think it was some aftermarket product, not the factory magazine.) If you're running or the weapon is getting jolted (which is surely going to happen in close-quarters combat), and the rounds stand a chance of rolling or tumbling inside the magazine, you can end up with a jam—and that is something you *do not* want to have happen. I had experienced that tumbling, and I didn't trust that sidearm, so I used the H&K. It never let me down.

We lost one of our guys, Cooter, in this training block for safety violations; he kept shooting the hostage target—and even swept one of us as we were going room to room. (This was, again, with live fire!) Cooter was a hard worker with a solid attitude, and because of that he wasn't tossed out. Instead, they rolled him and put him in a different platoon, where he had to start the whole workup again from the beginning. He did great and went on to make chief.

Outside the shoot house they had a gigantic tractor tire attached to a harness. If you threw a shot off a target or shot a hostage, then it was outside with you. You'd take off all your gear, strap into the harness, and drag that goddam monster for 500 yards, then run back to where you started, put your gear back on, and go inside and do it all over again—and get it right.

I did that tire-drag one time. Once was enough for me.

With all the focus on land warfare and diving, it's easy to forget about the *A* in SEAL, but mastering the skills involved in going airborne is a crucial part of the training, too. During this time I also did a block of high-altitude parachute training, starting with a week of work in the wind tunnel at Fort Bragg learning how to use our bodies as gliders, and then out to the perfect weather of Yuma, Arizona, to take it up into the air. Most of the other guys in the platoon had already picked up this training (and these days, it's automatically a part of the training pipeline right out of BUD/S), but I'd missed it, so they sent me out by myself now to make this one up.

For our first high-altitude jump they took us up in a little CASA C-212 twin-engine plane. When we reached 12,000 feet the ramp went down, and I caught my breath. What an absolutely stunning view. Beautiful and horrifying at the same time.

I'd done static-line jumping before, where a whole line of us jumped together and our chutes were automatically pulled for us. (We call it "dope on a rope.") This time, we were on our own and going solo. There was an instructor on board, but we weren't on tandem. Nobody would be connected to us when we jumped. We each had to throw ourselves out that door, and the rest would be up to us. Truthfully, I was nervous. The whole thing felt so counterintuitive, which is to say, insane. (As they say, you're throwing yourself out a perfectly good airplane!) One army classmate saw that ramp open and sat himself right back down, refused to jump. "That's it," he said, "I'm done with this shit. No way I'm throwing myself out that door. I quit." I understood how he felt, but then the whole SEAL thing kicked in. There was no way I was *not* jumping out that door. The next moment, I was flying.

Soon I was doing it again, only this time at night and on oxygen, at 20,000 feet. This was a whole new experience. Once we jumped we'd be airborne for a good thirty or forty minutes and land a good 40 miles upland from where we dropped. The idea is to have the aircraft drop while you're in clear space, and then you can ride the winds and fly under canopy until you're behind enemy lines, too small to be picked up on radar. We call them HAHO: high-altitude, high-opening ops.

I jumped. Up there it was even more beautiful than it had been at 12,000 feet—and cold as hell, well below freezing. Off to my left I saw an eerie series of lights in the distance: red, green, white, and one or two faintly strobing beacons. It was the navigation lights of a commercial aircraft. I was not alone up there, although the passengers on that craft (who doubtless had no idea a Navy SEAL was dropping by while they sat through their in-flight movie) were probably a lot warmer than I. *A lot less crazy, too,* I told myself and twisted my face into what I thought was a grin, but when your face is being pummeled by the full force of free fall, who knows.

It was one of the most flat-out exhilarating things I'd ever done. I absolutely loved it.

Not everyone felt the same way. We had two guys from Jordan in our class who never got over their terror of jumping. We'd heard they already had something like three hundred jumps behind them back in Jordan, but they'd been a total train wreck in the wind tunnel at Fort Bragg. Then we found out what their parachute training in Jordan had consisted of. They would be flown up and just tossed out of the plane with this helpful hint: "Make sure you pull your rip cord at 5,000 feet." No wonder these guys couldn't get stable in the wind tunnel; they'd been traumatized.

They didn't get any better when we started jumping, either. They would hurl themselves out of that plane and start tumbling head over ass, with no control or poise whatsoever. It was the weirdest thing. They'd always pull at 5,000 feet, right on the money, every single time—but up to that moment they'd be like frigging rag dolls tumbling down a staircase the whole way down. Poor guys ended up getting rolled into the next class. After they left, the instructor showed us a video of one of these guys in free fall, and he was screaming his head off, *Aaaahhhhhhh!!!!* as he tumbled through the air like a piece of furniture. We felt bad for them, but I have to admit, it was pretty hilarious.

Probably the most memorable "training" I received during the entire eighteen months of our platoon's workup was not an official training at all. I sure never got a certificate for it, but it made a lasting impression.

Not long after we met, Gabriele and I had a date set for our wedding. My family had spent good money on the preparations. For whatever crazy reasons kids do crazy things, though, around the second week of MAROPS, we decided we couldn't wait any longer. We quietly eloped—snuck off to Vegas and hit a chapel.

When we got back I said, "Look, my mom will kill me if I tell her what we did. She's planned this whole big thing. She'll be devastated." I swore Gabriele to secrecy. I couldn't let my mother find out, and since my sister, Rhiannon, was living right in the area and going to San Diego State, we couldn't let her find out either.

That same evening we went out to dinner at a nice place with the guys from the platoon, all there with their wives and girlfriends. Somehow the news leaked out. I suspect Gabriele just couldn't keep it to herself and took one of her friends into the ladies room and whispered it to her. The next thing you know I was tying myself in knots trying to defend this little white lie. "Hey," one of the guys said, "I heard you got married?"

"No," I said quickly, "someone doesn't know what they're talking about." I completely denied it. SEALs are resourceful, though. This was 1999, still the covered-wagon days of the Internet, but they went Web surfing and managed to find our Clark County marriage certificate online.

A few days later I was due to receive a conduct award at Friday quarters. This is something that typically happens every four years, if you have managed to stay out of trouble. Friday morning rolled around, we all mustered for quarters, and I heard my name called out. I went and stood in front of the whole team and our CO, Captain McRaven (Harward was gone by now), began reading out what I fully expected was going to be a conduct award. He started by reading my name, rank, and training history, and then he veered off into some pretty bizarre stuff, including a description of my sexual orientation, and then launched into a long list of "atrocities" I'd committed—concluding with how I had lied to my platoon. (I later learned that Chief Dan had written it. I wish I had a copy. It was a masterpiece.)

I was mortified and felt my face turn beet red. I had lied to my platoon, and now everyone knew it.

Reputation.

As summary punishment the whole team grabbed me and threw me in the ocean, which was pretty funny, except that I knew it wasn't over. There was a hazing in my future.

Every new guy had already gotten a basic welcome-to-the-platoon hazing out at San Clemente Island. That was bad, but we all knew it was coming and handled it well. It's a rite of passage that lets you know: *Hey, you may think you know something, and you may think you're pretty hot stuff—but you don't, and you're not.* I know it sounds harsh, but the truth is, most of us *did* think we were pretty hot stuff by that point, and maybe we did need to be cut down to size.

I also knew what normally happened to guys in the platoon who got married: They would get hazed. I once saw a newly engaged guy walking around innocently in downtown Coronado when a navy van with no license plates pulled up and a few guys in balaclavas jumped out and snatched the guy right off the street, threw him in the van, and took off. That was *normal,* but I'd withheld my news and then lied about it when confronted. I knew I was going to get it even worse.

They got me that same night. We had just come back from a beach training, about two in the morning. I was peeling off my wet suit, had it around my ankles—and the guys grabbed me and wrapped me up in something. Next thing I knew I was duct-taped stark naked to a metal cart we used for hauling equipment. They wheeled me over to the ice machine, dumped ice on me, then wheeled me into a gear storage area and started taping me up.

The CO happened to walk through and saw something out of the corner of his eye—but Chief Dan whispered something to him and he scurried off as if he hadn't seen a thing: plausible deniability.

They gave me a "lobster claw," duct-taping my hands into claws so I had no use of my fingers. Then they gave me a "happy hat," taping over the tops of my eyebrows, so I had a hard time seeing out from under the duct tape, then taping a handle onto my head so they could move it around like a marionette. They asked me, "Are you having a good time?" and then they nodded my head for me, *Yes, thank you.*

Chief Dan had a running commentary going, telling me that this was why I never wanted to lie to my platoon again. He interrupted himself to yell, "Go get the tequila!" A moment later, he put the bottle to my mouth and made me take a shot. It was the cheapest, worst tequila money could buy, just vile stuff, and I drank probably half the bottle by the time the night was over. Which was probably a good thing for me, because it did somewhat numb the experience.

Next they brought out a miniature handheld generator we use in demolition work, about the size of a small cell phone, called a miniblasting machine. You squeeze it four, five, six times in rapid succession, and you can hear it building up a charge, *rrrr, rrrr, RRRR, RRRR!!*—and then it lets loose with enough of a charge to set off a blasting cap. Only in this case, the wires weren't tied into a blasting cap. They were wired into me. Chief Dan had the guys screw a set of claymore wires into the handheld generator and hook the other ends up with alligator clips to my nipples.

I don't know how many volts go through that thing, but when that charge hits you, you lose all control, and that was exactly what I did.

Next, someone was ripping open an MRE, because every MRE contains a little bottle of Tabasco sauce. I strained to see who was doing this. *Oh, shit.* It was Krueger, the guy who took such pleasure in giving it to the new guys. *Not good.* Krueger opened the Tabasco sauce and poured it over my private parts. Now, I like hot food as much as the next guy, but having it on the outside is quite different than having it on the inside. When that Tabasco sauce hit my balls, I thought someone had dipped me in kerosene and lit a match.

The whole time, the senior guys were drinking beers, laughing and talking, tunes going on the radio in the background, while they gave the new guys orders. The new guys were getting pretty freaked out. Later they told me what was going through their minds at the time: *It's only a matter of time before one or more of us get thrown into the mix, too.* Meanwhile, Chief Dan continued giving me lessons on platoon ethics and the importance of holding your platoon above all else.

Now Krueger put on a pair of surgical gloves, took a pair of clippers, and started clipping off all my pubic hair. Then he put one hand over my eyes, took a can of spray glue that we use to attach targets on the shooting range, spray-glued my face, and sprinkled the clippings all over me.

Ah, perfect. Now I had a beard made of my own pubic hair.

I was freezing to death, nuts on fire, waiting for another shock any minute. Finally Chief Dan said, "All right, somebody call Gabriele and ask her to come get him." They called Gabriele from my cell phone, but she didn't pick up. I was supposed to have been home hours ago, and she naturally assumed I was out drinking with my buddies and just now getting around to calling her to say I was sorry, that I'd be home soon. She was too pissed off to answer.

I suspected they were making the call because they'd run out of beer, so they figured they might as well quit. I was right, but when she never picked up, Chief Dan just shrugged—and sent off one of the new guys to go get another 18-pack.

The torture lasted another thirty minutes. Finally they quit, leaving Glen and the Rat to untape me and help me through the shower. It took four razor blades to get my face clean, or at least mostly clean. I was picking off bits of spray glue for weeks.

That was the last time I ever got hazed, and it left an impression—not only on me, but on all the guys. They talk about it to this day. I'll tell you what, though: I never lied to the platoon again.

In the spring of 2000 our eighteen-month workup concluded with an Operational Readiness Exam (ORE), conducted off San Clemente Island, in which a small group of us simulated a covert tagging and tracking op on an enemy vessel. There were some tricky issues with water currents on the way back in, and things got sketchy. By the time we got back to rendezvous with our vessel, I had run out of air and had a headache, but we passed the exercise. GOLF platoon was certified and operationally ready to rotate overseas to serve in an alert status, which the platoon would do after a little downtime.

Before it did, though, something unexpected happened that changed the course of my career in the navy.

One day shortly after our ORE, Glen and I were called in to see our OIC, McNary. When we entered his office we found Tom, our platoon LPO, and Chief Dan there with him. Clearly something was up, something big, but we had no idea what.

Were we in some sort of trouble?

"Listen," said McNary, "you guys have done a really great job here, and we're short-handed on snipers right now. We want to offer you the opportunity to go to sniper school."

I was not planning to become a sniper. In fact, the thought had never occurred to me. Of course, we all knew the SEALs *had* snipers, and we all knew how difficult a course it was. The whole thing seemed fascinating, but I'd never for an instant considered that I might become one of those guys. All my life, I'd loved being in the water, and all my life I'd wanted to be a pilot, but a sniper? Not a chance. Now here it was, being offered to us on a plate.

We were stunned. We were thrilled. We were terrified.

It was unheard of for a new guy to get a sniper billet. There were some seriously seasoned guys on the team who had waited years to get a slot; that's how hard they were to get. We knew it was a fiendishly difficult school to pass, and the last thing anyone wanted was some wet-behind-the-ears new guy in there, because he'd just fuck it up and wash out. We also knew that everyone would be watching us, including our entire platoon, hell, our entire team, and that they would all be counting on us. If we washed out, we would be letting them down. If we said yes, we would spend the next three months under excruciating pressure.

We didn't hesitate for a second.

SIX

COLD BORE

There are some pretty difficult schools and training courses in the United States military, but none has quite the reputation of SEAL sniper training. It is one of the toughest programs anywhere on the planet. Even when compared to my combat tours in Afghanistan and later in Iraq, I count my time in sniper school as one of the most intense, grueling experiences of my life.

The SEAL sniper course is three months of twelve-plus hour days, seven days a week. Ironically, it is not all that demanding physically. After going through the brutality of BUD/S and some of the programs in SEAL Tactical Training, there was nothing in the sniper course that posed any real physical challenge. Nevertheless, it is extremely challenging mentally.

"First and foremost? *Intellectual capacity*." When people ask what it takes to become a Navy SEAL sniper, that's my first answer. Don't get me wrong: You have to be physically tough. Our training demands that every graduate be one of a unique breed, willing to snake his way through treacherous urban war-zone terrain or crawl the hot desert floor for hours, slow as a snail and often through his own bodily waste, sometimes withstanding days on end of unendurable physical hardship, to set up on his target. Still, the physical ability is maybe 10 percent of it. Most of it is mental.

Sniper school is one of the very few courses a SEAL will not be looked down upon for failing to complete. It's an unwritten rule that you don't give guys a hard time for washing out of sniper school. Because the course is known for its insane difficulty, just being selected or volunteering to go automatically elicits respect in the teams.

The students who entered the course were already the cream of the crop, but the attrition rate was still vicious. When I took the sniper course in the spring of 2000, we classed up with twenty-six guys at the start. Three months of continuous training later, only twelve of us would graduate.

A few weeks after our conversation in Lieutenant McNary's office, Glen and I, along with two dozen others, mustered at the SEAL Team Five quarterdeck in Coronado for our initial sniper school in-briefing. Though this would later change, at the time the different SEAL teams would rotate as course host, and it happened to be Team Five's turn.

They told us that there were two principal parts to the sniper training. First came the shooting phase, which would focus on learning our weapons, advanced ballistics, and, of course, the actual marksmanship training, during which we would work in pairs taking turns as shooter or spotter. Second was the stalking phase, where we would be trained in the arts of stealth and concealment.

We would be conducting the shooting phase at the Coalinga range, a private inland facility about a hundred miles northwest of Bakersfield, where we would camp out, receive all our instruction, and do all our shooting. In the event we survived the shooting phase, we would then go on to the stalking phase, concluding with our graded final training exercise (FTX) out in the California desert near Niland.

Being from Team Three, which at the time had charge over the desert theater of operations, Glen and I were already quite familiar with the challenges of operating in that ungodly terrain and how fucking miserable it could be there. We took comfort in the idea that this prior knowledge might give us some small advantage in the final phase. Assuming we made it that far.

We were led to the team armory, where we each checked out the suite of weapons we would be working with over the next few months. We each got a sniper M-14, a Remington .308 bolt gun, a Remington .300 Win Mag, and a .50 cal, along with scopes and ammo.

Once we had our weapons, we mustered back in the Team Five area to meet our instructor cadre.

At the time, the sniper school was run by a master chief named Jordan, who was just in the process of turning it over to Senior Chief Seth Carver. Seth was an ultramarathoner, one of those guys who runs 100-mile races but doesn't make any kind of big deal about himself. He was a total professional and highly respected by everyone there. A few years later I would end up working for Chief Carver as part of an advanced sniper training cell and would be on hand to see his life crumble to pieces and be salvaged by the goodwill of the team. We'll come to that story later. For now, Chief Carver was simply one of the good guys, one of those instructors we could count on both for his expertise and for his solid character.

That didn't apply in every case. Our instructor cadre consisted of several full-time instructors along with a few guys pulled from the different SEAL teams to help out and augment the staff. In terms of their shooting skills, these guys were all at the top of their game, but they were not necessarily good teachers. This is something we would change later on, when I became part of the team that redesigned the entire sniper course, but when we went through the course back in 2000, there wasn't much emphasis on teaching skills. It was a sink-or-swim deal: *Here's the training, and if you don't get it, tough.*

After meeting our instructors, we got the rest of our gear list and were divided into shooting pairs. Glen and I were happy to learn we had been paired as shooting partners. We had been working together in GOLF platoon for over a year by this point, had developed a good friendship, and trusted each other implicitly. As intimidated as we were, things were lining up in our favor. Now we just had to do the work—and do it perfectly.

We kicked off the course by going out to Camp Pendleton for a qualifying shoot. Just to *start* the sniper course, we had to be shooting on the standard navy rifle at expert level. They took us through a brief class to make sure we all knew how to set up and operate all our weapons, and then we were out on the range shooting.

We started off at 100 yards, doing a standing shot, then sitting shot, then standing-to-sitting rapid, then a prone slow fire, then a standing-to-prone rapid fire. Next we went out to 200 yards and shot another volley. Out of a perfect score of 200, we had to shoot at least 180 to qualify as shooting expert. We each got two tries. Some guys didn't make it, so we lost a few right then and there.

The rest of us saddled up and headed north for Coalinga, where we would spend the next six weeks camping out on the property of the Coalinga Rifle Club, a five-hour drive from San Diego up in California's Central Valley. When we arrived there, we found the place had a shower, bathroom facilities, a small kitchen facility, and that was about it. The classes would take place outdoors on picnic tables under the cover of a few shade trees. As we soon learned, it got hot as hell out there.

This place sports one of the largest shooting ranges in the West; the regional and state shooting championships are held there. It's also fairly isolated—far enough away from any distractions (read: women and beer) that it would force us to focus on the task at hand.

A few days after we arrived we were joined by guys from the Army Marksmanship Unit (AMU), the military's elite match shooting team. The SEALs are not known for their humility within the Special Operations community, but for what it's worth, we always strive for the best, even when that means going outside our community. In this case our instructor cadre was smart enough to bring in the best of the best. These guys could *shoot*. Most of them would go on to compete at the highest levels worldwide; some had Olympic gold medals to their credit. I quickly realized I needed to pay attention, take notes, and do whatever these guys suggested. This was some of the best marksmanship training I have ever received, and their training methods would not only stay with me throughout my time in the teams, they would also influence my teaching practices in the future.

We started out shooting iron sights, meaning without scopes, on the 7.62 mm M-14, a classic rifle that the U.S. military had relied on for four decades. Iron sights on a rifle consist of two elements, a rear sight and front sight, which you use to line up your view of the target. They are similar to the little notchlike sights on a pistol, except that the M-14 rifle sights provide knobs that allow you to dial in your windage (side-to-side adjustment to compensate for the effects of wind) and elevation (vertical adjustment to compensate for factors including distance).

The AMU sharpshooters taught us the fundamentals, including sight picture and sight alignment, breathing, grip, and trigger pull. They taught us about sight fixture: fixing on that sight post, which may be a centimeter wide on the front sight, visually splitting it in half and focusing on the top center edge. This requires an exceptionally tight degree of mental focus and concentration. A visual misalignment of even a tiny fraction of a millimeter, magnified by the distance you're shooting, can result in a complete miss, and the farther out you're shooting, the greater that magnification—in other words, the greater the need for complete accuracy in your sight alignment.

They taught us how to control our breath and how to work with our natural breathing cycle. Common sense might suggest that the best way to take an accurate shot would be to hold your breath. Actually, it's just the opposite. Instead of fighting your natural breathing cycle, you have to learn how to use it. When you're lying down, as you typically are when taking aim for a long shot, your rifle's sights slowly rise and fall with the movement of your chest expanding and contracting. What you want to do is time your shot so that it comes precisely during the lull of the natural respiratory pause at the bottom of your exhale, so your breathing doesn't affect the shot's elevation.

They taught us about something called natural point of aim: Whether you're kneeling, sitting, standing, or lying down, after you put your sights on the target, you scoot your body back and forth until you've put yourself into a position where you're naturally aligned with the target. If you have to swing your arm over to get on sight with the target, even if only slightly, that means you are using your muscles, which is not ideal. Instead, you want to be relaxed in perfect position such that that your alignment is naturally focused on the target.

We shot all the way back to 800 yards without scopes, except a personal spotting scope. We would have the spotting scope set up next to us so we could lean over, look through the scope, read the wind (for both direction and wind speed) and the mirage, estimate the windage (compensating horizontal adjustment) in minutes of angle (a minute is one-sixtieth of a degree), dial in a correction on our iron sight windage knob, then roll over and take the shot. Mirage is the heat-rippling effect you see when you look down a highway on a hot day. You can adjust your scope so it's visible, and it flows like a river, either to the right or to the left, showing which way the wind is blowing. Or it might flow straight upward, in which case we call it a boil, meaning that there is either no wind at all or that the wind is blowing straight toward you. You're also looking for any telltale signs, whether it's grass blowing in the distance or just the feel of the wind on your face. You get to be an acute observer of exactly what is going on in your environment and an excellent judge of how to apply that to your weapon.

There is a tremendous amount of science involved in making all these observations, but the art of it is bringing them all together into an extremely precise picture of the overall scenario. What is the weather doing at your position as the shooter? Looking down the range halfway to your target, what's happening at *that* position? Is that valley funneling the wind a certain way? What's happening 800 yards away, all the way down to where the target is sitting? Is the wind calm there, or moving, and if so, in what direction, and how strongly? Calculating all those factors, then assembling them all together to arrive at an estimation of exactly what you think is happening and precisely how it all applies to your weapon, and then making the perfect shot—it's incredibly complicated, and there is zero margin for error.

During the day we shot for five hours in the morning, then received instruction and testing until dark, went to sleep, woke up, and did it all over again.

In our second week on the M-14 iron sights we started shooting cold bore tests every morning at 6:00 A.M., and the stress levels escalated.

The cold bore shot is staged to simulate that all-important first shot taken in a combat situation in the field, when you don't have the luxury of taking practice shots and letting your rifle warm up. You need to be able to sight down a cold gun and take that first shot, right out of the box, with 100 percent reliable accuracy. That first shot has to be a kill shot— because if it isn't, you likely won't get a second chance.

The unique conditions of a cold bore shot are not simply a matter of human factors. Yes, that's part of it; we had to learn how to be at the top of our game instantly, with no opportunity to warm up and shake it out with a few practice shots. But there's also pure physics involved, because the bullet behaves very differently when the rifle is cold. As you shoot rounds through a metal chamber, it heats up, creating an increase in chamber pressure, which translates into a change in the bullet's trajectory. Put a bullet through a hot chamber and it may travel as much as a few hundred feet per second faster than when you put it through a cold chamber. Elevation—how far the bullet travels before succumbing to gravity and beginning its inevitable downward arc—is profoundly affected. This is why snipers are careful to track and log our cold bore data.

The night before, they would tell us, "Tomorrow morning, the whole class on the 500-yard line"—or whatever point on the range they'd selected for the following day's cold bore test. I would go to sleep with my single bullet next to me in my sleeping bag and my gun and kit all laid out and ready to go. I didn't want *anyone* screwing with my weapon.

We awoke early to head out to the range, taking only our rifle and a single round. Once we assembled at the prescribed location, they would give us our instructions: "Okay, you've got thirty seconds to sprint to the 300-yard line and engage your target from the standing position. Ready, *go.*" We took off at a sprint.

Right away, we were dealing with conflicting parameters. The faster you run, the sooner you get to your location and the more time you have to line up the shot—but the faster you run, the harder it is to control your breathing once you get there, which means the greater the chance that your breathing will screw up your shot. In those thirty seconds you not only have to reach your new location, you also then have to read the wind correctly, dial in the dope (the correct elevation data), identify your own target (nothing worse than shooting someone else's!), estimate lead if yours happens to be a moving target, do your best to slow down your heart rate, and in general get your shit together as rapidly as is humanly possible—and then take the shot.

And there were a lot of ways to screw this up.

Sometimes guys would forget to put their round in the chamber, or forget to dial in the right elevation. If we were starting out on the 500-yard line, for example, we would have already dialed that into our sights when we got there—but if we then sprinted to the 300-yard line and forgot to dial elevation down to 300, then we'd miss the shot. Sometimes guys would get everything right but be so nervous about forgetting something they would just blow the shot anyway.

The cold bore test was scored on a 10-point scale. If your shot landed inside the kill zone (head and heart), you received a 10. If you shot outside the kill zone but still within the human silhouette on the target, you got an 8. Miss the silhouette but still manage to hit the target and you scored a 7. God help you if you missed the target altogether, because you just landed a 0, and the other guys would then avoid you like the plague for fear your bad juju would rub off. Two or three goose eggs bought you a one-way ticket back to your SEAL team. This was made crystal clear to us from the beginning. The standard to beat was 80 percent, and if you didn't at least meet that standard, there was no drama about it, you were just gone. You made the cut, or you were out. I saw guys whose scores came in at 79 percent told to pack their bags. Every day was survival. As the saying goes in the teams, "The only easy day was yesterday."

Another part of the cold bore routine was edge shots. We would lie down in our lane and wait for the target, which would suddenly appear at some point in the next twenty minutes. We would have no idea when it was coming. All we could do was wait in a state of total vigilance. Take your eyes off the sight for even a moment—to wipe sweat off your brow, scratch an itch on your face, or take a drink of water—and you could miss it entirely.

I saw this happen. One morning, a guy a few lanes down from me looked down just for a second to wipe the fog off his shooting glasses—and he looked back up just in time to see his target lying down again. He had just missed it. "Noooo!" the poor bastard cried out. Brutal, but it certainly trained us to be patient and vigilant at the same time.

The cold bore shot was one of the most stressful events of the entire day. Hit or miss, that shot would stay with you. Make a good shot and you were a hero. Blow it and your own personal dark cloud hung overhead for the rest of the day.

I'll never forget the morning of my first cold bore shot. We ran out onto the range, got our instructions, hustled to our shooting line, threw ourselves on the ground, and scrambled mightily to get our shit together for that first shot.

ONE! TWO! THREE! FOUR!

One by one we counted off our lane numbers, right to left, so that we knew for sure which lane we were shooting in and wouldn't fuck up and hit someone else's target. I chambered my one and only round, got myself settled into my natural point of aim as best I could, target aligned and on sights, felt the tide of my respiration ebb to its lowest point, and in the short moment of that stillness squeezed the trigger—

And I missed the target completely.

Oh, man, I thought. Right off the bat, I was in the hole: a 0. I couldn't afford many more of those if I hoped to survive.

Fortunately for me, that was my first and only complete miss. I started out pretty rough in the cold bore tests, hitting mostly 7s. As the days went by I steadily improved my ability to control myself, and my scores slowly crept upward.

The stress of that morning cold bore shot got to a number of guys in the class. Sometimes they just could not bring the day's score up to 80 percent. Pretty soon the camp started thinning out as our numbers began to dwindle. It was eerie the way this happened. Guys would just disappear.

Nobody would ask any questions or make any comments for fear of jinxing their own chances.

The cold bore shot felt to me like the perfect expression of what it means to be a SEAL sniper, and it carried over into everything we did. We quickly learned that you can't always have the ideal circumstances, or even reasonably helpful circumstances. You can't always take practice shots. You have to be ready to perform at the very top of your abilities, instantly and without preparation, and under the very worst of circumstances, and do it over and over again—and do it perfectly every time.

Our third week at Coalinga, I woke up one morning with an ugly welt on my arm. I'd been bitten by a brown recluse spider as I slept. *Shit!* Brown recluse bites are no joke. They can rot right through your arm, and it happens fast. I tried to self-treat the bite, but infection had already set in. I was sent off to the nearest naval hospital in Lemoore, about an hour away, for some heavy-artillery antibiotics.

It wasn't much of a holiday. Brown recluse bite or no brown recluse bite, the scores on the range were not going to wait for my arm to heal. Within a few hours I was back out on the yard lines shooting M-14 iron sights.

During those long hours on the range, we were not shooting continuously the entire time. They would split the class in half, and while one half was shooting, the other half was down in the butts, pulling and marking targets for our classmates.

The butts was a secured bunker area behind the targets that provided a little shade and held the large target frames. When we rotated back to the butts, we would be in charge of raising and lowering the target frames on a pulley system in order to mark the bullet impacts and clean them off in preparation for the next round. Usually we would spell each other out there, half of us pulling and marking the targets while the other half goofed off. It was a good way to take a break from the intense pressure of shooting and give each other a hard time, something we were always fond of in the teams.

Never underestimate the shenanigans bored grown men are capable of perpetrating on each other. Once we ran out of stories (usually X-rated, and mostly true), we would come up with all sorts of crazy ways to occupy our time. One game I was especially fond of was Rock Duel; this one brought out the empty-lot rock-fight kid in me. Here's how it works.

Two people pair up. You each pace off 20 yards, perform an about-face, then shoot a rock-paper-scissors to determine who goes first. The winner proceeds to chuck a well-aimed, baseball-sized rock at the other person (no head shots, of course), who is forbidden to move or even flinch and stands as still as possible, hoping for a miss so he can then have his turn. The first person to score a kill shot is declared the winner, and the next two guys take their place and have a go. It was a great stress reliever.

We had some fun down there in the butts, but it was not without its hazards. Those metal target frames were huge, and the pulley system that raised and lowered them used 50-pound concrete counterweights. One day, as I stepped up to get into the bench seating area where we controlled the targets, someone yanked on a target. Between my inattention and his carelessness, the metal frame whacked me right in the head.

Oops. Suddenly there was blood everywhere.

This happened to be the day we were first sighting our .300 Win Mags. This was crucial: when first getting a new weapon we would have one day to dial it in, get all our elevations, and get the feel of the thing. I could not miss that day. I couldn't miss *any* day. So they ran me out to the doctor's, cleaned me up, slammed seven staples into my head, and ran me back to Coalinga. Within a few hours of the incident I was back on the range, sighting in my new weapon. My head was pounding with every shot, and it felt like someone was nailing a steel spike into my skull. *Tough. Deal with it.* Adapt and overcome.

A few weeks later, right after finishing the shooting phase, Gabriele and I had our official wedding ceremony and reception. (We had managed to keep the secret from my family.) Fortunately, my hair had grown in just enough so that the staples didn't show in my wedding pictures.

Along with the shooting drills, which kept us busy for up to eight hours a day, we also had extensive classroom work, which we did mostly during the heat of the day, sandwiched in between sessions on the range. We would get up early and shoot all morning, then do our classroom and practical exercises during the early afternoon hours, when the heat was at its height. In the later afternoon, we'd head back out onto the range and practice on the guns again.

Every few classes we would be tested on whatever we'd learned. As with the shooting tests, it was either pass or you're gone, no in between.

One of our classes consisted of a series of drills called keep-in-memory exercises, or KIMs. As a sniper, there are times when you have only a brief glance at a situation, and you have to be able to fix it all in your memory almost instantaneously. These exercises were designed to hone our capacity for accurate snapshot memory.

The instructors would lay a tarp over an array of objects, bring us in and stand us in front of the covered array, and then yank off the tarp, giving us thirty seconds to look at everything and memorize it all before the tarp went back to cover everything. Then we'd have to write it all down. Or they would scatter a series of objects over a hillside, and we'd have to scan it quickly with our binoculars and in that brief glance pick out everything that was out of the ordinary.

We also did very detailed target sketches, similar to the KIMs: In a given amount of time, we would have to sketch a target in detail and also record all sorts of data. From which direction was the sun shining? What were the weather patterns? Where were possible helo insertion points?

Helo extraction points? Exactly what was happening right around the area of the target? Digital cameras and laptops had not yet become the ubiquitous technologies they are today, and we had to do our field sketches and record all this information by hand.

Some of our most extensive classroom study was in the area of ballistics, including internal ballistics, external ballistics, and terminal ballistics.

Internal ballistics is what's happening on the inside of the rifle. When your firing pin hits the bullet's strike plate, it sets off an initial powder charge, and the exploding powder creates a rapidly expanding gas bubble, which propels the slug, or front portion of the bullet, through the chamber. It's very much a miniature version of a rocket ship launch. Just as the rocket discards its boosters once it's in flight, the rifle ejects the empty cartridge, sending only the relatively small front portion on its journey. In the rocket's case, that's the capsule that houses the astronauts. In the bullet's case, it's the death-dealing slug.

The inside of the rifle's barrel is inscribed with a series of spiral grooves, or rifling (where the term "rifle" comes from). This puts a fast spin on the bullet, giving it stability in flight, much the way you put a spin on a football when you throw it. Internal ballistics has to do with how many twists there are in the barrel and their precise effect on the bullet, how fast the bullet travels, and how it's moving when it exits the rifle.

This is where external ballistics takes over. Your bullet will start its journey at a velocity of over 2,000 feet per second. However, the moment it emerges from the barrel its flight path is already being influenced by its environment. Leaving aside for the moment the effect of wind, there is a universal drag created by the friction of that ocean of air the bullet pierces through in order to fly, combined with the downward pull of gravity. At a certain distance, different for different weapons and ammunition, your particular rifle bullet slows to the point where it passes from supersonic to subsonic. As it eats through the yards at rates of something like 1 yard every $\frac{1}{1,000}$ of a second, the integrity of its flight path becomes compromised. A .308 bullet traveling at 2,200 feet per second will lose its flight-path stability to the point where it starts tumbling head over heels by about 900 or 1,000 meters out.

External ballistics is also about exactly what that flight path looks like. When you shoot a .308 at a target 800 yards away, you're not shooting in a straight line; it actually makes a pretty big arc. Imagine throwing a football from the 50-yard line to the end zone. You don't throw it straight toward the goal. Instead, you know you have to throw it upward so that it arcs through the air, hitting its high point at about the 25-yard line and then curving back down to reach the end zone. The same thing happens with the .308 bullet. You're not shooting it in a straight line; you're really throwing it up in the air so that it arcs and comes down where you want it to. Understanding exactly how that works can have a make-or-break bearing on successfully hitting your target.

For example, let's say you're shooting at something 800 yards away. In the terrain lying between you and your target, you notice a low-hanging bridge. From all appearances, that's no problem. Your target stands at maybe 5'8"; you are lying on the ground, on your stomach; and the bridge is a good 10 feet off the ground at its lowest point. When you sight down through your scope at the target, you can see a clear pathway from you straight to the target. No problem, right?

Wrong. That bridge may not *look* like it's in the way—but when you take into account the arc your bullet needs to travel to land at your projected site, that bridge could be lying directly in the path of what we call the bullet's top arc. In other words, it could stop your bullet cold, halfway to your target. And in the kinds of circumstances a sniper will often be facing, you may not have the luxury of a second shot. You have to know your bullet's maximum ordinate, that is, the maximum height that bullet will reach on its path to your target, and calculate for that.

Once we had mastered the M-14 we moved on to other weapons, starting with the .308 bolt action Remington, a very solid weapon and quite capable out to 800 or 900 yards, in the right hands. This was our first look at a real scoped weapon—and right away, I knew had a problem. There was a Leupold scope on one of my guns that just didn't seem quite right. I pretty quickly realized that it wasn't maintaining at zero: it was slipping off. There was no way I could shoot with a scope that wasn't reliable.

These weapons are not delicate; they're made to withstand the rigors of combat. However, they are pieces of precision machinery, and they're not infallible. For example, the barrel of a .300 Win Mag is only good for a few thousand rounds, and then you shoot out the barrel and it starts losing accuracy. We were shooting thousands and thousands of rounds.

If your gun starts to malfunction in the middle of a shooting evolution, the instructor might assume it's you. In a lot of cases, he's right. In some cases, though, the weapon really *is* shot out, or there's some kind of equipment malfunction. We had a few guys who were excellent shots but got flushed out of the course because they had the bad luck of getting a weapon that didn't have a good log and was legitimately shot out, and they didn't yet have the skills or know-how to deal with it right away.

I was determined not to let that happen. My first shooting test was coming up. No way was this faulty scope going to flush me from sniper school. I told my instructors about it, and when they didn't do anything I kept bringing it up. I wouldn't let it rest. Finally they got an armorer out there from Crane, the navy's ordnance testing division. He looked at the scope and said, "Yeah, you have a bad optic."

Thank God. I easily could have flunked out in my first test because of a messed-up scope.

At the same time that we started working with scopes on the .308, we also started working in pairs, taking turns as shooter and as spotter. The shooter's job is to put everything else out of his mind, take the information the spotter feeds him, and make a perfect shot, period. As we soon learned, the spotter's job is in many ways more complex and more difficult.

As spotter, you are on the spotting scope, identifying and monitoring the target. Your job is to calculate windage and give target lead if necessary (that is, how much to compensate for the target's movement). As spotter you also watch the shot trace, which tells its own story and either proves the call dead-on accurate or gives important clues for correcting the next shot. Yes, even though it is traveling at speeds of 2,000 feet per second or more, you actually *watch* the damn thing. In most cases you can literally see those vapor trails all the way in to the target.

The spotter has to take all these considerations into account—and we had to learn it all in a hell of a hurry, or we would be going home.

Even aside from the fact that we were friends, Glen and I soon found that we made an excellent sniper pair. Glen is a naturally gifted marksman. I don't remember him ever missing a single shot, and most of his shots were perfect 10s. For my part, I seemed to have a natural gift for reading the wind and being able to calculate all the conditions and circumstances. Again, I think this had to do with my experience with navigation and having grown up near the water. Water currents and wind currents may be two very different things, but it is really the same basic concept, albeit in different media and moving at much different speeds. When you're sailing or boating, you're always thinking, *What's the weather doing? How is this affecting my point A to point B?* It's the same dynamic when you're preparing to fire a bullet. *I'm here, my target's there—what factors are affecting my getting from here to there?*

Reach your hand down into a stream or lake, and you might notice that it looks like it juts off as if your arm were suddenly bent at a sharp angle. Likewise, when you see a trout in a stream, it isn't located exactly where it looks like it's located. This is because the light is refracted by the body of water, creating an optical illusion. The same thing happens in the atmosphere. When the sun is low in the horizon, it creates the same kind of refractory optical illusion, and you have to compensate for that in your aim, maybe dial it down a minute of angle.

With my knack for spotting and Glen's natural gifts as a shooter, we made a deadly pair. Plus, we were both new guys, and we felt the same pressure to get this right. We'd have a few beers at night, but we didn't drink or carouse much. We were focused on staying locked on tight and getting through this thing.

Not that there was much in the way of nightlife anyway. Coalinga is a small town, with a prison, some farming, and not a whole lot more going on. On rare occasions we went out for a drink or got a bite to eat in town. Most often, though, we'd make a big bonfire right there where we were camping, drink a few beers, and tell each other crazy stories.

One guy, Ken, had a *Penthouse* magazine and would lie there at night in his sleeping bag jerking off, thinking he had all the privacy in the world. Unfortunately, he had this head lamp switched on so he could see his damn magazine, and as a result he would unintentionally be giving the whole camp a shadow-puppet show on the wall of his tent. "Goddammit, Ken, quit jerking off!" we'd yell out. "Or at least turn off the damn light!"

The range had a nice little grass campground complete with a kitchen and a restrooms/shower area. All the students were instructed to bring a tent and kit. Most of the guys traveled pretty light. I take just what I need, and it all fits in my pack. Guys in the teams had a saying, "Pack light and mooch." My saying was "Don't pack light—pack right." Not Glen, though. As I soon learned, Glen liked to travel in comfort, which meant plenty of extras. He was like a one-man gypsy camp. He must have gone out and bought the biggest tent he could find at the local Kmart; that thing could have slept a family of ten. He had three fuel-burning lanterns, a radio, a coffeemaker, a generator—it was out of control.

We were partners, so my tent was right next to his. I love Glen like a brother, but this was torture. That son of a bitch would be up and about for a solid hour before the rest of us in camp even started thinking about opening our eyes, and once he was up it was nearly impossible to stay asleep because his gypsy encampment lit up the whole side of my tent. First I was awakened by the blinding white glow and steady hum of his Coleman-exploration power lanterns. Then the sounds would start: his percolating coffeepot, then some sort of eighties rock music blaring through his earphones, which he thought we couldn't hear but in fact only made him even more oblivious to the extent of the racket he was making, messing around with all his stuff, clattering around and getting his coffee ready, burping and farting but not hearing himself because he had those earphones in, then followed by his electric toothbrush, endless loud gargle, and the invariable lengthy punctuating spit that made us all groan. After a week or so of this daily routine, the guys began referring to Glen's morning ablutions as "Chernobyl."

If I had my choice, I would pull myself out of sleep maybe twenty minutes before we had to muster up, giving myself just enough time to brush my teeth, throw some water on my face, and grab my gear. But no. I tried for days, but it was not possible. Finally I succumbed and started letting Glen be my alarm clock.

Soon we had our first graded test on the .308.

As pairs we shared a combined grade, so we knew we would sink or swim together as a shooter/spotter pair. Glen and I scored in the nineties on that first test, but by that time we were both feeling completely frazzled and harried.

Still, we knew we had developed into a solid shooting pair, and we seemed to handle the stress better than many of the other guys. During that first paired shooting evolution, we could see the tension level in some of the other pairs simmering; by the time of that test, a few of them went through complete meltdowns.

Typically what happened was that the spotter would make a bad call or, even worse, not make a call at all and leave his shooter partner hanging. One or two of these scenarios and the honeymoon would be way beyond over. We saw guys actually throw down and get into a knock-down, drag-out fistfight because a buddy had fucked up multiple calls. Needless to say, this constituted a guaranteed ticket home.

Pretty soon it dawned on us that the steadily escalating stress we were seeing was no accident. Not only was it intentional, it was being carefully orchestrated. Our instructors were constantly watching, pushing, and testing us to see who could handle the stress and who could not.

One day, while I was spotting, Glen took a shot that I could clearly see had struck the target—but our instructor marked it as a miss.

"What?" Glen exclaimed. I knew what he was about to say next: *That's total bullshit!*

"Don't worry," I told him, "you're fine. It was a hit."

We continued on with the evolution unfazed. Later we learned that the instructor had called down to the butts over the radio and told the students who were working our lane to mark his hit as a miss. Why? Just to fuck with us and see how we would handle it.

We were fortunate. By this time Glen had developed total faith in my spotting, making us killing machines on the range—and we had already realized that the instructors were playing games with us to see how well we handled adverse situations. Some guys didn't get this, and they would self-destruct, carrying the falsified missed shots into a testable evolution and failing miserably.

They gave us two kinds of tests on the .308, starting with a snaps and movers test.

Snaps and movers involves targets that suddenly appear out of nowhere, snapping upright in a variety of locations and at different, unpredictable time intervals, and targets that move continuously, left and right, in random and unpredictable order. These are full-size E-silhouette targets, a flat panel with a sort of bottle-shaped silhouette on it that represents a human torso and head. Typically we had three head snaps and three moving targets on each yard line, positioned at the 200-yard, 400-yard, 600-yard, and 800-yard lines.

Working with snaps and movers was where we learned how to lead a moving target. This is tricky, because you have to take into account what the wind is doing and calculate for the distance that you have to lead ahead of the target as it moves. It can feel counterintuitive at first, because often you shouldn't aim where common sense tells you that you ought be aiming.

I remember the first time I put my crosshairs directly on the target, even though it was obviously not stationary and everything in me was screaming at me to move the crosshairs a few degrees off in the direction the target was moving—in other words, to lead the target. According to what we were learning, however, the wind would push my bullet out of its attempted straight path and, over the course of its arc toward the target, actually blow it *into* the target and cancel out those few degrees of lead. If this sounds like some kind of bizarre funhouse-mirror maze of calculations and competing factors, that's exactly what it felt like—and it all had to happen on a time scale of thousandths of a second. It felt completely wrong, but the logic of external ballistics told me it was right on the money.

I squeezed the trigger and *ping!* The target went down.

Next was an unknown distance test. For this, they laid out a series of steel targets in each lane at various elevations and distances, all the way from 50 yards to 900 yards, which was right at the outer limit of effective range for the .308—only we didn't know exactly what any of these elevations and distances were. This was where we started really learning how to use our scopes and, in particular, learning range estimation using the mil dot scope reticle.

The reticle, or crosshairs, in a sniper rifle scope is outfitted with two series of tiny dots, called mil dots, that run horizontally and vertically through the field of vision and allow us to measure the approximate height and width of sighted objects by making some simple visual calculations.

If we saw that our target measured, say, 1.5 mil in height in the scope, and we knew the target's actual height in inches, then we could plug that into a formula that would give us the target's distance. As long as we had a known measurement to work with, we could work out the exact range. Practically any kind of known measurement would do. We learned to ask questions like "What's the standard dimension of a Middle Eastern license plate? What's the height and dimension of a standard STOP sign in the Middle East? What's the standard window height?" We learned to record this information carefully, knowing that sooner or later, we would be in a situation in some Middle Eastern country and need to know how to calculate the range of a target so we could dial in the correct elevation before taking the shot—and do it fast.

We also have laser rangefinders, of course, which give us these measurements directly, but in the sniper course we had to learn how to make these calculations the hard way. To tell the truth, even with all the new technology, it's still smart to know how to do this by hand. You don't want to count on always having a laser rangefinder handy—as I would find out firsthand in the midst of split-second, life-or-death circumstances in the mountains of northern Afghanistan.

We practiced ranging these targets, and once we ranged them we shot to verify that we had ranged correctly. Then we'd make slight modifications, if necessary, and shot again. We had ample opportunity to perfect the process in practice tests, but when the final test day came, our shit had to be seriously dialed in, because then it was *game on* and no second chances.

After we spent weeks practicing and testing with the .308, they put us on the .300 Win Mag, which packs more power than the .308 and can therefore shoot to ranges up to 1,000 yards and beyond. Each of these has its own character and idiosyncrasies, and by the time the shooting phase was over we had come to know them both like old friends.

We also started doing some longer-distance shooting with the .50 cal sniper rifle. The .50 cal bullet is a monster, about twice the size of the .308, and it can shoot way out past 1,000 yards to 1,500 or even 1,800 yards. It's also a more stable bullet with a little more powder and oomph behind it, and it serves more as what we call an area weapon, meaning that we would typically use it for things like shooting out an engine block in a vehicle or the propeller system in a Scud missile.

And here something strange happened. When we started getting out to a certain distances with the .50 cal, we started seeing effects we just didn't understand. We were shooting out to 1,500 yards, shooting at tanks and other big targets, and I wondered, *How come I'm holding for a 10 mph wind that's coming in from the right, but the bullet's still not on target—and I can see the trace doing something weird. What the hell is going on?*

What was going on, I eventually learned, was the Coriolis effect, which refers to the influence of the earth's rotation on bodies in motion. Yes, incredibly enough, on top of all the other environmental and ballistic information a sniper keeps in his head, the *earth's frigging rotation* is yet one more factor to bear in mind. Here's why:

While my .50 cal bullet was in the air, the earth's rotation would cause the planet's surface and everything on it—including my target—to slip slightly eastward, so that by the time the bullet landed, nothing was exactly where it had been when that bullet's flight began. Because the earth is so large and the local impact of its rotation so subtle, it's practically impossible to detect this without scientific instruments, until you start looking at motion over large distances—like 1,500 yards.

Shooting out to 200 yards, 500 yards, even 800 or 1,000 yards, the impact of the Coriolis effect is so negligible that you can get away with ignoring it. Once you're shooting out to some serious distances, though, it can move your bullet's trajectory by as much as several inches, enough to cause you to completely miss your target.

It was all such a massive amount of information to synthesize, and I soon learned to use my brain as a lens to bring that entire universe of variables to bear on the tiny circle of focus inside my scope. This also meant blocking out any distractions, such as when the instructors intentionally messed with us to get us flustered and throw us off our game, or our own fears about not passing the course, and pouring every atom of concentration into that focal point.

We had learned to use the PEQ laser sight that projects a visible red dot on the target. (Another version of this scope projected an infrared red dot visible only through night-vision technology, allowing us to sight targets without giving our position away. Today these two functions are combined into one model.) That red dot came to represent everything I was learning, compressed into a pinpoint of brilliant light.

It was as if I were standing *inside* a minuscule red circle, hurling the bullet to its destination by an act of sheer mental concentration. In those moments on the range, everything else disappeared and my world shrank, like the near-infinite compression of matter in a black hole, into that red circle.

At the same time we were learning the various weapons and going through snaps and movers and unknown distance testing, we continued with those cold bore tests—which our instructors somehow managed to make more stressful every day. They had a truly devious genius at doing this, as they ably demonstrated on one of our classmates, Bill.

Bill had a brother going through BUD/S training while we were in sniper school. Although none of us knew this at the time, it turned out that Bill's brother had thrown in the towel and rung that brass bell, which meant his class helmet had been put out there on the ground along with all the other quitters' helmets, their names facing out for all to see.

One of our instructors managed to get this guy's helmet and affixed it to Bill's cold bore target. The poor guy had no idea his brother had quit BUD/S until the moment when, out of breath and under the extreme pressure of the morning's cold bore shot, he zeroed in on his target as it popped up—and saw his brother's name on that helmet. To his credit, he scored a clean head shot, dead center. I heard later that his brother wasn't too happy about it, but we were all quite impressed with the shot, and we proceeded to give Bill plenty of credit for it, along with an equal amount of shit about his brother quitting BUD/S.

As tense as our tests were, our instructors did not leave it to circumstances to apply the pressure. They found all kinds of creative and diabolical ways to tighten the screws. For example, you think you're going to take your test eight hours from now, in the cool of the evening—and suddenly the instructors inform you that you're taking it in fifteen minutes, right here at the blindingly hottest point of midday. Or you're on the range, testing on movers and snaps—and you suddenly realize your moving target is tilted because it wasn't put up all the way.

Tough. Deal with it. Adapt and overcome.

The more we learned, the more we practiced, the more we tested, the more grueling it got. All the while, our class size shrank as our classmates dropped away, one by one. Finally six weeks had gone by and it was time for our final test.

Before the test itself, the instructors sat each of us down for a brief conference, telling us what our grade was so far, where we were strong, and where we needed to focus to improve. I appreciated the fact that they did this. Unfortunately, that moral support stopped there. Once we got to the test itself, we found we had Dick Slattery as the test instructor. Slattery was a genuine asshole. Some of our instructors were harsh and strict, but we always knew they really wanted us to do well. For example, when Jordan, the outgoing master chief, was hard on us, it was clear that he was being hard on us for our benefit. Not Slattery. He treated us like dirt—especially the new guys, which included Glen and me. With Slattery, we never got the sense that he was tough on us for our sake. He just didn't give a shit.

The test was again a combination of snaps and movers and unknown distance. Again, as a sniper team, we not only took every test together, we also combined our individual grades so that we were graded as a team, not as individuals. It's a good thing, too: If not for that, one of us would have left the range and gone back home.

On the .300 Win Mag snaps and movers, we did well, both shooting into the 90s. Then we moved to the unknown distance.

I went first. We ranged the targets; then it was time for me to shoot. We had a time limit of twenty minutes for this part of the test, so we had to keep it moving along—but we started having some trouble. Glen was experiencing a little bit of difficulty reading the wind and putting me on the target. As the shooter, my job was to focus on making a good shot. As the spotter, it was up to Glen to control me with his instructions. "Okay, dial in X for your elevation," he would say, "and hold X for wind," and then I would take the shot while Glen watched closely to see the bullet's vapor trail so he could make any necessary adjustments for the next shot. In this case, the spotter was also responsible for keeping track of time, since we were on the clock.

We were on our third lane, with two more lanes to go, when I got an uneasy sense that we were running out of time. "Hey," I said to Glen, "how much time do we have?"

"We're okay," he assured me. "Plenty of time."

I let it go and put all my focus on the next target. Glen continued on, methodically evaluating the conditions so he could put me on the next shot—and suddenly Slattery called out, "Time!"

I stared at Glen. "What the hell?" I had eight bullets and two lanes' worth of targets left. We were out of time.

Glen stared at his watch, devastated. "Dude, I don't know what happened."

Slattery just stood there grinning and laughing at us.

I was furious—not at Glen, because I knew there was no way he would have intentionally messed this up, but I was stunned. *What the hell happened here?* To this day, I don't know what went wrong. Glen was keeping track on a bezel watch rather than a stopwatch and maybe put his bezel to the wrong number. Whatever it was, it had happened, and we were screwed. I had scored something like a 60.

Fortunately for us, we had hit every target we'd shot at, so we hadn't dropped any rounds, and because we were combining our grades, we still had a chance. Now it was Glen's turn to shoot and my turn to spot, which meant we were both about to play to our strengths.

"Okay, listen," I said, "we have to get you a score of 95 or higher."

That would net us a combined score that would squeak us by this test. It meant Glen could miss one shot, and only one shot. The rest would have to be perfect 100s. This was our last test before leaving the range and moving on to the stalking phase—if we did move on. If we didn't score a 95 or higher on Glen's shoot, then at least one of us would *not* be going on to the stalking phase. Glen might or might not be out, but I definitely would be history.

Meanwhile, Glen was still beating himself up.

"Dude," I said, "we need to let this go. We need to clean this test. Let's just do this thing."

So we did. Ignoring Slattery's jackass chuckling, we switched places and slid over to the next lane. I was like a machine, calling that wind. I put him on every shot, and he took every shot. We both put everything else out of our minds, climbed into that red circle, and put ourselves on the top of our game. Glen shot a 95. When they did the scoring, Glen had tied another guy, Mike Bearden, for the highest score of the day.

Just before we left Coalinga to move on to the stalking phase, we held a shoot-off to see who would win a brand-new shotgun that a manufacturer had donated. It came down to those two, Glen Doherty and Mike Bearden.

Mike, whom we called the Bear, was not only a crack shot, he was also a great guy, someone that everyone just naturally loved to be around. The Bear was paired up with a guy named Sam who had been in my BUD/S class, and who earned the nickname Happy. (Sam and I are good friends to this day, like two of Snow White's seven dwarves: Happy and Dirty.)

It was a great contest. They used the .300 Win Mag, which shoots almost 1,000 feet per second faster than the .308 and has a much flatter trajectory. Glen and the Bear matched each other, shot for shot, right out to 1,000 yards. Finally, at the 1,000-yard mark, Glen missed the shot—and Mike hit it, edging out my partner by a hair and winning the shotgun. The Bear had triumphed. Of course, I was rooting for Glen, but I didn't begrudge the Bear his win; he was just too damn likable not to feel good about it.

The way things turned out, I would always be especially glad that the Bear left Coalinga with that victory under his belt—but I'm getting ahead of myself.

Having cleared the hurdles of the shooting phase, we headed off to the Niland desert for the second half of the sniper course, the stalking phase. Now that we had all these skills on the gun, it was time to train us in the arts of camouflage and stealth so that we could with 100 percent consistency and reliability place ourselves in the necessary position to use those skills. It doesn't matter how good a shot you are if you can't get close enough to take the shot in the first place.

Once we got camped out and settled in, the instruction began, starting with classes on stealth and movement. We learned how to use natural vegetation to our advantage, especially in outfitting our ghillie suits.

The ghillie suit traces back to the Scottish Highlanders who served in the British Army in World War I as Lovat Scouts, forerunners of the modern sniper. Many of these men had been gamekeepers in civilian life, often called ghillies (from the Gaelic term for "youth" as they served as hunt guides for the wealthy); they had cultivated the art of weaving bits and pieces of local flora into their loose-fitting robes to help them blend into their surroundings. Their unique skills were later taught at the British Army sniper schools, which were attended by Americans once the United States entered the war.

For our ghillie suits we started out with a base outfit with a neutral desert pattern, then clipped on scraps of vegetation growing in our immediate environment. We also used scraps of burlap in different shades, which we learned to vary depending on the specific environment in which we'd be stalking. This sounds simple, but it is amazing to see the degree to which this art can be perfected. When you look at a photo of a Navy SEAL sniper in a ghillie suit out in his environment, it's almost like those "hidden pictures" you may have pored over as a child: You look and look, and all you can see is trees and bushes. The sniper completely disappears.

They taught us how to make a veg fan, clipping branches from manzanita bushes or whatever happened to be around and zip-tying them together. We learned to hide behind this ad hoc camouflage as we would slowly rise up in the middle of the bushes, eyes just peeking over the top of the fan, using either our binos or the naked eye to peer through the veg clippings and get an idea of where our target was, then slowly melting back down again.

They taught us how to use what they called dead space, which proved to be one of our most important lessons. Imagine standing on the street, next to a car at the curb. If someone is looking in your direction from the sidewalk and you crouch down below the back of the car, suddenly you disappear. You're using the dead space of the car to cover your signature. You can do the same thing with bushes, boulders, even a few feet of rising or sinking elevation, like a dirt mound or shallow ditch—anything you can put between you and your target.

The terrain in Niland didn't provide much in the way of natural cover. It's pretty flat, desolate scenery. But even there in that cracked-earth desert, you can find dead space if you look for it. There are tumbleweeds and other desert bushes, slight dips and rises in elevation, rocks here and there, even an occasional scraggly tree. Find even a little gully, and if you can slip down in there, you've got dead space.

They also taught us how to camouflage our rifles when setting up in our final firing position (FFP), and how to make sure we had cleared the muzzle by tamping down the firing area or using veg clippers to clip away vegetation surrounding the muzzle, so that when we took that shot, the pressure wave wouldn't cause any movement in nearby trees or grass. The last thing you want to do is take a shot and have it create a big signature. Even if you are completely hidden and unseen when you take the shot, if someone whips around and looks to see where that sound came from and sees some grasses swaying or branches moving, he might make your position and nail you.

We also practiced building hide sites. We would dig into the ground, sometimes using mesh or chicken wire we'd brought with us, but mostly using whatever natural terrain we might find on-site. It was almost like becoming a burrowing animal. In the desert, especially, it provides not only cover but also a bit of relief from the intense heat. If you build it right, someone can be standing right next to you and never even realize you're there. You might have four guys living in this thing for days on end, watching the target, radioing back to base until they give you authority to take the shot.

This skill would prove extremely useful in the mountains of Afghanistan, as I would discover before long.

Then we started practicing in stalking drills. To give you a sense of the experience, I'll describe a stalking drill.

They take you out to some location out in the desert and say, "Okay, your target is roughly 2 to 4 kilometers in that direction. You've got two hours to get to within 180 to 220 yards of the target, set up, and take your shot."

Off you go, crawling on your belly, you and your gun and your drag bag, which you've hooked to your belt at your crotch and now drag along behind you, inching along in the sweltering heat. A half hour goes by, then an hour. Some guys around you go to the bathroom in their ghillie suits. What else are they going to do? You can't stand up, that's for damn sure. You have to get within that range—and you aren't allowed to use laser rangefinders, so you have to use your scope to measure your target and then figure out exactly what point you have to reach in order to be within about 200 yards.

Two instructors are waiting for you in the command tower, scouring the area with their high-powered binos, looking for you and communicating by radio with three or four walkers on the ground. The walkers are instructors who walk the field; they are not there to hunt you but to act essentially like robots, carrying out commands from the tower. If an instructor detects movement, he'll radio the walker who is nearest to that spot and say, "Hey, Eric, I've got movement, I need you to run 20 meters to the right . . . Okay, stop, left face, now take three steps forward, stop. Stalker at your feet." If that walker is standing right next to you, he says, "Roger that," and you're busted. You've failed the stalk.

The whole idea is to make this as difficult as possible. By the time you are in firing position, you're only about 200 yards from the tower. You're up against two trained sniper instructors who know exactly what direction you're coming from, know exactly what area you have to set up in, and have not only high-powered binos but also a laser rangefinder. They know you're coming and would love nothing more than to bust you.

If you've made it this far, now comes the moment of painstaking patience, as you slowly pull out your gun, then pull out your scope, and get everything into place. You can't let your scope give off any kind of reflection or glint of sunlight, so you might cover it with fine mesh, then slowly move into position, get your sight positioned on the target, and squeeze off your shot.

For that first shot, you shoot a blank, which essentially announces that you have made it to your FFP. The walker approaches to within 3 feet of you, then signals the two instructors in the tower that he is in your vicinity. The instructors take a look, peering in your direction with their high-powered binos. If they see you, you fail. If they aren't able to see you, then they get on the radio to the walker and say, "Okay, give him his bullet."

Now they turn away for a moment, so they can't see the walker come up and hand you your live cartridge. They set up a target right where they had been sitting moments earlier, and clear out. Now you take your shot and hit the target—you hope.

There's a lot that can go wrong. If your bullet path isn't completely clear and your bullet even lightly grazes a small twig or branch as it hurtles through the air, that can easily be enough to throw its trajectory off and result in a complete miss. And you're lying down, remember: There might be a small mound of dirt in the way that you hadn't noticed.

If you do everything right and hit that target on the chest or the head, you score a 10. Hit just anywhere else inside the silhouette, and you score a 9; just hitting the target scores you an 8. Miss, and you've earned a 0.

Then you get up, walk back to the truck, and wait for everyone else. And by the way, after you take that shot you better not leave a trace. We had guys who stalked all the way into position and got off a very decent shot but then left behind a piece of brass, a zip tie, or a veg clipper—and failed the stalk. You can't get cocky.

We started doing several stalks a day, a long one (2 to 4 kilometers, which might take four hours or more) in the morning, and then a shorter 1-kilometer stalk (about two hours) in the evening. The heat of the day, thank God, was set aside for classes. As with our shooting work up in Coalinga, we would practice for a few days and then be tested.

My first stalk, I ran out of time before I even got to my FFP. It was humiliating. Missing the shot would have been bad enough. I didn't even get to *take* the shot. I made up my mind right then and there, that was not going to happen again.

I quickly learned that the first priority was to get eyes on the target. Once you have eyes on the target, then you own it: You know exactly where the enemy is, but he doesn't know where you are. From that vantage point, you can set about planning your exact route to your FFP.

Jack Nicklaus, the legendary championship golfer, used to say that when you're making a difficult shot, 50 percent of it is the mental picture you create, 40 percent is how you set it up, and 10 percent is the swing itself. In that respect, sniping is a lot like golf: 90 percent of it is how you see the picture and get your shot lined up.

I realized that a lot of the other guys were getting down on the ground and just taking off, crawling in the general direction of the tower without first having gotten eyes on the target. As a consequence, they wouldn't really know exactly where it was they were going, and they would run out of time—just like I did.

For my second stalk I figured, *Hey, this is practice—let's push the limits and see what happens.*

Instead of getting down on the ground, I set off at a bold stride in the direction the instructors had told us the target was located. I passed guys who were crawling on their bellies on the hot Niland ground, slowly and painfully, and they looked up at me bug-eyed, with expressions that said, *My God, what the hell are you doing?* I figured there was no way the instructors would see me; I was still almost half a mile away, and besides, they wouldn't be really looking yet, because they wouldn't be expecting any of us to start getting close nearly that soon.

I kept going until I had eyes on the target—and then immediately got down into a low crouch and started checking out every detail about the terrain between me and the target. Once I had my route planned, I got down on my belly and started crawling the 300 yards or so I still needed to cover in order to get to my FFP. Moving as quickly and as stealthily as I could, it took me maybe thirty minutes to low-crawl into position, set up my firing point, get everything dialed in, and go.

From that point on, it started to click for me. I would find a little high ground and make sure I had eyes on the target, and as soon as I knew exactly where it was, I would map out my approach, put a big terrain feature between me and the target, and then just walk right up on it. I started taking down 10s, perfect stalks every time.

It drove some of the guys nuts that I caught on so fast, especially those who had come from the country and grown up hunting. There was one guy from Alabama who had spent his whole life hunting in the woods and who was beside himself that I was cleaning his clock. How the hell was this California surfer kid who'd never hunted a day in his life outstalking them?

Again, I think it was all the time I spent spearfishing. The thing that clicked for me was the concept of dead space. That was the key to these stalking exercises. Put that dead space between you and your target, and you can literally run up to them without them ever knowing you're there. Although you could hardly come up with a greater contrast in environments than underwater versus the Niland desert, that didn't matter. The concept was exactly the same: Find the dead space and use it.

People often assume that sniper stalking is all about getting down on your belly and crawling along incredibly slowly. Yes, that's part of it—but the greater part of it is strategic. It's a very mental process.

One day Glen approached me and said, "Dude, I'm not doing well on my stalks. Can you help me out?" By this point I had a reputation for my bold, crazy stalks, and Glen was worried that he was going to fail. I told him, of course I'd help him.

The following day, on our late afternoon stalk, we set out together. I described how I saw our stalk path laying out, and how if we went this way and then that way, we could basically walk in and set ourselves up over there in this little tree we could just see in the distance, and from there, we'd be all set to take our shots.

Glen peered into the distance and then looked at me like I was nuts. "That tree? I don't know . . . I'm not so sure that can really work."

I didn't blame him. It must have looked like a pretty crazy idea. He wasn't used to my version of a stalk, which was to do it like a blitzkrieg—sneak up fast and be the first one there, take them by surprise. Besides, this was no big oak tree; we were talking about a pretty scrubby, miserable little thing. I thought it would be perfect.

I'd also learned that there was another strong tactical advantage to getting to your FFP fast. There was already so little terrain to work with in the bleak Niland landscape that whatever did exist was automatically prime real estate. If you were one of the last guys showing up in the setup zone, all the best spots would be already taken. It's no fun showing up at 200 yards and finding there's nothing left for you but flat, featureless desert.

But Glen was not ready for a Webb blitzkrieg and an FFP up in a tree. "You go ahead," he said. "I'll be okay."

I said, "Glen, you sure?"

He nodded. So I took off, scurried up there along the path I'd sketched out in my mind, hopped up into that tree, and got myself set up in a nice standing position, with my stock resting on a branch. I clipped out a little circle of small branches so I had a clean hole to shoot through, and *blam!* I took my shot. We were about fifteen minutes into the stalk.

The instructors freaked out. "Goddammit, who AD'd?" I heard one of them yell. Shooting off your weapon by mistake—an accidental discharge, or AD—is about as serious a sin as you can commit, and they wanted to know immediately who had done it so they could boot that guy's ass off the range right then and there. It didn't occur to them that someone could have actually taken a legitimate shot. Not within fifteen minutes of start time.

The walker closest to me got on his radio. "It wasn't an AD, sir. It was Webb. He's in position."

In other words, I had taken my blank shot, and now I was coming for them.

When the instructors heard that, I could tell they wanted my ass. By that point in the course I had taken down some pretty good scores, and that alpha-male, head-butting energy was in the air: They really wanted to nail me. I started hearing all this chatter over the walker's radio. Neither of the instructors could see me, but they didn't want to give up. They started scouring my vicinity, searching for me like crazy.

"Hey, man," I said to the walker, "what the hell? Can I take the shot, or what?"

Finally he told the instructors he was giving me my bullet. He handed it over, and I took the shot. As bad as they wanted me, they didn't get me. I scored a 10.

I started walking back, and as I neared the start point there was Glen, crawling on his stomach. "I'm an idiot," I heard him mumble.

After that I helped a few other classmates who were having a hard time getting the hang of it. We were coming down to the very last stalk, and there were three guys who had racked enough poor scores that they now needed to get a perfect score, or else they wouldn't pass. All this time and effort, and it was coming down to this one last stalk that would decide whether or not they would become SEAL snipers. The level of tension was inhuman.

These were really good guys, and I badly wanted all three of them to make it. On our last stalk before the final test, I went with them, doing everything I could to help them get themselves a clean, fast pathway into the zone for a solid FFP. In the process, I didn't pay enough attention to what I was doing myself and hung myself out a little too far. I got busted—and failed the stalk. I didn't mind, though. I had enough margin in my accumulated scores to make it through even with a 0 on that one. When the final stalk came, two of them made it. The third went home.

Here was the funny thing: When they read out those final scores, another guy and I had tied for first place—and after that came Glen, right behind us in second place.

I looked over at him and said, "You bastard! What do you mean, you were in jeopardy of failing? You were doing *fine*. You almost passed me up in points, you bastard!"

But that's Glen: He's an absolute perfectionist. He always wants to do better. It's one of the traits that makes him great.

We left Niland and headed back to Coronado to take some brief instruction in how to waterproof our weapons and how to take care of them when going in and out of the water. After graduation we would go on to spend another week doing some two-man contact drills and over-the-beach training, but for all practical purposes, we were done. We'd made it.

The graduation ceremony took place in the Team Five compound on June 12, 2000, my twenty-sixth birthday. The COs from all the different teams showed up. It was a proud moment for everyone in GOLF platoon.

Our personal triumph also translated into bragging rights for them and enhanced the reputation of the whole team. Glen and I were on Cloud Nine.

My SEAL sniper certificate carries the signature of Capt. William McRaven, who at the time was serving as commander of Naval Special Warfare Group One. More than a decade later, now a four-star admiral, McRaven would be credited with organizing and executing Operation Neptune's Spear, the Special Ops mission that took out Osama bin Laden in May of 2011. The following month he was confirmed as the ninth commander of SOCOM, the entire U.S. Special Operations Command, taking the reins from Admiral Eric T. Olson, another Navy SEAL.

It was ten years almost to the day since my dad threw me off our family's boat in the South Pacific. Then, I'd been a scared sixteen-year-old kid. Today, I was a Navy SEAL sniper.

Our platoon would deploy soon, but first I had some leave coming, which I took with pleasure. It was good to decompress a little, to surf for hours and spend time with Gabriele.

A little more than a month after graduation, I decide to go look up the Bear.

Right after graduation, Mike and I had made a horse trade. While I was part of Team Three, he had been assigned to a cold-weather platoon in Team Five, and we each had extra pieces of equipment that the other coveted. He had an extra cold-weather sleeping bag I thought might come in handy, and he agreed to trade it for a desert tan assault vest of mine. I had already given Mike the vest, but he still owed me the bag, and I wanted to collect before heading out to wherever I was going next.

I showed up at Team Three, expecting the bag to be sitting there waiting for me, as Mike had promised it would be. It wasn't there, and frankly, I was a little pissed off about it, but I figured I ought to give Mike the benefit of the doubt. I knew he must have a good reason.

I called up his platoon hut at Team Five to give him shit. One of his platoon mates answered the phone.

"Hey," I said, "is the Bear around? And can you tell him to come to the phone so Brandon can kick his ass over the wire, just for now, until I have a chance to come over there and kick it in person?"

There was silence on the other end. It lasted only a second or two, but in that short gap I felt my stomach drop out from under me. Something was wrong.

"Yeah . . ." the voice said. "Actually, no. Mike was in an accident."

That didn't sound good. I instantly felt like a complete ass. "What the hell? What happened? Is he okay?"

He was not okay. On July 12, just a few days earlier, the Bear had been in a freak accident while in parachute training. During a free-fall exercise, his main chute got tangled with a secondary chute and failed to open. He didn't make it.

The Bear left behind a gorgeous wife, Derinda, and a beautiful little two-year-old boy, Holden.

I couldn't attend his funeral because by that time I was already deployed and on my way toward the Persian Gulf. A few of my friends did, though. They told me later about that day, and about Holden walking up to them because he recognized the gold SEAL Tridents on their uniforms, just like his dad's, and asking them if they knew where his daddy was. One friend said there were at least a few guys who could barely keep it together at that point. Most had to go off for a solid cry.

Mike's death shook everyone who knew him, and it hit me pretty hard. He was the first of many friends I would lose over the years.

SEVEN

WHEN EVERYTHING CHANGED

In the late summer of 2000 our platoon embarked on a trans-Pacific run, headed for the Persian Gulf by way of Hawaii, Australia, and points west. Our first deployment. Thank God, we were finally getting out of here! We were attached to the USS *Duluth,* a troop transport ship, or amphibious transport dock. The *Duluth* was a fine old vessel, the last ship to be launched from the Brooklyn Navy Yard in the summer of 1965 before the yard's closure.

The *Duluth* departed from California on August 14, 2000, with most of our gear aboard—but not us. We skipped the boat and boarded a plane for Hawaii. Rather than having us waste a lot of time on board, our command would fly us ahead to the ship's next destination, where we could put in additional days of training while waiting for the vessel to catch up. This was a pattern we followed for most of the trip west. During those times we did spend on board we got a lot of kidding from the rest of the navy personnel, because in their eyes all we did was train. (They said the acronym SEAL stood for Sleep, Eat, And Lift, as in lift weights.)

In Hawaii we did some combat diving, paired off for a little hydrographic survey work, and occupied ourselves with the various ways SEALs continually train and retrain. In the daytime, that is. Once evening hit we'd go have fun. The single guys all chased girls, and we married guys had good times out with the boys. Chief Dan and I had both brought our surf boards along, and we'd meet up early in the mornings and surf for a few hours before joining the rest of the guys for our workouts. Later on, at other ports of call on our westward trek, we found a few days to peel away and go on surfing outings together. We got some pretty odd looks at various customs stations. (SEALs with surfboards? What were we going to do, take out bad guys by outsurfing them?)

The Hawaiian port where we put in was one with a unique place in American history. It was at Pearl Harbor that we had been attacked on our own soil nearly sixty years earlier. Being there on that historic site almost made you wonder: *That could never happen again . . . could it?*

Leaving Hawaii, we hopped on a C-130 transport plane and headed for Darwin, Australia. I have to tell you, flying in a C-130 is an absolutely fantastic way to travel. We could stretch out, go do push-ups in the corner, or do pretty much whatever we wanted. We brought our own food, had hammocks strung up all over the back of the plane, went up to the cockpit to shoot the shit with the pilots for a while, or rocked out to our headphones. I'll take that over commercial flying any day of the year.

We made a few brief stops on our way to Australia, including one night in the Marshall Islands on the beautiful little atoll of Kwajalein, where a small contingent of defense personnel was stationed. This place was like paradise, and it made me think of Hiva Oa, the little island in the Marquesas where I had fallen briefly in love with a girl whose name I

At thirteen with my catch, a ten-pound lobster.

At sixteen on Captain Bill's dive boat, the *Peace*, with a nice Calico bass.

Boat crews in BUD/S. *(I'm on far R.)*

The O-course cargo net, BUD/S First Phase, class 215.

Hell Week in BUD/S First Phase. Notice the telephone poles used for log PT, with "Ole Misery" near the end.

My first "stacked duck"—two Zodiacs tied together with G-12 parachutes, about to be tossed out of a plane.

I am a new guy on exercises in Niland with an M-60 machine gun and 1,000 rounds.

GOLF platoon in Niland. *(I'm third from R.)*

With my sniper partner Glen Doherty, getting ready for a 1.5-mile swim this past summer.

My graduating sniper school class. *(Front row: I am third from L; back row: Mike "Bear" Bearden, second from L; Glen Doherty, fourth from L.)*

ECHO platoon doing perimeter patrol on the USS *Cole*. Notice the ship's gaping wound, dead center.

ECHO platoon patch that I designed in late 2001.

Taking prisoners: Our nighttime takedown on the Persian Gulf.

On the eastern outskirts of Kandahar, driving into the city.

Meeting up with a group of indigenous "friendlies" outside Kandahar.

With two "friendlies."

ECHO platoon in one of the Task Force K-Bar compounds at Kandahar Airport. *(Front row standing: Osman and I on L, Lt. Cassidy second from R.)*

Processing incoming POWs at EPW camp at Kandahar.

Tarnak Farms: On this exact spot a SEAL was later killed by a land mine. *(I'm on the R.)*

Contraband found in the caves at Zhawar Kili; mostly ammo (a mix of American, British, and Russian).

More contraband found in the Zhawar Kili cave complex.

Zhawar Kili: an Al Qaeda recruiting poster (created pre-9/11).

Weapons cache found at Zhawar Kili; notice the debris spread everywhere from air strikes.

Cooking chickens at the deserted village that ECHO platoon used as base of operations in Zhawar Kili. *(L to R: Osman, I, Chief Dye.)*

Destroying a weapons site in the Zhawar Kili area.

Demolition at Zhawar Kili.

ECHO platoon at Bagram Air Base, after returning from Zhawar Kili.
(Back row: Lt. Cassidy, tenth from L; Chief Dye, eleventh from L, Osman
twelveth from L; front row: I am fifth from L.)

ECHO platoon at Kandahar, after the Zhawar Kili mission, with JDAM our mascot. *(With Lt. Cassidy, front row, fourth from L.)*

Lt. Cassidy scanning the area at Prata Ghar.

Major Mike *(far R)*, our German brothers' OIC.

At Kandahar, before the Prata Ghar mission. *(Back row from L: Lt. Cassidy and I; front row on L: Heath Robinson.)*

Ahmed Kheyl exfil; the red smoke is a marker so the exfil helo can see both our location and ground wind direction.

With two German KSK buddies, flying the Afghan colors at Ahmed Kheyl checkpoint.

A moment of silence at Bagram: commemoration for our fallen brothers immediately after the Roberts Ridge incident.

Instructing a sniper school class on the basics of stealth and concealment.

Sniper setting up for a shot at 200 yards from the target in the distance.

Sniper students in the stalking and concealment phase of training.

SEALs conducting a Gas and Oil
Platform (GOPLAT) takedown.

In Iraq, supporting "the Client" in urban
intelligence operations.

never knew. Ten years earlier I had been not far from this very spot, being booted off the family boat at Papeete. And now here I was, a U.S. Navy SEAL sniper, being deployed on a troop transport ship to the Persian Gulf to help keep the global peace. I still have a hand carving I picked up on our stopover in Kwajalein. Call it a keepsake, a reminder of a more innocent time—a time before everything changed.

We continued south and west through a week's stay in Australia, three days of a humanitarian assistance operation off East Timor, brief stops at Singapore and Phuket, Thailand, and eventually north through the Indian Ocean into the Persian Gulf, where we put in at the little island country of Bahrain, which had a fairly liberal culture as Muslim countries went. By now we were into October.

We were there in Bahrain to conduct some training exercises with the neighboring Saudis. As an unofficial rule, we don't train these guys in the Middle East too thoroughly. I mean, we're there to help—but at the same time, when the sun comes up tomorrow in that part of the world, you never know for sure who's going to be arrayed against you. After a few days we got back out onto the *Duluth* and into the Gulf, where we planned to spend a few days engaged in ship-boarding training exercises.

That's when we got the call about the attack on the USS *Cole*.

To much of the world, September 11, 2001, was and still is "the day everything changed," and it's easy to understand why. In the summer of 2001 the public's attention in the United States was focused largely on the debate over stem cell research and the latest political scandal about whichever congressman had been most recently caught with his zipper down. (In case you're wondering, it was California Democrat Gary Condit.) The reality of war was mostly a fading memory, the topic of nostalgia. Stephen Spielberg's made-for-TV World War II epic *Band of Brothers* had just premiered on HBO, on Sunday, September 9.

It had been a decade since the fall of the Soviet Union. The Cold War was over, a new century had begun, and it was easy to be lulled into a sense that the kinds of global conflicts that had convulsed the twentieth century were already archaic relics of a distant past. We had left behind a world defined by the opposition of two vast global forces, Western capitalism and Eastern communism. But we hadn't yet come to grips with what came next. For most of the world, what came next was suddenly, starkly defined that sunny, clear-sky New York morning in the fall of 2001.

Not for me. For me, it came eleven months earlier, on October 12, 2000.

Going into that fall, there was no significant conflict for our military forces to focus on. Still, the whole Mideast region was a political and military tinderbox that always loomed in the background. At the time, SEAL Team Three was involved in reinforcing United Nations sanctions against Iraq, and Saddam was smuggling out an awful lot of oil. We were expecting to participate in policing the area, which would mean doing a significant number of ship boardings on noncompliant vessels. The Iraqis would send these tankers out onto the Gulf to make a run for Iranian waters, where American and other NATO personnel could not legally pursue. Our job would be to catch up with them and intercept them while they ran that brief gauntlet through the narrow international shipping lanes.

This was a mission we were hoping to rotate in on. We had just gotten back on the *Duluth* and were mobilizing to get our equipment and go participate in that ship-boarding detail when we suddenly got word that an American destroyer, the USS *Cole*, had been hit in the nearby Gulf of Aden just off the coast of Yemen, and hit bad.

That morning, the *Cole* had put in at about 9:30 local time for a routine refueling stop. By 10:30 refueling had commenced. At 11:18 a small craft loaded with about a quarter ton of homemade explosives and manned by two individuals approached the ship's port side and made contact. The explosion killed seventeen sailors and injured thirty-nine others, putting a 40' × 40' hole in the hull in the process.

Wait—*what*? Two guys in a speedboat? How the hell had *that* happened?

We took off and were on-site within shooting distance of the Yemeni coast within eight hours, putting our fast boats over the side. The marines had an outfit in Bahrain they called the Fast Company, and they earned their nickname: they were on the scene a few hours ahead of us and had already established a security command post on the injured *Cole* by the time we arrived. We immediately set up a 500-meter perimeter incorporating both the pier and the surrounding water. We were also directed to set up a sniper team on the bridge of the ship itself to monitor the situation, glassing the entire perimeter constantly to ensure that no other bad actors got into the mix.

This was where Glen and I came in. We set up two teams to rotate on round-the-clock sniper watch, twelve hours on and twelve off. We had a .50 caliber sniper rifle and four LAW rockets on the bridge. Our task was to protect both the ship and the rest of the crew while repair and containment efforts were under way.

It was a tense situation. Our relationship with Yemen was not great, and there was a powerful current of anti-American sentiment in the little country. Standing there on the bridge of the crippled destroyer, we were acutely aware of all the nearby Yemeni weapons that were trained on us. It had the anxious, volatile feeling of a standoff. Our orders were simple: Anything or anyone who breaches our perimeter, take them out.

Although no outright hostilities broke out, the perimeter was in fact tested a few times. Each time we saw a vessel encroaching on our perimeter we radioed the guys in the boats: "Hey, I've got someone coming in close at ten o'clock. It doesn't look serious, but they're on the fence."

Meanwhile, crews were furiously at work pumping bilge out of that gaping hole in the *Cole*'s flank. It was a constant battle just to keep the vessel afloat, and for a while there it was touch and go. We nearly watched that destroyer sink.

It was a nasty scene. The suicide bombers had rammed the ship right where the galley is located, and just at the time of day when a large numbers of sailors were lining up for lunch. The carnage was awful. It was now nearly twelve hours since the explosion, and in the insufferable humid Middle Eastern heat we had both dead bodies and all the food in the ship's hold decomposing rapidly. The stench was unbearable, and the trauma among the living compounded the nightmarish quality of the whole scene. When we first arrived, the guys who greeted us all sported the famous thousand-yard stare that reflects an intimacy with the horrors of combat casualties. Now night had fallen, and much of the crew had set up to sleep in cots out on the deck in what looked like a shantytown of shell-shocked catastrophe survivors—which was exactly what it was.

I talked with a few of the survivors to try to find out exactly what had happened, and how this absurdly low-tech assault had penetrated the *Cole*'s security in the first place. The answer, in essence, was "Security? *What* security?"

When they described their security posture, I was appalled. The lack of preparedness was ludicrous. Here we were, docked just off the coast of a hostile nation with an openly anti-American sentiment that included a history of kidnappings and sponsorship of terrorism—and as protection they'd set up a few guys to stand on the ship's rail with M-14s. These soldiers had had no training on the M-14 and, in fact, did not even know what kind of rifle it was they were holding. And to top it off, there were no bullets in their magazines. I need to repeat that last point. They were protecting a billion-dollar vessel by standing on its deck brandishing weapons they were not familiar with—*and that were not loaded*. Really? What, as if the sheer appearance of force would be sufficient deterrent to any potential aggression?

As I soon learned, this was not an exceptional situation; it was widespread. For all intents and purposes, it was standard. At least it had been up until now. After the *Cole* was hit, things changed fast. Soon the military was making it mandatory for at least 30 percent of every ship's crew to be actually trained in force protection, as opposed to the previous requirement, which was 0 percent.

It's easy (and, frankly, justified) to jump all over the Clinton administration for this lax condition, but at the same time it's also important to see the bigger picture. In a sense, this was part of a cycle that had gone on for decades—hell, for centuries. We had our forces in a high-security posture right after World War II, and then again after Korea, and then again after Vietnam. In the years in between, our sense of urgency would fade every time, and as a nation we would gradually be lulled into a false sense of security. Then all of a sudden something would go *bam!* and military readiness would once again become relevant.

Incredibly, earlier that year there had been a failed attempt on another U.S. vessel in the very same port. The would-be attackers had even used a similar crappy little boat and made a similar run up to one of our ships as it pulled into port, but in that instance their explosive-laden boat had sunk before they could consummate their deadly rendezvous. We had been lucky—but we had also been warned. So what happened? The incident was treated like so much background noise in the larger picture of global intelligence and sloughed off. Now we had paid for our complacency with seventeen American lives, thirty-nine more injured, and hundreds of million dollars' worth of damage.

I've mentioned a number of times how fanatical about training we are in the teams. It's not really fanaticism, though, it's realism. If you want to become not just competent, not just good, but *outstanding*, you have to train like a maniac at whatever it is you're intending to excel at—and then train some more. In his 2008 bestseller *Outliers*, journalist Malcolm Gladwell does a great job documenting the secret behind the accomplishments of such outstanding achievers as Bill Gates, Mozart, and the Beatles. Turns out, surprise of surprises, they all worked their asses off training. Gladwell coins what he calls the 10,000-Hour Rule, which says that outstanding (outlying) success in any field is largely the result of a shitload of practice, like twenty hours a week for ten years, which translates into 10,000 hours. Amp that pace up to eighty hours a week and you'll get it done in two and a half years—and that right there is one reason SEALs can do what they do.

I may have had a crazy childhood, wild and undisciplined in many ways, but one thing I'd always known was the rush that comes with pushing yourself hard, the thrill of seeing endless practice gradually producing a capacity for excellence. Whether it was wrestling or skiing as a kid, becoming a rescue diver on the *Peace* under the watchful eyes of Captain Mike and Captain Bill, or suffering through BUD/S with Shoulin, O'Reilly, and the rest of those crazy slave drivers, I'd always known what it means to train hard. If I could do anything significant to serve my country, it would probably be through sharing that capacity to train. Though I didn't know it yet, even beyond my own service in Afghanistan and the Gulf, my contribution to training a new generation of twenty-first-century warriors would become the crowning achievement of my career. All I knew at this point was that this tragic fiasco was a failure of training, and specifically of the people in *charge* of the training.

When Glen took position on the bridge and I rotated off-watch, I went down a few floors to look around. I found a used coffee mug, washed it out, and brought it back up on deck to the temporary food station they'd set up at the back of the boat, where I used it to get a cup of hot coffee. I was just starting to get some of that hot java lift into me when I noticed one of the sailors staring at me.

"What?" I said.

He pointed wordlessly at my coffee mug. I turned it around and looked on its reverse side. I hadn't noticed, but the guy whose mug it was had written his name on there.

It was one of the guys who'd been blown up in the attack.

Maybe some would have been spooked and set that thing down in haste. For me it was just the opposite. This sailor had been one of the first to give his life in a war we didn't even know what to call yet. It was an honor to drink from that man's cup. I kept that mug and used it for the rest of our tour.

We were there on the *Cole* for about seven days. The ship was eventually boarded onto a huge Norwegian craft designed to carry offshore oil-drilling equipment and hauled back stateside, where after fourteen months of repair work it was returned into service.

The attack on the USS *Cole* opened my eyes to how ill prepared we were for the threat that existed everywhere around us. An Arleigh Burke–class guided missile destroyer, crewed by nearly 300 sailors, weighing close to 10,000 tons, and costing more than $1 billion to put in the water, was crippled and nearly sunk by two guys in the kind of motorboat you might see out behind a New England summer lake house. When it was all over, the destroyer would require about $250 million in repairs. This was not just a catastrophe, and it wasn't just about whether we were adequately prepared for surprise attacks. There was a fundamental shift happening here, a shift in the very nature of military conflict, and this attack off the coast of Yemen was arguably its clarion call.

At the time we were still thinking in terms of the Cold War massing of NATO versus Soviet forces, which was a logical extension of how we had viewed warfare for centuries and longer. War had always been a matter of hurling masses of men and matériel against one another, from the phalanxes of Xerxes and legions of Rome to the endless troop lines of the Blue and the Gray lowering bayonets to charge after exhausting their weapons' single shots. That kind of pitched battle of the masses reached its apotheosis in the midtwentieth century with the tank battalions of Patton and Rommel pounding each other in the North African desert.

This passage from Lee Child's 2004 Jack Reacher thriller *The Enemy* beautifully captures that core sense of twentieth-century warfare:

What is the twentieth century's signature sound? You could have a debate about it. Some might say the slow drone of an aero engine. Maybe from a lone fighter crawling across an azure 1940s sky. Or the scream of a fast jet passing low overhead, shaking the ground. Or the *whup whup whup* of a helicopter. Or the roar of a laden 747 lifting off. Or the crump of bombs falling on a city. All of those would qualify. They're all uniquely twentieth-century noises. They were never heard before. Never, in all of history. Some crazy optimists might lobby for a Beatles song. A *yeah, yeah, yeah* chorus fading under the screams of their audience. I would have sympathy for that choice. But a song and screaming would never qualify. Music and desire have been around since the dawn of time. They weren't invented after 1900.

No, the twentieth century's signature sound is the squeal and clatter of tank tracks on a paved street. That sound was heard in Warsaw, and Rotterdam, and Stalingrad, and Berlin. Then it was heard again in Budapest and Prague, and Seoul and Saigon. It's a brutal sound. It's the sound of fear. It speaks of overwhelming advantage in power. And it speaks of remote, impersonal indifference. Tank treads squeal and clatter and the very noise they make tells you they can't be stopped. It tells you you're weak and powerless against the machine. Then one track stops and the other keeps on going and the tank wheels around and lurches straight toward you, roaring and squealing. That's the real twentieth-century sound.

But that "overwhelming advantage in power" Child describes, that arraying of massive forces that had been so effective even as recently as Desert Storm, was no longer the trump card in the warfare of the new century. As weapons of war go, it doesn't get much more massive than a billion-dollar destroyer—and one of those had just been nearly sunk by two guys in a dinky little speedboat.

We had entered the age of asymmetrical warfare.

We were no longer dealing fundamentally with huge ground forces rolling across the desert. We were up against tiny terrorist cells, a decentralized kind of guerrilla warfare on a scale we had never seen before. There's a certain convenience to calling it al Qaeda, as if it is one centralized, organized entity run by a single central command, like Moscow's Soviet Union or Hitler's Third Reich. The truth is probably a lot messier and more complicated, and therefore more difficult to deal with. There are a lot of other nonaffiliated terrorist groups that have sought to jump on the al Qaeda bandwagon, perhaps for the perceived clout that gives them. Whether you call them al Qaeda or Taliban or disaffected extremists in the West or Somali pirates, what it boils down to is that you have armed and fanatically dedicated combatants pursuing an entirely different sort of combat than we used to fight in the days of trench warfare or tank battles.

It was a new kind of war, and over the next few years it would prompt a radical shift in the makeup of our Department of Defense—especially in relation to Special Operations.

In the long story of war, Special Operations forces—the British and

Australian SAS, the American Green Berets and Army Rangers, the Navy SEALs—were exactly that: *special,* something you don't use every day. Spec Ops forces were kept on the shelf and brought out for deployment only in certain circumstances. In modern warfare, those of us in Spec Ops were the icing on the cake of massive destruction, the period at the end of a sentence of overwhelming forces. Special Operations were the bastard child of conventional forces, there mainly to support the larger mission.

Now that equation has changed. Today the relationship has been turned virtually on its head. Over the first decade of the twenty-first century, the entire strategy of American military organization has shifted toward one in which our massive assets, such as destroyers, aircraft carriers, and nuclear submarines, are reconfigured to support small field teams and tiny units. The Spec Ops warrior of the twentieth century was fundamentally an outsider who worked on the periphery of military strategy. Today he stands at its core.

Shortly after that experience in the Gulf of Aden I was talking about it with a friend, Thomas. "We really don't understand the world we're living in," I said. "It's totally different than we think it is—and a lot more dangerous."

Thomas nodded.

"We're in for it, you know," I added.

He asked me what I meant by that.

"Sooner or later," I mused, "there's going to be a major hit, right here on U.S. soil. We're not ready for it."

After I got back from that deployment on the *Duluth,* two big changes were in store for me on a personal level. I was about to become a father, and although I didn't know it yet, I would also soon be leaving GOLF platoon. Both changes would have a major impact on my life for years to come. They were also related, in a way. The reason I made the move to leave GOLF platoon, frankly, came down to a matter of family finances.

I was soon coming up for reenlistment again, which meant I had a cash bonus coming, something like $40,000. The problem was, reenlisting while stateside would mean I'd be heavily taxed, with a significant California tax on top of the federal bite. If I reenlisted in a tax-free combat zone, I would get the whole bonus. This would amount to a difference of something like fifteen grand. My wife was now pregnant with our first child, and fifteen grand can buy an awful lot of diapers.

It's not uncommon for command to send a guy overseas for a short deployment to help him out in circumstances like this, so in July I went to talk with our ops officer, Keith Johnson, about the possibility of getting myself sent overseas. (The ops officer is typically a senior lieutenant, about to make lieutenant commander, who runs operations for the team, working directly for the commanding officer and executive officer.)

After hearing me outline my situation and what I was looking for, Keith thought for a moment, then said, "Look, Brandon, we've got a situation with ECHO platoon. Frankly, they're a bunch of fuckups and we've just shaken the whole thing up. We fired the chief and OIC, cleared out the whole leadership team to wipe the canvas clean, but kept most of the guys."

He hadn't gotten to his point yet, but I knew where this was going, and I didn't like it. He was talking about sending *me* to join this screwed-up ECHO platoon.

We had great chemistry in GOLF platoon, which is as crucial on a SEAL team as it is on a pro ball team. You can train all you want and have the most qualified guys in the world, but if the chemistry doesn't click, the team won't work. When that happened in a SEAL platoon, they would break the team up and reshuffle all the guys to other teams, much as you'll see in pro sports. This is what had happened to ECHO platoon. Obviously, command was hoping to rescue this misbegotten team by bringing in some new blood, and Keith was on board with that plan. My coming to him with my tax-or-no-tax bonus problem happened to play right into the situation at hand.

"You should join ECHO," he said. "They're the next ones up to deploy, and you'll get your tax-free bonus."

I did *not* want to join this godforsaken platoon. They had a terrible reputation; everyone in Team Three knew they were a mess. Guys used to joke about them in the halls—and he was asking me to become part of this joke of a team? I had hoped there'd be some other avenue for getting me overseas, maybe joining DELTA platoon or some other excellent fighting force. Keith was selling it hard, though, and now that he'd proposed it to me it was going to be hard for me to wangle any other option. I realized it now came down to a choice: I could go join ECHO platoon or stay with my team at GOLF and give up the fifteen grand. GOLF platoon had a great reputation, and I pretty much had my pick of jobs there. Ultimately, though, I decided to put my family first and agreed to join ECHO platoon.

It was a move I would soon regret.

ECHO platoon was then at the tail end of their workup, doing some VBSS training operations, so I flew out to join them on the aircraft carrier where they were staged, about a hundred miles off the coast of San Diego. When I got there, I met up with Chris Dye, who had just taken over as the platoon's new chief in the command's efforts to rehabilitate the outfit.

Chief Dye was legendary in the SEAL community. A decade earlier, when he was at SEAL Team Two, he and his dive buddies had participated in a Special Op called Operation Nifty Package, part of Operation Just Cause, the United States invasion of Panama. As part of the op Chris and his dive buddy Randy Beausoleil planted the explosives that sank Noriega's private boat. (You can read a riveting account of the whole mission in the excellent book *SEALs: The US Navy's Elite Fighting Force,* written by my BUD/S classmate Chris Osman and Mir Bahmanyar.) A few weeks after this first meeting, I was helping Chief Dye move one day, and I noticed a plain stainless steel wheel among his stuff. It was about two feet in diameter, six spokes coming off an empty hub. Looked like maybe a steering wheel for a yacht or something.

"Hey, Chris," I said, "what are you doing with this old wheel?"

"Oh, that," he said. "I'm just hanging on to it. That came off Noriega's boat." He had personally salvaged it off the wreck of the ship after planting the bombs that sank it. This dude had seen some interesting action in his time.

Finding out that Chief Dye would be running things at ECHO cheered me up quite a bit. Maybe this wouldn't be so bad. The two of us were not really acquainted personally, but we knew each other by reputation, and I had been tagged with the role of general go-to guy to help him put things in order.

Chief Dye met me when I landed on the aircraft carrier where they were staging for their workup exercises. "Oh, man, am I glad to see you," he said. "Welcome to ECHO. We have our work cut out for us."

He told me they were planning to go out the next day to do some fast-roping off a couple of helicopters as part of a maritime ship-boarding op, and they were short one castmaster. The castmaster is in charge of rigging up the setup inside the helo, deploying the guys out on the rope, and making sure it all goes properly. He's the last guy out. I wondered how the hell they'd been planning to go fast-roping with two helos and one castmaster, but I didn't say anything. Chris would have figured out a way to do it. It might not have been exactly legal, but it would have worked. In any case, I was certified as a castmaster, so that was no longer an issue.

The next day we got out there up in the air and started the exercise. I was serving as castmaster in the second bird, watching the guys go out the door: one, two, three—and suddenly there was an MP-5 rifle flying through the air in free fall.

I nearly shit my pants. I could not believe what I was seeing. A SEAL team fast-roping out of a helo—and somebody *dropped his frigging weapon?*

It was downright embarrassing. Everything is supposed to be slung in and tightly attached—that's rule one. When we say, "That guy has his shit wired tight," this is *exactly* what we're talking about. Working around water and heights, you *always* lanyard your gear to your body. I've seen guys lose night-vision gear off their heads: Turn, whack the door of the helo cabin, the night vision pops off—and if it's not tied in to your body, it's going over and into the drink. Losing an expensive piece of night-vision equipment is bad enough—but losing a *weapon?* In career terms, that's suicide.

The moment that MP-5 hit the deck, the guy who'd dropped it scooped it up and kept right on going. Chief Dye was in the other bird, so he didn't see it and didn't have to suffer this humiliation in person. Nobody else on our craft even noticed that it had happened, but I sure as hell did.

Nothing like this would ever have happened in GOLF platoon, and if it had, the guy perpetrating the misdeed would have been sent back to the fleet with his trident ripped from his chest. I'd seen it happen. When we reached Pearl Harbor on our way to the Persian Gulf the previous summer, for a day or two we had one weapon unaccounted for. For a SEAL, this particular brand of carelessness is one of the worst offenses you can commit. It turned out to be Chuck "Liberty Risk" Landry's fault. After that episode a few years earlier when Landry had gotten drunk and wrangled with the base security guards, they'd given him a second chance. Losing track of that weapon in Hawaii was strike two, and there would be no strike three. The weapon did finally turn up, but Landry got sent back home. Brutal, but that's how we did things—at least in GOLF platoon.

I held my tongue throughout the rest of that fast-roping exercise, but once we got back on the aircraft carrier at the end of the day to debrief, I let them have it.

"Look, guys, I know I'm brand-new here, but I have to tell you, that was inexcusable. Who the hell dropped that gun? That thing could have easily gone over the side, and if it had we would be in some serious shit right now!"

A big guy named Gilroy Jones raised his hand. "It was me."

This was my introduction to the realities of ECHO platoon. Jones was a tough dude but a complete train wreck of a soldier. First time through BUD/S he got to Third Phase and then came up against a domestic violence charge for hitting the lady he was with. He made it all the way through his second time, went to Team Three, and screwed up there. It was amazing to me that he hadn't been fired from the team—and now, he had screwed up our exercise. Turned out, he had made some sort of jury-rigged sling for his MP-5 out of surgical tubing, and in the course of the exercise it got hung up and broke.

It wasn't just Gilroy Jones. These guys were a mess in general. It was so clear that they had never had any really good leadership. They'd had no one to look up to or learn from.

We had a 90/10 rule in the teams: 90 percent of the guys on any given team are going to be solid, and 10 percent will be guys you hope will get kicked out or transferred to another team. That's just the way it is, and you can live with that. The problem with ECHO platoon was that we had far more than our fair share of 10-percenters. In a platoon of sixteen guys, 10 percent means one or two fuckups at most. Right away I identified half a dozen guys there as weak links, including our third officer and AOIC (assistant officer in charge)! Oh, great. Even our second and third in command were misfits. (Hadn't Keith said they'd shit-canned the whole leadership? What did they do—replace them with guys who were worse?)

I felt like I had been yanked from playing on a World Series team and kicked downstairs to a farm league. I wanted to go back and beg for my old place on GOLF team again. Screw the fifteen grand—I wanted to be back with my guys.

During that same fast-roping exercise I'd noticed that our corpsman, Jackie, had his entire med gear with him. Jackie was a really quiet guy and would speak sort of under his breath so you couldn't quite hear what he said.

When I saw that he was lugging along this huge pack, I said, "Hey, Jackie, why are you fast-roping with this big pack?" He said something back, although I have no idea what, so I elaborated. "All you should be bringing on a jump like this is basic trauma gear. You need to shit-can that whole bag."

Christ on a crutch. I wasn't even a medic, and here I was telling him how to pack his medical gear.

Jackie wasn't bad, though; he was just wet behind the ears and hadn't had strong leadership. In fact, he ended up becoming a solid citizen in the platoon and going on to join a tier-one unit and have a solid career in the community. A handful of the others were consistent screwups, though. A few of them would very nearly get me killed in the mountains of Afghanistan.

Not that ECHO platoon was all bad. Our breacher, Shawn, had been a BUD/S classmate of mine and was a very solid guy. After this disastrous day of fast-roping I took him aside and said, "Shawn, what the hell? How can you stand there and let these guys be such a mess?"

"I know," he said, "but I didn't think it was my place to tell them what to do." I understood his point. Thank God Chris Dye was our chief; this was a guy I could work with. There were quite a few other solid guys there, too. Patrick had joined the platoon only recently and therefore had not suffered through the previous "leadership" at ECHO. It was clear right off the bat that Patrick was very sharp and an asset to the team. Heath Robinson, another guy who was fairly new to the platoon, also had his shit wired tight. A few years later, on an op where a group of SEALs took back a merchant vessel from some Somalian pirates, one of our men was jumped by a hiding pirate, the clinch too close for anyone to shoot. Heath pulled out his knife and cut the guy's throat—one of the few SEALs since Vietnam to have a certified knife kill to his credit. Then there was Garrison, who joined at the same time I did. Garrison had been a marine before going through BUD/S and had been through some solid experiences with the Corps. Garrison was squared away, although with his marine background it took him a little doing to get accustomed to the SEALs and our, shall I say, lack of military bearing.

Over the weeks after I arrived, things gradually started looking better as a trickle of additional guys joined us after finishing whatever workup they were on, further helping shore up the platoon. Two of these, like Shawn, were BUD/S classmates: Ali, our senior corpsman, and Chris Osman.

Osman and I went way back, all the way to that moment on the beach in Third Phase when he became an accidental hero. Throughout BUD/S I couldn't stand him, but during our time together in Team Three we gradually became friends. Soon we would also work together closely as the platoon's two snipers, and our time in the Gulf and Afghanistan would cement the friendship.

A former marine, Osman was an excellent SEAL and a very squared-away dude. He can also be a frigging nightmare to be around. He is an intense guy and has a personality that can grate on you. Spend much time with him and chances are you'll end up either loving him or hating him.

Osman was also something of a legend among the marine scout snipers. When he and Patrick went through the marine sniper course together, as part of their final training exercise they developed a mission plan that included monitoring the Camp Pendleton residence of the marine two-star general in charge as a surveillance target. Osman took the exercise a little further than planned: He broke into the guy's house, snapped a bunch of pictures of its interior, and took the general's starched camouflage uniform with its two stars from where it hung in the closet and sneaked it back out with him as plunder. The marine sniper instructors were terrified shitless when they found out what he'd done, and everyone tried to hush it up. Osman wore the purloined uniform for his class graduation photo. For years afterward I would run into Marine Corps snipers in the fleet who would ask me, after learning that I was in SEAL Team Three, "Hey, do you know that crazy SEAL, you know, the guy who broke into the general's house and pinched his cammies?"

Osman never went through the SEAL sniper course himself; as a former marine, he'd done that marine course instead. Because of this, one could make the plausible argument that he wasn't technically a true SEAL sniper, something I proceeded to have a lot of fun giving him shit about. "Hey, Osman, how hard is that Marine Corps course?"

Don't get me wrong. The Marine Corps has great shooters, and they're some of the best marksmen in the military. Osman also could shoot.

With Osman and Ali joining the platoon, it was starting to feel like a minireunion. Those guys were happy to see me, and I was sure as hell glad to see them. I started feeling a bit better about my situation. Maybe life in ECHO platoon would be tolerable. I sure hoped so.

EIGHT

INTO THE WAR ON TERROR

One fine fall day not long after wrapping up that workup with ECHO platoon, I got up at the crack of dawn to go surfing. Our platoon was about to rotate overseas (the whole reason I'd joined them in the first place), so I would soon be back out on the Persian Gulf, where we were scheduled to participate in the interdiction of oil-smuggling boats coming out of Iraq—the same mission I'd been hoping to participate in when the attack on the USS *Cole* tossed our plans out the window. That was still some weeks off, though. Gabriele was now eight months pregnant, and my command had granted me permission to stay stateside long enough to be there for the birth of our first child. After that I would go rejoin my platoon. For now, I was enjoying the R & R.

I knew this would be my last day of surfing for a few days, so I made the most of it. The next day I was booked on a flight to Texas for a Stinger missile school at Fort Bliss that would last a few days. Always training.

After an hour or two of surfing I returned home exhilarated and ready to start my day. Even after all the years and all the crazy things I'd done, from Dräger-diving underneath gigantic tankers to jumping out of planes at 20,000 feet, there was still no experience that beat being out in the surf in the chill of the early California morning, nothing but a sleek plank of lightweight foam like a membrane between my bare feet and the surging elements. It's one of the greatest feelings in the world. I love it to this day.

When I got in, I found Gabriele sitting not five feet from the television, enormously pregnant, staring at the screen. It was early still, barely six o'clock, but she was already up. She turned to look at me, her face pulled into an expression of speechless horror. I sat down next to her and started watching the live broadcast from New York City, just in time to see the second plane hit the South Tower. The attack on U.S. soil that I'd worried about after standing watch over the crippled USS *Cole* was no longer an abstraction.

Within days I had joined my platoon on a nonstop flight to the Middle East. By the time our son Jackson came into the world on the last day of November, I was in the Persian Gulf and headed for Afghanistan.

We left North Island Naval Air Station in a big C-5 cargo plane, stopped off in Washington state to pick up some Army Rangers, made a short refueling stop in Iceland and then a brief overnight somewhere in Spain. Barely twenty-four hours after leaving San Diego we were receiving a briefing at Camp Doha, the principal U.S. base in Kuwait, where we were told we would be participating in, yes, the interdiction of noncompliant vessels in the Gulf.

Ironically, this was now a bit of a letdown. A year ago I'd been looking forward to exactly this mission. Hell, just a month ago we would have been thrilled to be on this assignment. *Finally, some action!* we'd have thought. Now everything had changed. Our country had been attacked in a brutal and unprovoked strike that slaughtered thousands of civilians. It was payback time, and we were champing at the bit to get our asses where we could do some serious damage in the name of our people back home. Interdiction of Saddam's oil smugglers, until recently a cherry assignment, now seemed like a time-consuming detour.

Still, this was a perfect mission for SEALs, and we'd had teams in there supporting the operation for years, ever since Desert Storm. In violation of U.S.-led sanctions, these maritime operators were feeding a huge black market, getting illegal oil on the cheap and selling it on the open market for millions in profits. Some were Middle Eastern nationals; others were British sea captains gone rogue. I'd met a number of both varieties in the back-alley bars in Bahrain. Another term for these characters would be "pirates."

These ships were coming out of Iraq sealed shut and tight as drums. To prevent being caught by boarding teams, these guys would literally weld themselves in so nobody could get to them. When the regular navy tried to board a vessel like that and take it over, they would be completely stymied and unable to get inside.

That was where we came in. We knew how to get on and into these boats silently, quickly, and effectively, boarding in minutes. We also didn't screw around. If the metal ship doors were welded shut, we'd cut our way in through the roof with an acetylene torch. But we'd have to move fast, because the moment the smugglers realized they were being boarded they would take aggressive action and haul ass for nearby Iranian waters—and if they made it, that was game over. Once they were outside that narrow channel of international waters, there'd be nothing anyone could do but clamber back off their damn boat and head back empty-handed. So when it came time to take down a smuggler's boat, we knew we had to move like lightning.

This was where that VBSS (Visit, Board, Search, and Seizure) training we did off the coast of San Clemente Island paid off. There's a reason SEALs train constantly, and this was it. We nailed those guys.

Typically there's a lot of adrenaline pumping during a maneuver like this. You're going out in the middle of the night, coming up alongside a vessel doing 15 to 20 knots, keeping your craft even with it and trying your best to put your whole team on board before the bad guys are even aware you're on them. Even in normal circumstances, this is an exacting and exciting procedure. Now everything felt heightened. With the events of 9/11 just weeks behind us like a fresh and gaping wound, the air crackled with an angry electricity. We would quietly shoot the shit to keep ourselves occupied, but none of us were feeling casual about what we were doing here.

Our platoon was outfitted in black from head to toe, wearing balaclavas, those Ninja-style masks that conceal the entire head except the eyes. A few of our guys who spoke Arabic had dubbed our team *Shaytan abyath*, "the White Devils," after overhearing crews captured from a few of the smugglers' ships we'd taken down muttering the phrase in our direction. We embraced the name, and I used the idea of it in a patch I designed for our platoon: an image of a white devil on a black background underneath "3ECHO." In addition to our platoon patches, we also had NYFD patches sewn onto our uniforms to pay homage to fallen heroes back home. To say that we were in the mood to kick some ass is to put it mildly.

The platoon would leave at sunset for its late-night operation on a small high-speed Special Ops boat called a Mark V. The Mark V is a modern marvel of design, equipped to take sixteen SEALs out some 500 miles from source to staging; its angular shape and low silhouette reduce its radar signature, making it hard to detect. Once out in the middle of the international shipping lane, the platoon would sit there silently in the dark, staging for minutes or hours, waiting for the word to go. Meanwhile, the platoon's sniper would be nearby in the helo, quietly trolling the area and looking for targets.

As a sniper, you have the big picture in the helo; you orchestrate the silent, deadly nighttime dance. It's the sniper's job to identify targets using the helicopter's forward-looking infrared system (FLIR) and pass critical target information to the platoon. In the helo, we are the eyes of the operation; the FLIR, a glass bubble on the bottom of the craft, has a range of over 50 miles. Nestled in the back of the Sea Hawk, you sit there watching that 18-inch green screen with a clear view of what's happening miles away down on the Gulf's surface. Once the team begins boarding the ship, you are the one passing real-time intel on all onboard activity to the team leaders. It's also your job to take out any targets that threaten the operation, if it comes to that, though this is a rare occurrence.

As Glen and I had done on the bridge of the crippled USS *Cole,* Osman and I shared this role. As sniper on duty, we'd participate in the nightly helicopter crew briefing, then hit the deck and take off in the bird to go cruising for targets. The rest of the platoon was stationed onshore at Camp Doha, and they would ride out every night in the Mark V, spend a few hours out on the Gulf, and then, about 3:00 or 4:00 A.M., ride back in to Kuwait for the night. Not us. Because the helo deployed directly off the deck of the destroyer out in open waters, one of us would live all week on board the ship right along with the helicopter squadron. They set up a cot for us in the weapons hold area where we would sleep with our guns. (We preferred to keep them on our person. What better way to know they were secure?) For all practical purposes, when not out on a mission we lived in that room.

We did this for weeks. Osman and I rotated out, trading off being on sniper watch and being part of the boarding teams. During the month or so we spent out there, we took down about half a dozen smuggling vessels. It was fun work, though not especially dangerous.

One day we got a briefing from some guys from the National Security

Agency (NSA) about a terrorist transport boat they'd been keeping an eye on. They thought it might be coming out of Iraq soon with a substantial cache of weapons and HVTs (high-value targets) on board. Whether "high-value targets" meant a known terrorist, hostile intel asset, or other person of interest, I didn't know, didn't need to know, and frankly didn't care. Whatever or whoever was on that boat, it was important. They described the target vessel's profile and gave us its identifying mark: Alpha-117.

This was the same ship, they said, that had been used by al Qaeda operatives to smuggle out the explosives that had been used to blow up U.S. embassies in Tanzania and Nairobi back in the summer of 1998, while I was just finishing up my Seal Tactical Training and preparing for my Trident. Those attacks had killed more than two hundred people, including a dozen Americans, and injured over four thousand more. That was the terrorist attack that had put bin Laden on the map (and the FBI's Ten Most Wanted list) for the first time.

This was no measly oil-smuggling operation. This was for real. These guys were serious bad actors who had spilled American blood, and they would be armed. The intel guys were briefing all American assets in the region, they said, and then they gave us the rules of engagement for this particular situation. "If you guys see this target," they told us, "you're authorized to take it down." Period.

A few days passed, and Osman rotated out to the team while I took his place on sniper duty. As much fun as it was being part of the team in a smuggler takedown operation, I looked forward to being back on sniper watch. I have always loved flying, and this gave me the chance to go out every night in a bird. The nights when we didn't see any noncompliant vessels, the crew on the surface would have nothing at all to do, but even on those nights, up in the helo I was kept relatively busy manning the helo-based surveillance equipment, and I enjoyed it.

My first night back on watch, I sat in the back of an H-60 Sea Hawk helicopter, shooting the shit with the crew over our comms as we made our way in slow, lazy arcs across the water and back. I didn't know which had a more soporific effect: the monotonous, high-pitched whine of the helo's rotors or the sweltering thickness of the Middle Eastern air. We kept the helo door open as we cruised, which provided a slow, muggy breeze. To pass the time and keep ourselves alert, we talked about everything we could think of, from sex to our taste in music to war stories of our training days. It was a few minutes after midnight.

An hour earlier I'd been on the flight deck of a U.S. destroyer a few hundred miles away in the middle of the Gulf, sitting in on the helo crew's briefing and adding my own input before takeoff. I'd grabbed my kit, and the four of us had saddled up—two pilots in front, the rescue swimmer/ sensor operator (the role I was originally trained for before going into BUD/S), and me—and made our way toward our rendezvous with the rest of my platoon. Now here I was, crouched in the back of our blacked-out Sea Hawk in the murky nighttime atmosphere over the Port of Basra off the southern tip of Iraq, trolling for smugglers.

Chr chr chr chr chr chr . . . The Sea Hawk rotor chopped relentlessly through the hot, soupy atmosphere as we swapped stories in the sweltering moonless night.

I'd been staring at the FLIR screen for a while when I saw something that made me sit up straight. I glanced down to scan my notes from that intel briefing a few days earlier. What was that boat's call sign again? I looked back up at the FLIR and murmured, "Holy shit." Right there on the pale green screen I could see the identifying numbers on the boat's stern: ALPHA-117. I was staring at the target the NSA had briefed us on, the ship that had supplied the explosives that had taken out our embassies in Nairobi and Tanzania.

In our nightly game of maritime poker, it looked like we had just drawn the joker from the deck.

This was hot. We thought we'd been sidelined while another platoon went ahead of us into the action in Afghanistan. Now it looked like maybe we were going to be the first to see serious action after all.

I radioed Lieutenant Chris Cassidy, our platoon commander on the Mark V, and told him I had the target ship on the FLIR. "Solid copy, stand by," he replied and then clicked off. I waited, knowing that he was radioing command on the destroyer a few hundred miles out on the Gulf. Word would come back almost instantly. Sure enough, a few seconds later my comm crackled back to life. "Sniper One, this is Echo One, good copy on all. We are taking her down, get us good eyes on."

Cassidy's a good man, I thought. Just weeks from now he would be leading us through a complex reconnaissance mission in Afghanistan, and he would later go on to become a NASA astronaut and complete three space walks. Right now I felt good knowing he was in charge of the crew on the Mark V. I'd seen some bullshit leaders, and Cassidy wasn't one of them. I was confident this would go smooth and fast.

Cassidy clicked off again to alert the platoon, knowing that I'd be back on comms in a moment.

Now I briefed the helo crew. Up to this point these guys knew nothing whatsoever about Alpha-117. As far as our intel went they were on a need-to-know basis, meaning I wouldn't pass on any information unless something happened. Well, something was happening. We were ready to get it on, and it was time to read them in on the situation. I keyed up my ICS (internal communications system) mike.

"Guys, here's the situation. We have a terrorist-sponsored vessel dead ahead. These are serious bad guys on board, and are most likely armed. This is the real deal. Time to go to work."

I heard a murmured "Holy shit" from the pilot. My thoughts exactly.

This was a much different situation than taking down a bunch of smugglers. Typically Navy helo crews do not see much in the way of combat action. Don't get me wrong. They have a tough job, and flying over these hostile waters in the dead of night at a bare few hundred feet off the surface is no joke. There's no putting down on land and walking away from the mission on one of these maritime interdictions. As I had nearly experienced myself years earlier during maneuvers over these same waters under the "leadership" of Lieutenant Burkitt, that bird can easily be in the drink and upside down in seconds, taking its crew straight down to a briny grave. There was no margin for error here, and these guys were good—but they hadn't been in this type of situation before, and they were clearly nervous. We were going in to take down a hostile terrorist ship, and if those characters saw us coming they wouldn't be welding themselves in and waiting to see what we did. There were weapons on that boat for a reason. They'd use them on us.

I went back to Cassidy and started feeding him the information he needed to mount our silent attack. In this instant his concerns were pure physics and logistics. *How do we get on board fast and clean? What class of ship is it? Where's the superstructure located—midship? foreship? aft? What's the ideal point on the ship to board? How long will it take the team to scale and board—how many feet of freeboard are we looking at?*

In an operation like this, stealth and accuracy are everything. Unless you want to have the other guy's arsenal start unloading in your direction, you need to strike with the speed and accuracy of a snake. This is the quintessential sniper's task: instantaneous calculation, integration, and delivery of critical information, complete and with 100 percent accuracy.

I emptied my mind and focused my faculties like a laser sight. Right now I had to function as a precision instrument for surveillance and calculation. I started passing Cassidy the data he needed.

"Hull length 300 feet. Vessel speed, 18 knots. Twenty feet of freeboard . . ."

Eighteen knots is about 20 mph. Freeboard is the vertical distance from the water line to the hook point on the edge of the rail. Twenty feet is a pretty high freeboard, meaning there was a significant vertical distance to travel in order to put the team on board. This boarding would have to be surgically precise.

"Superstructure's aft, with direct access to the bridge. I'd say hook on aft. Nobody on deck—looks like we can double-hook."

This was good. If we could get two simultaneous hooks going, we could send two teams up and over at the same time, one on each side of the ship.

Cassidy spoke quietly into his comm, briefing the team. They hopped into two RHIBs—rigid-hulled inflatable boats. The RHIB is a very fast craft, with twin diesel engines delivering 1,000 horsepower. You come up alongside the ship, matching its speed, and pin your RHIB right up against the hull. This is a precision stunt, something like pulling up in a Hummer next to a bus going 60 mph on a highway and maintaining your position in perfect tandem while eight guys step over you and board the bus in full gear. One simple misstep can screw it up, and here that would have lethal consequences.

Now I communicated to the pilots our optimum standoff distance, and the choreography began. I had to be careful not to put the helo on scene too soon, because if the crew on the tanker was alerted by the sound of the approaching helo, we would lose the crucial element of surprise. I had to time it to the split second and coordinate the procedure precisely with the platoon on the water and pilots up front in the helo. Training, training.

Just as the RHIB teams reached the ship, port and starboard, we slipped the bird into position on the tanker's port flank, hovering 150 feet off the surface. Our helo was completely blacked out. I was on night vision with the door still open, staring out into the black, silent scene below me.

Now we swung into the diciest part of the operation.

Up to this point I'd been giving Cassidy the playbook on how to board the ship. Now my role slipped into its most acute phase, because I had to deliver a stream of real-time intel as the situation began to unfold. If I saw someone emerging from below, from the wheelhouse, the engine room, or any other area of the ship, I'd need to let the right person on the team know instantly—"I've got a guy coming out of midship on the port side, heading your way"—so they'd know what they were dealing with.

And it was not all a matter of pure reconnaissance. I was, after all, a sniper. If a serious threat showed up, I was there to take it out.

It all happened fast.

In movies you see assault teams swarming over boats or buildings with someone in charge shouting "Go, go, go, go, *go!*" But this was not Hollywood, and in the waters off Iraq at midnight the assault sequence played out in a surreal silence, broken only by momentary brief murmurs into comms as critical bytes of information were passed on. From point man to breacher, every member of the team knew exactly what he had to do.

As I scanned the tanker's deck for signs of discovery, one of our guys in the portside RHIB swung up a tall carbon fiber pole. Atop the pole sat a surgical tube quick-release mechanism attached to a titanium double hook, in turn attached to a narrow titanium caving ladder, some ten inches wide. The pole hooked the rail and popped off the quick release, and the ladder was in position. The same operation was happening in simultaneous mirror image starboardside. On each side of the vessel, while the designated ladder man held tension on the ladder, the other guys scurried up the 20 feet of freeboard, over the rail, and onto the ship's deck.

This was a delicate step. I vividly remembered an event that had occurred a few years ago off the surly California coast during our eighteen months of training workup. As we had gone through exactly this type of operation, Shawn, our breacher, scuttled up a caving ladder outfitted with his acetylene torch and 60-pound tank. Some rookie was at the helm of the RHIB and accelerated too fast. The ladder suddenly snapped taut and twanged hard, sending Shawn, off and into the drink. Loaded with torch, full gear, and body armor, he sank a full 30 feet before he was able to shuck off enough equipment to start fighting his way back up to the surface.

It was a damn good thing this had happened to us in training. Because it had happened then, it didn't happen now, and the operation went off like a precision electronic instrument. As the members of the assault team scrambled up the narrow ladders and slipped silently over the rails, I sat up in the helo, peering out the open door, scanning the length of the terrorist boat, scrutinizing the scene through my night-vision goggles for the slightest trace of movement.

There was no one on deck. We had caught them completely off guard.

I watched as one team headed for the wheelhouse and another peeled off to head below for aft steering. In moments the ship would be effectively taken over—if all went well. And it had to go well. Once you go internal the risk escalates, because in a firefight you can get ricochets.

Suddenly I saw a searing flash of light, nearly blinding in the pitch black. Explosively bright bursts of light streamed out through the wheelhouse windows, accompanied by sharp reports.

The helo pilot yanked on his stick, pulling us off station, ready to bank and haul ass out of there. I knew what he was thinking: *We're taking fire!*

"Hold station!" I barked at him as the bird jerked hard left, nearly tossing me out the door. "No—don't worry!"

It *looked* like hostile fire, especially on night vision—but it wasn't. Our guys were just using standard hostile room-entry tactics, using flashbangs, a type of grenade simulator SEALs employ in operations like this. The flashbang is an effective (albeit somewhat dangerous) stun grenade. You crack open the door and roll this baby into the room, it goes off with a loud *crash* and burst of light, and everyone in the room is momentarily stunned and blinded, giving you a few seconds to move in and take them.

Our helo pilot put the bird steady back on course, and we watched the scene unfold below. *Crash! Crash!* Cabin after cabin they fanned out, scattering their explosive seeds and harvesting each roomful of stunned prisoners, clearing and securing area after area.

Without firing a shot, our guys had taken the ship.

One group immediately started a reclear, methodically going back through the entire vessel, room by room, making sure there were no stragglers. I heard it all happening over my comm. One of our guys had grabbed the hat off the ship's captain's head and now wore it himself. He lit up a cigar he must have found on the ship (the thing was loaded with illegal smokes) and started running from cabin to cabin reclearing the vessel, El Capitán's chapeau perched on his cranium, chomping on his cigar and brandishing his M-4. Jesus, what a character.

Meanwhile, the rest of the crew were hauling our prisoners out onto the aft deck, about thirty of them in all. Typically guys captured in a slam-bang operation like this will be so frightened they will be pretty submissive at this point, but occasionally you'll get someone who decides to go aggressive. An incident like that had occurred back in 1999, when a guy from SEAL Team Three got into a scuffle with one of his team's prisoners. His weapon went off and he took a round in the leg. Another SEAL patched him up. (No doc. Ouch.) Since then we'd started wearing weapons catches; we would slip our primary weapon to the side and into the catch so it would be fixed and not go flopping around (as had happened with Gilroy Jones on my first day with ECHO platoon).

I could see there were some pretty belligerent characters here, and our guys appeared to be giving them some tough love.

"Hey," I said to the sensor operator, "move the FLIR forward of the superstructure." *And let these guys do their job*, I added to myself. The image on the FLIR was being streamed back to the command post on the destroyer, and I wanted to keep these guys out of trouble. There was no outright abuse or wrongful conduct happening here, but our guys would do whatever it took to contain this situation fast and hard. This was not a time for waffling or second-guessing.

In a few hours we would be turning the boat over to a Maritime Interdiction Force, a specially trained navy crew who would steer it down to a holding area off the coast of Dubai, where it would be turned over to one of the alphabet-soup intelligence agencies. From that point on we would never know what happened or exactly what these characters were up to. But it didn't take a high-level clearance to see that they were up to something big—and not good.

All told, we'd taken about thirty prisoners, a bunch of fake passports, over a hundred grand in U.S. dollars, and a *lot* of weapons. From start to finish, we pulled off this high-threat takedown in about five minutes, with maybe another ten to comb the ship and make sure everything and everyone was accounted for.

It was a textbook boarding.

In late November, not long after that successful nighttime op in the Gulf, about half our platoon was flown down to stage on Masirah Island off the coast of Oman, to the southeast of the United Arab Emirates and the easternmost tip of Saudi Arabia, where they would spend a few weeks modifying some army Humvees to ready them for us to use in Afghanistan. Because of my air quals, I stayed behind in Kuwait to pack up all our gear. I knew how to build a pallet, how to label all the hazmats, weight it all correctly, and work with the aircrews to make sure everything was safe and to spec. I got everything packed and all our pallets loaded onto a big old C-130 and boarded it to make the roughly 1,000-mile flight to Oman.

Once on the plane and nestled safely among the pallets, I settled in to grab some sleep.

A short while later, I woke up. Something was wrong. The plane was humming along, but at an odd pitch. I jumped up and headed for the cockpit to see what was going on. Didn't take long to find out. We'd lost an engine.

I woke up our crew chief and told him what was happening. He freaked out. It was the middle of the night, and we were rapidly losing altitude over the Persian Gulf. Warning lights were going on all over the cockpit. I woke up the rest of the guys and briefed them in a few sentences. We had work to do.

To help compensate for the plane's awkward angle and the resulting shift in its center of gravity, we had to move our gear. A crew of us got behind one big pallet and started pushing that sucker forward. It was mighty heavy, and because of the plane's tilt the push was all uphill. We moved it about 10 feet and locked it into place, then got to work on another one. Pretty soon we had the plane leveling out, and the pilot made a successful emergency landing in Bahrain, about halfway to our destination, where we spent the rest of that night before giving it another try the next morning.

It was a mighty inauspicious way to start a mission into one of the deadliest places on the planet. It was a good thing I didn't believe in omens. Or at least, not as much as I believed in our guys and our training.

The next day we and our C-130 made it the rest of the way to Oman, where we joined the rest of our platoon at a large staging area. By this time operations in Afghanistan were well under way. On October 7, while my buddies and I were boarding oil smugglers off the coast of Iraq, President George W. Bush and Prime Minister Tony Blair each announced the commencement of Operation Enduring Freedom, a joint effort between the Afghan United Front and U.S. and U.K. forces to oust the Taliban and al Qaeda influence and destroy their terrorist training infrastructure in Afghanistan. That same day, American and British air forces began massive aerial bombardment of Kabul and a few other key locations in Afghanistan. By the time our platoon was staging in Oman, the Taliban's control over Kabul had been decimated, and our guys were starting to establish a foothold.

We knew there was a lot going on over there and that we would be joining the action sooner or later, but we didn't know exactly when or exactly where, or what we'd be doing when we got there. In fact, we didn't know much of anything. They did their best to brief us in Oman, but information was sketchy. Maps of the area, for example, were either a mess or nonexistent. We had some old Soviet-era maps, but they were next to worthless. Our briefings covered the current political situation and the latest intelligence, both of which were in a state of constant flux. It was amazing just how little we knew about Afghanistan.

A lot of our C-130 gunships were based there in Oman. They would take off from our staging area and fly northeast across the mouth of the Persian Gulf and then through Pakistani airspace until they were over Afghanistan, where they would wreak havoc on Taliban enclaves.

The C-130s videotaped these raids, and the gunship crews would invite us over each day to watch their videotapes from the night before. We watched hours of this footage, and it was one of the most bizarre things I'd ever seen. It sounds trite to say it looked like nothing so much as a video game, but that's about the size of it. There would be a basically blacked-out screen, dotted with dozens of tiny little green trails zipping around. These, we knew, were the heat signatures of people running for their lives into the mountains while the C-130s continued pounding them from the sky. These gunships fly at 20,000 feet with their howitzers trained on the ground below. They are so high up, those poor bastards on the ground couldn't see or hear a thing up there—all they knew was that death was raining down on them. We called it Murder TV.

We watched them wipe out hundreds of enemy forces. *Holy shit*, I thought, and I was pretty sure the other guys watching were thinking the same thing. *This is no joke.* I knew one thing: I did *not* want to be a little heat signature on the end of that kind of firepower.

Meanwhile, we pitched in with the rest of the platoon, helping to get all our gear together and convert those Humvees, ripping off their doors and getting everything customized to save weight. This was not Desert Storm terrain or the relatively flat Somalian plateau of Mogadishu; Afghanistan was home to a section of the frigging Himalayas. As little prepared as we were for the terrain, we were similarly unprepared for the weather. Temperatures could be up into the high 90s and higher during the day and plummet to below freezing at night. More on that topic later.

Soon the word came down: We were heading to Kandahar Airport, one of the first bases we were establishing on the ground. Kandahar International Airport had been occupied by the Soviets at the beginning of their ten-year siege starting in December 1979 and was severely damaged during that decade. In recent months it had become one of the toughest Taliban strongholds, but the Taliban forces there had been squeezed by Afghan loyalists (tribal fighters) led by Gul Agha Sherzai, the pre-Taliban governor of Kandahar, and Hamid Karzai, who would later become the first democratically elected president of Afghanistan, and U.S. forces had ramped up the effort. An expeditionary force of marines was sweeping in from nearby Camp Rhino to the south, the Coalition's first ground-based stronghold, to take the airport.

Kandahar Airport would now become the base of operations for Task Force K-Bar, the Spec Ops group we would be joining. One of the first ground assault teams in the U.S.-led invasion, Task Force K-Bar was composed of Special Operations forces from eight different nations: Australia, Canada, Denmark, Germany, New Zealand, Norway, Turkey, and the United States. Here also was some interesting news: Task Force K-Bar was being run by none other than Captain Bob Harward—our second CO at SEAL Team Three, the guy who had taught me how to take the lead in a beach run by tying up the other guy's boots. *Good*. Harward was an animal, and I mean that in the best sense. He would pull no punches.

At Oman they went over the current rules of engagement (ROE) with us, and this was a surprise. The ROE seemed to boil down to this: *You see any dark-skinned male of fighting age, i.e., fifteen years old or older, and you're cleared to engage.*

Now *that* was highly unusual. Normally the ROE for combat missions are pretty complicated and quite strict. If anything, SEALs can tend to feel frustrated and operationally hampered in combat situations by what often feel like unnecessarily restrictive (and perhaps more politically than strategically motivated) ROE. (For example, read Marcus Luttrell's *Lone Survivor* with an eye out for this point, and you'll see exactly what I'm talking about.) But they were not messing around here. This was something like the conditions that prevailed on the damaged USS *Cole*. At the time of that attack, the forces on the deck had felt hamstrung by ROE. By the time we got there eight hours later, the ROE had drastically changed by presidential order: *Anyone gets within 500 feet of this ship, you kill him.*

We got the general impression that there were Taliban and al Qaeda running around everywhere, and it was often difficult to know who was who and who was on which side. Some of these tribal leaders were smart fuckers, too, and knew how to take advantage of our own lack of clear orientation. They would tell Coalition forces, "Those guys over there, across that ridge, are Taliban," and then U.S. troops would go wipe out those guys over there, across that ridge—only to learn later that they had just wiped out a rival warlord that the first guys had been battling for decades, and that it had nothing whatsoever to do with al Qaeda or Taliban. I did not learn about this latter complication until we'd been in-country for a while, but we did get the general impression that it was chaos over there.

We didn't know what to expect. We'd seen all this footage from the C-130s, and it looked like a free-for-all, like the Wild West. I asked Chief Dye exactly what he thought we were walking into. "Man," he said, "I don't know. All I can tell you is, we're going into the shit."

·   ·   ·

Before we left Oman, an unfortunate episode occurred. Two Air Force Combat Controllers (also called Combat Control Technicians, or CCT) had been assigned to our platoon. They would go along with us on missions once we were on the ground in Afghanistan and be in charge of calling in whatever air support we needed.

Air Force Combat Controllers are fantastic, and we were glad to have them. All these guys do is comms, and they're really good at it. Unfortunately, as we soon realized, these two particular Combat Controllers were quite young and inexperienced. Actually, I'm being nice. It wasn't their lack of experience that was the problem, it was their attitude. Chief Dye wanted to make them feel they were part of the platoon and tried to get them to roll up their sleeves and participate, but they just did not play ball. They'd been in Oman for a while, and they were not that focused on what we were doing. They never offered to help out. We'd tell them, "Hey, guys, we need you here tomorrow morning to help us work on these Humvees," and they wouldn't show up.

Finally Chief Dye caught them playing grab-ass with some of the air force girls on base. That was the last straw, and he fired them, saying we would get some more mature air force guys once we got over into Afghanistan.

When the two guys came over to pick up their stuff, one of them tried to get back a pair of boots he'd traded to Chris Osman. Osman wasn't about to give up those boots and was not that interested in whatever this guy's problem was. In the course of the exchange the guy said something insulting to him.

Now, dissing Osman to his face is not a wholesome plan. The guy can go from zero to seeing red in seconds. He very calmly set down the MRE he was eating and quietly said, "Okay, you and me, we're going outside right now." He said it so evenly that the guy didn't quite understand what he meant, but he immediately got uneasy.

"What," he said, already backpedaling.

"You just insulted me in front of my guys," replied Osman.

"Okay," the guy said, "but what do you mean, we're going outside?"

"Well," Osman explained as he slowly got to his feet, "we're going outside, and I'm going to kick the shit out of you, and then I'm going to come back in here and finish my MRE. That's what's going to happen."

The guy literally started to tremble. It was sad. "Look," he stammered, "I—I—I don't want any trouble—you can have the boots, I'm out of here," and he was gone.

The two air force guys felt they'd been embarrassed by the whole episode, and they were not happy about it. Months down the road, this would come back to bite us. It planted a seed of resentment that ended up costing me a medal and getting Osman sent home.

In the middle of December our boots hit Afghan soil for the first time. Rolling down the ramp of the C-130, hitting the ground and looking around, it felt like being dropped onto the set of a classic Vietnam movie like *Platoon* or *Apocalypse Now*. Helicopters filled the air; equipment was moving everywhere. Chaos. There was clear evidence of that initial firefight in which the marines had wrested control of the airport from Taliban forces: broken glass everywhere, and bloodstains all over the place. Our buddies from the Corps had clearly kicked some serious Taliban ass taking this place.

The first guys in hadn't yet quite figured out our footprint here, and EOD (Explosive Ordnance Disposal) teams were still working to clear the perimeter, which was no small task. When the Soviets had been here years earlier, they had blanketed the place with land mines. In fact, Afghanistan is one of the two or three most heavily land-mined countries on the planet. The morning after we landed, a marine went out walking and veered too far off perimeter. He stepped on a mine and blew his leg off. One of the

SEAL corpsmen, Marco Gonzalez, put a tourniquet on the guy and patched him up.

That first week at Kandahar Airport things were pretty crazy, as our command structure worked to set up a tactical ops center and hammer out some kind of order in this place. Meanwhile, we got settled in as best we could. We constructed a homemade shower, built a fire pit, and a sort of lounge (though there was no alcohol on the premises, or at least there wasn't supposed to be), and carved out little rooms for ourselves in some of the outer-perimeter airport buildings. We had taken over a set of buildings right next to the Army Special Forces unit where we had our compound, which looked like nothing so much as a little shantytown.

We set up camp with stuff that we foraged in those areas that had been cleared by the EOD team. It was like a treasure hunt, and we found all sorts of wild and crazy stuff. There were old Soviet tanks and MIGs rotting away on the tarmac. A few guys found AK-47s wrapped in rags and hidden in the bathrooms, locked and loaded and ready to go. We found torture rooms, including boards outfitted with leather straps that clearly had been used for some kind of prisoner interrogation, and not the polite kind.

Kandahar Airport also served as our prisoner-of-war staging camp. As the Afghanistan effort proceeded, all the Taliban, al Qaeda, and others who were captured in the field would be brought to Kandahar to be processed and interrogated before being flown to Guantánamo. By the time we got there, people had already set up a large prison camp facility that bore a striking resemblance to the POW camp I'd been incarcerated in at SERE school: guard towers, barbed wire, the whole package. Surreal.

On Christmas Day 2001, we went out on our first patrol in Afghanistan. We spent all afternoon packing our gear and were ready for anything. We had the Mark 41 automatic grenade gun, which launches a series of mic-mic

(40 mm) grenades. It's like shooting a machine gun, only instead of bullets, you're firing a string of grenades. We had rocket launchers and LAW rockets strapped all over our vehicles, as well as a .50 cal and an M-60 machine gun. Our comm antenna was hooked up so our comms guys could link into satellite, and we were all outfitted with night-vision gear. We were, in other words, loaded for bear.

The environment was not the sand desert of Kuwait but a rough, high desert terrain. Just outside Kandahar it was more plains than mountainous, the largely flat area far more manageable for our vehicles than what we would experience later on, farther up north. We had two EOD guys with us, Brad and Steve, as well as our new Air Force CCTs, another Brad and Eric, who were solid, mature guys and fit in right away. Chief Dye had clearly made the right move firing the younger pair back in Oman.

On the ride out we didn't encounter anyone, but the journey was a little hairy nevertheless because we kept seeing red rocks everywhere, which we assumed signified mines, or at least the possibility of mines. We'd stop, our EOD team would dismount and scope everything out, then they'd get back in the vehicle and we'd keep moving forward. Progress was slow and tense.

We had set out in the early evening, maybe 2000 hours (8:00 P.M.). After six or seven hours of this halting progress, we'd hit all our checkpoints and hadn't seen anything worth noting. By now it was two or three in the morning, time to lay up for the night and get a few hours' sleep. We had just come to a river and were looking for a good spot to cross. On the other side, we could see a series of massive, beautiful, dark red sand dunes that rolled on for miles. They were gorgeous, like something you'd see in an epic film.

Right in the middle of the dunes I noticed a small cluster of trees. I was in Cassidy's vehicle, and I saw that he was focusing on this cluster of trees, too. Alarm bells went off quietly in my head. This was something we'd been taught in sniper school: It's human nature to gravitate to an object of note in an otherwise featureless stretch of landscape. If you're looking at a wide open stretch of beach, for example, and you see a cluster of rocks and not much else, you'll automatically gravitate to those rocks. That was exactly what was happening with Cassidy and that little cluster of trees nestled into the endless stretch of sand dunes.

As snipers we were taught two things about this. First, it's a natural tendency to be drawn to that unique feature. Second, fight it! Do *not* give in to the obvious. Not only do you not want to be predictable to the enemy, you also don't want to be accidentally compromised. If you are drawn to that landscape feature, other people will be, too—and those other people might be there right now. Or they might be drawn there once you're settled in and starting to relax.

I sidled over to Cassidy and said, "Hey, LT, that's not a very good option. No doubt other people have been there and will use that place to hole up. We'd be better off going out into the open, setting up our own camouflage netting and camping out on the sand dunes."

He fought me on it. "No," he said, "we'll go own that area. We're out in the middle of nowhere. There's no good reason to think that there'd be anyone else holed up there."

I didn't like it. I mean, why would we want to take the risk? Sure, we could bring serious firepower to anyone we might run across—but still, why do that when there was an entire open desert available to us? I could see that everyone was tired and wanted to get some shut-eye, and yes, choosing that cluster of trees as our site for the night would make setting up camp quicker and easier, which would translate into getting to sleep sooner, which might even translate into getting a slight bit *more* sleep. I understood all that—but I still thought that none of this was any reason to take the easy route.

We had a short, heated discussion. "Point taken," Cassidy finally said, "but this is the decision we're making." After fording the river, we headed for the cluster of trees.

As we started setting up, I shone my flashlight on one spot on the ground—and sure enough, there at my feet was a fire pit. I nudged Cassidy and pointed with my flashlight beam. "Hey, LT," I whispered, "there ya go." It was as if we had followed *Fodor's Guide to Terrorist Afghanistan*. It wasn't just that one fire, either. There were fire rings everywhere, a few days old at most. Some forces, God knew who, had recently stopped by these trees and camped out exactly where we were standing right now. Fortunately there was no one there at that moment. But there easily could have been.

"Goddammit," said Cassidy, and he nodded. He knew I was right. We set up a watch and pitched our camp.

I relate this not to toot my own horn but to make the point again about our training. Sniper school simply makes you into a better operator. It trains you to pay attention to things others might miss, even other Navy SEALs, and it trains you to pay attention when others might get lazy. Sniper school squeezes the lazy out of you. It forces you to make good decisions even when you're tired. I saw similar things happen many times over.

One thing about Cassidy I really appreciated: He wasn't afraid to admit when he'd been wrong. To me, this is one of the strongest marks of great leadership. Nobody is always right. Great leaders use that to learn and improve, instead of fighting it.

The patrol was otherwise uneventful, and we headed back the following day, patrolling as we went, and worked our way back to camp by evening. Although nothing much happened, it was good to shake out the cobwebs and get ourselves moving out in the field.

A few days after Christmas, an event occurred that shook us up and showed us how little margin for error there was here—and how far we still had to go to get our shit sufficiently together if we intended to come out of this place alive.

About a thirty-minute drive from the Kandahar Airport there was a place called Tarnak Farms, where the 9/11 attackers were said to have trained. (Tarnak Farms was also believed to have been home to bin Laden for a while and was the site of a narrowly missed opportunity to take him out a few years earlier.) Shortly after the 9/11 attacks, the news channels had run a captured video clip of terrorists-in-training running an obstacle course and monkey bars at a training camp. That was Tarnak Farms.

The place had now been completely leveled by Coalition bombing raids, but it was still a useful training site. We had set up a mock shooting range there and would go out to test weapons, check our explosives, and blow off captured enemy ordnance. We had been out there not long before Christmas and had used the site to sight our .50 cal and grenade launcher and do some basic weapons training.

Now, a few days before New Year's, we headed out there again to do some more testing on our weapons and make sure our zero was good. We didn't have a lot of the technology we've developed since then. Today I wouldn't need to go anywhere to confirm my rifle's zero; I could just plug my local coordinates into my software and it would correct for that part of the world, with its particular elevation, degree of latitude, and environmental conditions. Back in 2001 we didn't have that sophisticated software, and nothing could replace getting out on the range and physically testing the weapons. We also had a bunch of enemy ordnance we wanted to take out there to blow.

About half the platoon went out this time, maybe eight guys including our two EOD guys, and we took just two vehicles. We arrived and parked, and as I stepped out of the Humvee I'd been riding in I happened to glance down at the rear tire. My eye caught a glimpse of something that looked like a pink pig's tail sticking out from under the tire. I bent down slowly to get a closer look. Damn, that looked an awful lot like det (detonation) cord.

It *was* det cord.

Shit. I froze. "Hey, Brad?" I called out to one of our EOD guys. "You want to take a look at this? It looks a whole lot like det cord to me."

Det cord looks much like an M-80 fuse, only bigger. I'd done enough demolitions to know what I was looking at, but when you have an expert handy it never hurts to get a second opinion. This was a situation where it would certainly pay to be sure.

Brad stepped over cautiously to where I stood and angled in close for a good look. "Holy shit," he murmured, and he looked around at the other guys. "Okay," he said quietly, "everybody slowly step back."

Everybody slowly stepped back.

Brad called over his buddy Steve, who slipped over to Brad's side to become part of our tableau. Brad and Steve very slowly, very carefully, checked the whole scene out, inch by freaking inch. I heard Brad let his breath out, and it was not from relief. It was from the need to maintain maximum control, which you can't do effectively when you're holding your breath. "Okay, guys," he said, "here's the situation. We have parked directly on top of an antitank mine. Which happens to be tied into three antipersonnel mines."

It did not take a degree in physics or expertise in demolition specs to know that the shit our Humvee was sitting on was enough to blow us all to Pakistan.

We stood in place while Brad and Steve dismantled the whole mess, wondering how on earth we hadn't set the explosives off. I mean, we didn't just lightly brush the damn thing. We parked a frigging Humvee on it. Why were we still standing here, left alive to tell the tale? Not that we were complaining any—but it was weird not knowing. Was the thing a dud, or were we just ridiculously lucky?

Our answer came soon enough. Brad came over to us after they'd finished their work and said, "Whoever set this thing up missed one step. They didn't set up the drum correctly. As a result, the pressure plate didn't rotate properly and failed to initiate the charge. Which, all things considered, was a good thing."

We couldn't argue with that. Without that one human error, the thing would have gone off and taken all of us with it—us in our Humvees with no armor and no doors.

I still have a picture of that little det cord, and with it, another picture of me standing in that same area initiating a charge later that day on some of our captured ordnance, and in this one you can see a bombed-out blue minivan in the background. We'll come back to that second snapshot again, because that blue minivan took on new significance to me about three months later.

Here was the really freaky thing about our close encounter of the nearly fatal kind: Only a few days beforehand, an EOD team had been out there and cleared the whole area. So how was it we'd just driven in and parked our Humvee square on top of an economy-sized Armageddon, when the whole place had already been scoured and pronounced clean? There were only two possibilities. Either our EOD guys had completely missed this series of mines, which was extremely unlikely—or else someone was out there surveilling the area and had slipped in and booby-trapped the place *after* the EOD guys left, figuring that we'd be back. I was pretty sure it was the latter.

Three months later, I would be 100 percent sure of it.

NINE

IN THE CAVES

Shortly after New Year's Day we learned we would be going on a mission up north to the province of Khost, a few hundred miles northeast of Kandahar and nestled in the mountains right up against the Afghanistan-Pakistan border, home to the infamous Zhawar Kili cave complex, the location where Osama bin Laden is said to have officially declared war on America in 1998.

The second-largest known training camp in Afghanistan, Zhawar Kili was an elaborate training complex of caves and tunnels built into the mountainside. The Soviets had used it during their occupation in the eighties, and the Taliban had now reclaimed it as their own. This place was a key strategic flash point. The entire area was riddled with caves and tunnels and was one of the prime regions where al Qaeda and Taliban leadership was believed to have fled after we heavily bombed their cave hideouts at Tora Bora, some fifty miles to the north. It was also a major corridor to Pakistan.

Hard information on this cave complex was sketchy at best. We knew there was a base camp consisting of three large tunnels, with an unknown number of rooms, caves, and subtunnels. We also knew there was an extensive system of caves and tunnels built into the mountain ridge above the base camp. This cave complex was a frigging warren, encompassing arms depots, communications, hotel-like residences, a mosque, a kitchen, a medical facility—an entire terrorist town drilled into the face of a mountain, with room for some five hundred people at a time.

The place was also a fortress, and damn near invincible. The Afghan government had tried to take it when it was held by mujahideen (rebels) and failed. The Soviets were slightly more successful, but only slightly: They bombed the hell out of the place and forced everyone inside to flee, then went in and planted mines everywhere. Three weeks later the mujahideen were inside again and back in business. The site had been hit by U.S. air strikes shortly after hostilities commenced on October 7, but to little effect. In order to really nail this place, we needed people on the ground exploring the caves themselves on foot and coming back with the specific coordinates that would allow precision strikes.

That's where we came in.

Our air forces were going to launch a massive air strike, pounding the area with JDAMs (Joint Direct Attack Munition) to soften the target. Our SEAL platoon would go in the following day to bat cleanup.

This was not originally meant to be our mission. The Zhawar Kili site was too large and complicated for a single platoon. Originally it had been allocated to a larger team of Green Berets, but a recent incident had thrown a wrench into those plans. The unit that had been slated for Zhawar Kili was sent on a direct action mission to take a Taliban-controlled compound.

Someone got jumpy, and they ended up killing virtually everyone in the place—who all turned out to be not Taliban at all but members of Hamid Karzai's anti-Taliban forces. It was an unmitigated disaster. You never heard about it in the media, and you probably never will; it was not exactly something the military wanted to publicize. The ODA (Operational Detachment Alpha) team that had screwed up was sent home, and now the task of combing through the remains of Zhawar Kili fell to us.

Our platoon of sixteen was going to need some reinforcements, so our numbers were appropriately goosed with the addition of a ground unit of about twenty marines. These were young guys, in excellent shape, well trained, and highly motivated. I've always been impressed with the Marine Corps and their military bearing. When it comes to standing watch, these guys don't mess around. With marines, from the top officers right down to the basic foot soldier, you know you're dealing with high-caliber personnel. You definitely sleep well at night knowing these guys are on the perimeter.

We also had our two Air Force CCTs, Brad and Eric, who were damn good at their job and always seemed to have close air support at their fingertips the moment we needed it, and our two EOD guys, Brad and Steve, who had saved our asses at Tarnak Farms and were obviously strong assets. For this mission we were also assigned two guys from the FBI to provide forensic expertise and DNA-sample collection from enemy gravesites, one more from the Counterterrorist Intelligence Center (CTIC), and a chemical weapons expert from the army's Chemical Reconnaissance Detachment (CRD), for their expertise in combing through whatever we would find out there.

The plan was for the marines to insert with us, then split off and set up a defensive perimeter higher up on the ridge, making sure our backs were covered while we combed through the dozens of caves and tunnels, doing BDA (bomb damage assessment) and documenting whatever was left behind. We would get into the valley, spend eight to ten hours on-site once we made our way to the cave complex, then extract and report back. It would be a solid one-day op, no vehicles, all on foot. Twelve hours from start to finish, max.

At least, that was the plan.

Less than an hour before we were to board the C-130 to fly up to Bagram Air Base for a few days of final briefing and prep, we got an addition to our team. A lieutenant commander, Commander Smith, joined us and said, "Hey, guys, I'm going out there with you." Actually, that was a slight oversimplification. He was not just coming with us, he was coming with us as ground forces commander.

Now, Commander Smith was an intelligent officer and a nice guy, but he had very little situational awareness here. At the time he was an officer with one of the SDV (SEAL Delivery Vehicle) teams, and the guys in the delivery vehicle community drove underwater subs; it was a completely different sort of mission. He hadn't been operational in some time and was rotating over here to get some theater experience. Jumping in to join our mission at the last minute was fine, but in my opinion, he'd been out of the game too long to be in charge of tactical decisions on the ground.

A few of us glanced at each other warily. He could see the apprehension in our eyes and quickly reassured us. "Don't worry, guys, I know Cassidy's in charge. I won't get into the decision making here. I'm not going to get in your shit." Okay. *Let's hope not,* I thought.

We resumed with our preboard preparations—and sure enough, within five minutes Commander Smith was in our shit, big-time. He told us he wanted us to go in fully suited up, Kevlar body armor and all.

I raised my hand. "Look, sir, none of us are acclimated to working at

7,000 to 12,000 feet elevation. We're already carrying a pretty heavy load." In addition to our weapons, we would also be carrying breachers and explosives, in case we had to blow ordnance or breach our way into a cave. "Plus we have to hump 12 klicks just to get to where the op starts," I added. The place was likely crawling with hostiles, so rather than insert directly at the mouth of the cave complex, we were going to start out a good distance away, under the cover of darkness, and then hump the distance silently to our destination. "We're in mountain country, and if we overload ourselves we're going to be a wreck by the time we get to the site."

This was not a direct action mission, where you fast rope in and *boom!* you're on target. We were going to be patrolling 12 kilometers out—that's about 7.5 miles. When you carry a heavy load for that long, your situational awareness starts to shrink. At first you keep yourself acutely tuned to everything around you, but after a while your attention starts to flag. Soon you're just staring at the next footprint in front of you. I'd seen it before. In GOLF platoon and sniper school I'd learned that for a reconnaissance mission like this, it makes a lot more sense to pack light and go fast.

Smith wasn't budging. "No, this is my call, and everyone wears armor."

He was already making tactical decisions for us—and he'd just made a bad one. Chief Dye sided with me privately, but what could we do?

"Check," I said, "got it."

We started suiting up to go, everyone putting on all their battle armor. I quietly took out my armor plates and left them behind. Call it gross insubordination if you want, but this was fucking ridiculous, and I was damned if I was going to do it.

SUNDAY, JANUARY 6

It was about a three-hour insert by helicopter from Bagram Air Base to the Zhawar Kili complex. We were let off in the mountains well before dawn, about 4:00 A.M. We set up a quick perimeter, checked in with the marines (who had arrived a little ahead of us), made sure we were verified for where we were so our air support team would know we were friendlies and wouldn't take us out, and set up our rendezvous points for extraction at the end of the day. Then we set off, patrolling our way in the direction of the cave complex.

A few kilometers in I looked over at Shawn, our breacher, who was carrying a hooligan (a big metal breaching tool) on his back along with a ton of explosives. Brad and Steve, our EOD techs, had all their explosive equipment, too. Casey, our AOIC, carried photographic and video equipment to document whatever we would find. These guys had to be miserable. We still had miles to go, and we were gaining altitude. I was so glad I didn't have my armor plates.

About an hour in, we took a water break. I sat down on the ground next to Shawn. "How you doin', brother?" I felt so bad for him.

"Dude," he said, "right about now I would welcome stepping on a land mine."

Soon we were back on our feet. Everyone else was already tired and sweating. I was set to go, feeling alert and nimble. Shawn's focus was like a flashlight beam on the ground in front of him. By the time we got within proximity of the site everyone was completely worn out, even Cassidy. I saw Cassidy and Smith huddling up for a couple of minutes.

Then Cassidy came over to us. "All right, everybody," he said, "we're going to ditch our armor and stash it. We'll cache it right here and pick it up again on our way out." He quietly took me aside and said, "Okay, you were absolutely right. We fucked up. So go easy on me."

"Forget it," I said. Then I added, "But fuckin-A, I told you so."

Everyone started shucking their plates. Cassidy looked over at me. "Hey, Webb. Aren't you going to stash your plates?" I shook my head. "Nope. I didn't wear any." Cassidy looked at me for a moment with no expression, then grinned. "You son of a bitch."

I wasn't just trying to be a smart-ass. To my way of thinking, this was critical strategic thinking. Look at the kind of enemy we were up against: Here was a dude running around in the hills carrying nothing but a wool blanket, a wool hat, an AK-47, and maybe a little water and bullets. Not only did this guy have the advantage of knowing the terrain like the back of his hand, but he was also fast on his feet, running through the hills like a mountain goat—and here came a group of American soldiers trudging along, loaded up with God knows what. We needed to modify our equipment load to make us way more nimble if we wanted to have any hope of matching pace with the guys we were hunting.

On the way to our destination we passed a few villages that seemed deserted, nothing but empty buildings and a scattering of animals left behind. As far as we could tell, everyone was gone; no doubt they'd taken off once the aerial bombardment started the night before.

By the time we reached the cave complex, the sun was coming up. We started in at the base camp, taking a cave at a time. Our planes had pounded the hell out of the place. There had been quite a few people in these caves the night before, but there was nothing there now but bits and pieces of bodies, hardly anything even identifiable. It was a scene of pure carnage.

Inside the caves up on the ridge it was a whole other story. As we started penetrating into the mountainside, it quickly became clear that our bombing raid hadn't done shit. This place was in mint condition. These caves were so deeply burrowed into the mountain that many of them were still completely intact. Hell, some went back a good half mile. Some of the tunnels were reinforced by steel beams and lined with brickwork, with plenty of evidence of Soviet craftsmanship left over from the eighties.

This place *was* damn near invincible.

We started in, using a procedure similar to the way we would clear a house. Four of us would go in to clear a cave, then come out and report, then move on to the next, and the next, making sure each cave was clear as we went. One cave was an ammo bunker; the next was a classroom, then living areas. It was an extensive network, with some of the tunnels interconnected, and it went on and on.

The caves were so deep that we couldn't see very far into them. Our night vision was severely limited in effectiveness, because to use night vision you need at least a small bit of ambient light, and it was pitch black in the caves. We had an infrared floodlight function, but this proved to be not very useful. We ended up inching through the caves using the paltry beams of illumination thrown by the small lights mounted on our weapons and clearing around corners with our good old-fashioned SureFire white-lens flashlights.

Those first few hours going deep into those caves and tunnels were intense. We had no idea exactly what we'd find in there. We didn't know if we would run into anyone, or if there was possibly an ambush lying in wait for us, or if the caves were booby-trapped. We had no idea where the hell we were going, or what—or whom—we might run into.

Fortunately we did not encounter a single person—but we were stunned at how much we found in the way of matériel. There were massive amounts of ordnance, ammo, and fuel, stacked floor to ceiling. They had stocked up on some big hardware, too, including tanks and other Soviet-era combat vehicles. These guys had prepared for quite the campaign.

We found some American-made Harris 117-Delta radios with what appeared to be internally embedded crypto, which completely freaked us out. These were highly proprietary, highly sensitive tools of the U.S. military. How the hell did these characters lay their hands on such things? Many years later, speaking with a gentleman who worked with the company who manufactured these radios, I learned that they were originally sold to the CIA, who in turn gave them to mujahideen forces to help them in their efforts against the Soviets. Geopolitics is a fickle business. We found a bunch of Stinger missiles, too, more fruit of Uncle Sam's largesse;

fortunately the batteries on Stingers are completely drained after a few years, so none of these suckers were operational.

We found classrooms with posters on the walls, sporting anti-American slogans. On one the artist had cobbled together a photo of bin Laden in the foreground with two planes crashing into the Twin Towers in the background. I stared at this freakish piece of propaganda nearly open-mouthed. This thing was created as an al Qaeda recruiting poster for the mission it illustrated. In other words, it had been put together *before* the event it was depicting had taken place. Standing there deep in the bowels of this godforsaken mountain on the other side of the world, staring at a picture of the attack on New York City that was composited and hung here before the attack itself actually occurred—it was one of the eeriest experiences I've ever had. I still have that poster.

It was hot, tedious, nerve-racking work. Within about four hours we had the whole place cleared. Fortunately, we hadn't run into any resistance.

Now that we knew we were alone and had a general sense of the lay of the land, we went back through the whole place a second time, gathering up intel, collecting the smaller items that we could bring back with us, and planting demolition in areas we would later blow. Brad and Eric recorded the exact GPS coordinates at the entrances to each cave so our guys could follow up with more accurate air strikes, since the shotgun approach of the night before had missed so much. The FBI guys had DNA kits as part of their mission, which was to ID whatever bodies we might find. As we worked, Casey and some of the others documented everything with video and tons of photographs.

Meanwhile, we were constantly reporting back to Harward, who was following the entire operation so closely it felt like he was looking over our shoulders the whole time. It was believed that some key Taliban or al Qaeda leader in the area had been killed recently, and Harward had a hard-on for the DNA evidence. We had found some extensive gravesites, but they were a few weeks old, and the forensic team didn't think they would yield much of significance. Plus, we were on the clock. The complex had been more extensive and the total cache far larger than we anticipated. We had a date to keep with a crew of helos at our extraction point, so we were wasting no unnecessary minutes.

After gathering everything we could take with us, we got it all ready to blow. We blew up the radios and a ton of ordnance. The explosion created a huge fireball that nearly consumed half the mountain. The secondaries cooked off for probably four to six hours. It was January 6, but it sure looked like the Fourth of July.

Daylight was starting to fade, and we got the hell out of there. We picked up our stashed armor (all except me, since I didn't have any) and started the long hump back to the perimeter for our rendezvous. We were still on a good schedule. The plan was for us to be extracted in the evening, under the cover of darkness. We finally reached our extract point and got on the radio to base. One CCT was talking to the inbound helo coming to get us; the other was talking to Harward at the TOC (tactical operations center). We were thirty minutes out from our scheduled exfil.

Nothing to do but sit and wait.

One of our EOD techs, Steve, started dumping his water. He'd been carrying extra bottles of water that they would use to shape blasting charges, and he figured now he wouldn't be needing any of it. That seemed crazy to me. That was potable spring water! When you're out in the field on any kind of recon, water is more precious than gold. He'd already dumped out several bottles when I saw what he was doing and stopped him.

"Dude!" I said. "What are you doing?"

"I'm tired of carrying around all this extra water," he said. "I'm just shedding some weight." For such a big guy, he sure did complain about the weight of the stuff we carried.

"Hey, dude," I said, "give me the rest. I'll take all that." He had eight bottles of water left, and he gave me all of them. I drank four, then started filling up my CamelBak bottles with the remaining four.

Just then we heard the distant but unmistakable sound of the transport choppers, probably five to ten minutes away. They were coming to get us. At that moment Brad, our CCT, called out quietly to one of the FBI team, holding the radio set out to him, "Captain Harward wants a word." Harward wanted to know if the FBI team had dug up the graves we'd found and conducted any forensics there. They hadn't. Harward wanted them to go back and look for DNA evidence. One of the FBI team, who happened to be a former SEAL, spoke a few crisp words and handed the radio set back to Brad. "Jesus Christ," he muttered, "that grave is old. We're not going to find anything new there."

But Harward had latched on to this thing like a dog on a bone. The DNA business was a very big deal, especially from a public relations standpoint. If the forensic evidence revealed that we'd taken out any of the bigwig bad guys from the top of the al Qaeda food chain, that would be a significant victory to wire back home, and everyone from military top brass to Congress to the White House could get serious mileage out of it. It was more than the DNA, though. Out in those caves we had found a treasure trove of enemy resources that exceeded even the most optimistic expectations, and there seemed to be good indication that there was more out there for the finding. In for a penny, in for a pound: Now that we'd cracked open this prize, Harward wanted us to stay out there and see how much more we could dig up.

Now Harward had Cassidy on the radio. I could see from the set of LT's face that he wasn't thrilled at what he was hearing. I saw him nod, say a word or two, and sign off. The sound of the helicopters briefly hovered, then slowly started to diminish. With our extraction just minutes away, Harward had turned them around. Word came down: We weren't being extracted after all.

We were out there, on our own, for at least another day or two.

Steve looked at me in horror as I smacked my lips, having just polished off the last water bottle. He was devastated. What could I say? Hey, that's why you don't pour out your water, *ever*. You just never know what's going to happen.

So here we were, out in the middle of nowhere, deep in enemy territory, on our own for the night—and the temperature had already dropped to around freezing. You burn up a lot of calories humping around all day. These were not good conditions. We needed a plan.

Cassidy, Chief Dye, myself, and a few of the other senior guys huddled together to figure out what we were going to do for the night. Commander Smith, apparently still in the shit-getting-into frame of mind, said, "Well, I guess we'll just go into the hills and lay up in the bushes."

Chief Dye and I looked at each other in disbelief. We hadn't brought much in the way of extra warm clothes because we hadn't planned to be out overnight, and it was quite hot during the day. In fact, we'd been murderously hot while working the caves. But the clothing that felt suffocating during the afternoon now offered little protection against the frigid high-altitude desert nighttime. When you're pushing up above the snow line, it gets cold as hell.

Even if we *had* thought to bring it, we didn't have the cold-weather gear back at camp that we wanted to have anyway. Back when our platoon had first landed in Afghanistan we had put in a big cold-weather-gear request list. Evidently one shipment was sent, but it got lost somewhere on the way. Whether they'd sent a replacement, nobody knew. We kept hearing, "It's coming . . . it's coming next week," but nothing showed up. For the moment, we were all going with what whatever we each had with us, along with the promise that we'd have better stuff as soon as possible.

On our own, most of us had bought ourselves some pretty decent gear. The SEAL teams are among the best-equipped fighting forces anywhere in the military. We had smart wool-blended socks, good boots from REI, good

North Face jackets, that sort of thing. I had a $300 pair of Italian leather mountain boots, and I'd brought along a neoprene shell and wool cap. It wasn't much, but at least it was something.

The marines, however, had it much worse. These poor bastards didn't have shit for cold-weather gear, just standard-issue crappy desert boots and cheap white socks. True to their spartan culture, these guys were not going to complain at all, but they were in for a world of hurt with the subfreezing temperatures coming our way. And Commander Smith wanted us to *lay up in the bushes*?

I spoke up. "Hey, that's a bad idea. These poor marines are already freezing, and it's only going to get colder. We're sure to have some cold casualties if we do that."

Smith shook his head and said, "We gotta do what we gotta do. We're just going to have to suck it up."

Suck it up. This was his brilliant tactical plan? The man was definitely getting in our shit now. It was one thing for us to suck it up, but we had twenty marines we were responsible for, too. They would absolutely suck it up if that's what they were told to do—but that wasn't going to prevent our having some cold casualties on our hands.

Chief Dye was having none of it. One of the villages we'd seen during the day lay up at the top of the valley at the end of a ridge, and I knew he had that place in mind as a strategic fallback position. It was on high ground, you could see the entire valley from there, and it was well protected as a fighting position.

Chief Dye turned to Smith and said, "All due respect, sir, your plan sucks. Here's what we're going to do. I'm going to take Brandon and a couple other guys, do a recon, clear and occupy that village so we have a place to stay where we can start a goddam fire, get warm, and set up a perimeter for the night."

"No," said Smith, "we're not doing that."

"Yes," said Chief Dye. "We are."

Now Lieutenant Cassidy spoke up. "Got it," he said. He nodded, and that was the end of that.

My respect for Cassidy was already high, but it had just gone up a notch. He was our officer in charge, but he also knew he wasn't the most tactically experienced guy there. Like a good leader, he was the first to defer to the person with more experience, which in this case was Chief Dye.

You'll find officers who think, *I'm the highest-ranking officer, I should have the best ideas,* but that's not necessarily so. Being an effective leader doesn't mean you have to be the smartest guy in the room or always have the best idea.

Years after returning from Afghanistan I was introduced by my friend John Tishler to Dr. J. Robert Beyster, the nuclear physicist who founded SAIC (Science Applications International Corporation), a billion-dollar, Fortune 500 employee-owned defense contractor. In the course of a project I was working on in the private sector, Dr. Beyster took me out to lunch. Later we spent some time in his office, where I noticed a sign on his wall:

NONE OF US IS AS SMART AS ALL OF US.

J. Robert Beyster is one serious genius, and one reason he's gotten to where he is is that he understands this core leadership truth: No matter how smart you are, you'd be stupid not to listen to the experts around you. Cassidy understood that, too. Smith, not so much.

Five of us took off and started moving quietly up the hillside: Chief Dye, Patrick, Heath, Osman, and I. It took us about an hour to get up there. When we got close to the village, it was pretty clear that the place had been completely deserted. Probably whoever had been there left as soon as those bombs started falling the night before. Still, caution dictated that we assume nothing. We snuck around behind and approached from the rear.

The place consisted of several buildings, all mud hut construction, and looked to be a multifamily living situation with a little stable for some goats, chickens, and a couple of donkeys. The doors were secured with some flimsy lock-and-chain assemblies, easy to kick in. Osman and I went through the place with the standard two-man room-clearing procedure while the others stood sentry. Once we'd cleared every room and made sure the place was secure, the others stayed while Osman and I went back down to pass the word and lead everyone back up there.

There was no question Chief Dye had made the right call. In terms of our tactical position, we had excellent visibility (or at least we would once daybreak came), it was very defensible, and we were up high so the radios would work well. Plus, the place had wool blankets, fireplaces and fire-wood, and plenty of adequate shelter to keep us out of the wind. To us it was like walking into the Ritz-Carlton. The marines were pretty stoic, as always, but you could see the looks on their faces: *Thank God*.

Right away we set up our comms and called in our location to base camp via sat radio. The last thing we needed was for some gunship flying 20,000 feet over our heads to see our heat signatures and make us the fea-tured guest stars on this night's episode of Murder TV. Meanwhile the captain in charge of the marines set them up, half to go get warm and get some sleep and the other half to stand the perimeter.

We figured we would use this place as a kind of forward operating base the whole time we were out there, however long that would turn out to be. It was a smart decision—because we would be out there in the wild for a lot longer than one or two days.

MONDAY, JANUARY 7

The next morning we split up. Part of the platoon went out with the forensics team to go dig up those gravesites and see if they could bring Harward some fresh, juicy DNA. Four of us—Cassidy, Osman, Brad, and

I—went out before dawn to patrol a site where a C-130 gunship had engaged some forces the night before, to see if we could find any bodies.

We reached the coordinates we'd been given just moments before the indistinct grays of predawn resolved into the pastels of daybreak. Before we could do any serious searching, we heard voices coming from some nearby caves above us. The four of us instantly hit the ground and waited. As we watched, a spill of enemy fighters started pouring out of one of the caves—twenty, at least, and all armed.

If this were happening in the movies, we would all just leap to our feet and blow these guys away, but in real life it doesn't work that way. We were outnumbered at least five to one, and we were not exactly armed with machine guns. This was not the OK Corral, and if we leapt to our feet we would all be mowed down in short order. There was no hiding until they were gone, either: These guys were headed our way. We would have to call in an air strike, and do it fast.

There was a B-52 nearby; Brad got it on the radio. It was my job to give him the coordinates—but there was a snag. The only way to ensure that the team in the B-52 dropped their fireworks on the other guys and not on us was to give them exact coordinates. Typically we would do this using a high-powered laser rangefinder hooked into a GPS so that when it ranged the target it would give us not only distance but also the target's GPS coordinates, which we could then pass on up to whoever we were calling for air support. These bombers are extremely accurate with their ordnance, like vertical snipers in the sky.

We'd only planned for a simple twelve-hour mission and didn't have all our usual equipment. Typically, for a full-on recon mission, I'd have at least a good sniper rifle. We didn't have even a decent rangefinder.

Training, training. As a SEAL sniper I'd been taught to estimate distances on the fly even without all the usual tools, using only my five senses and my gut, but typically I'd be shooting a 10-gram bullet from the muzzle of a rifle. In this case, we were shooting a 1,000-pound "bullet" out of a 125-ton aircraft, flying 20,000 feet above us at near the speed of sound, at a target less than 500 yards away from where we sat—I had to get it right.

Range estimation. This was something else we covered in sniper school: You visualize a familiar distance, say, a football field. *That's one football field, two football fields, three football fields* . . . but this can be risky when you're not on level ground. Here I had to sight up a rugged, rocky incline. And daybreak lighting can play tricks with distances.

Those twenty-plus al Qaeda, or Taliban, or who the hell knew who, were trickling down the slope heading straight for our position. They hadn't seen us yet, but it would be only seconds before they did. If we were going to do this thing, it had to be *now*.

"Brandon!" Cassidy hissed. "You need to Kentucky-windage this drop!" "Kentucky windage" is a term that means basically this: *Wing it. Give it your best shot*. I gave Cassidy a bearing I estimated as 100 meters *past* the group. If I was going to be off at all, better to guess long than short, and if I was balls-on accurate, a drop 100 meters behind them should at least buy us a few seconds to adjust and drop a second time.

Now the enemy cluster was so close we couldn't wait any longer. We were concealed but not covered; that is, they couldn't easily see us, but once they knew where we were, our concealment would give no protection against incoming fire. We quickly moved to cover—and that's when they spotted us. There were a few alarmed shouts and then the sounds of small-arms fire.

There is nothing quite so galvanizing as the distinct *crack! snap!* of semiautomatic weaponry being fired over your head, the *crack!* being the sound of the initial shot itself and the *snap!* being the bullet breaking the sound barrier as it zings past you.

We returned fire. I sighted one guy wearing a black headdress, dropped him. Quickly resighted and dropped a second, this one wearing the traditional Afghan wool roll-up hat. Sighted a third—then glanced up and saw vapor trails in the sky. The B-52 was flying so high it was invisible to us, but I knew exactly what was happening up there: They were dropping the first bomb.

When you are this close to a big explosion it rocks your chest cavity. You want to make sure your mouth is open so the contained impact doesn't burst your lungs. Brad got the call: We were seconds from impact. We opened our mouths, dropped and rolled.

The Joint Direct Attack Munition is a big bomb and extremely accurate. When the first set of JDAMs hit, it shook the mountain under our feet, throwing rubble everywhere.

I whipped around and glanced back up the incline to assess the strike. Perfect—about 100 yards behind the target. I rolled again, adjusting numbers in my head, and quickly shouted the new coordinates to Cassidy, who gave them to Brad to relay up to the bird. In moments like this your senses go into hyperacute mode and seconds seem to stretch into minutes, hours, a timeless series of discrete snapshots. I focused on my breathing, making it slow and deliberate, feeling the cool morning air mixed with the distinct smell of explosives teasing my lungs. I knew my numbers were accurate and that the men shooting to kill us would themselves be dead in seconds. For a brief moment, I was at peace. And then an unexpected sound sliced through the strange silence: the wail of a baby crying.

My stomach twisted. I had a five-week-old baby boy at home whom I'd not yet held in my arms; hopefully I would survive this war to meet him face-to-face. Someone up on that hillside had a baby they would never see or hold again.

I knew these people had made the decision to bring their families out here to this godforsaken fortress, knowingly putting them in harm's way. Sometimes, I'd heard, they even did this intentionally, using their own children, their flesh and blood, as living shields to prevent us from attacking. *It was their choice,* I told myself, *not ours.* But I'll never forget the sound of that baby's cry.

We opened our mouths, ducked and rolled. The second drop took them all.

We continued our patrol but never did find anything from the previous night's air strike. We were at the exact coordinates they'd passed to us. Maybe they got the GPS coordinates wrong. We headed back for our new base of operations, and on the way we came upon another little village that appeared deserted. We started doing two-man house clearings, room by room. There was a well there, so we collected some water to bring back with us, since we were already running out of supplies at our impromptu base camp. Before hauling it, we treated the water with the iodine tablets we had on us as part of our standard survival supplies.

Even though we had planned to be out in the field for only twelve hours, SEALs are well acquainted with Murphy's Law. We wouldn't think of going out on any mission, no matter how brief, without certain critical supplies. Before inserting the day before, for example, we had been supplied with updated maps, such as they were (which wasn't much), and had each gotten an updated blood chit. A blood chit is a map of the area you're going to be patrolling that has a notice written on the back, in this case in both Arabic and Pashtun, promising a substantial cash reward (I think it was $100,000) to anyone who gives assistance to the bearer. Each of us carried an escape and evasion kit, which included a piece of flint, water purification tablets, and a knife, along with our blood chit. If we got into a situation where we had to ditch everything, this was what we'd keep as last resort. Some guys sewed their blood chit into a hideaway pouch tucked into their clothing, so that if everything but their clothes was taken away from them, they'd still have it on their person.

The last room we cleared led out into a stable area. Cautiously, I made my way in to check it out. There was nobody inside except a single donkey. I slid up onto the donkey's back. It's SOP when you exit a room after clearing it to call, "Coming out!" so you don't surprise anyone. I called out, "Coming out!" then smacked my mount on the ass and emerged from the stable like a gunslinger in a Western, except that my steed wasn't exactly a tall white horse. Poor thing could barely support my weight. The other guys cracked up. Someone said, "Which one's the jackass?"

In one of the houses we found caches of suitcases filled with passports, money, and clothing. Evidently this was a safe house for Taliban and/or al Qaeda in their war against the infidels. After taking GPS coordinates, we left; a subsequent air strike reduced the building to rubble.

When we got back to camp, the other guys were returning from blowing up some more caves, not only to destroy more matériel they'd found but also to do their level best to make the place uninhabitable.

We were now feeling the pinch of our lack of supplies. We had each brought with us a single MRE, and that was long gone. We decided it was time to start slaughtering some of the animals there. The marines were reluctant to do this. These guys count their bullets and do inventory after every operation. We had no such scruples. Osman and Patrick pulled out their guns and *bang!* shot a few chickens dead, followed by one goat, then started dressing it all up to cook and eat. The captain of the marines seemed a little freaked out. "Holy shit," he said, "you guys don't mess around."

Still, there were only so many chickens to go around. With our twenty marines and our platoon of sixteen now swollen to twenty-five, we had a crew of forty-five mouths to feed. In addition to food, we also needed fresh batteries for our radios. We radioed in and were told we'd be getting resupplied the following day.

When two big H-53 helos landed the next morning with our resupply, they had brought a few large cases of radio batteries—enough to last a month of talking twenty-four hours a day. Then they kicked out one case of water and one case of MREs and took off.

We stood there staring at the case of MREs. "You've got to be shitting me," someone said. The warehouse at Bagram was full of these things. A case of MREs is ten meals. Ten. That was not even enough to feed a single meal to one in four of us. How were we supposed to divide these things up? It was like chopping up an M&M into thirty pieces.

This was a classic case of military communication. (It's worth noting that the terms SNAFU, "situation normal: all fucked up," and FUBAR, "fucked up beyond all repair," both originated in the military during World War II.) Someone had probably passed on our request: "Hey, those guys up at Zhawar Kili need some food and water." So they'd sent us some food and water. We hadn't specified *how much* food and water.

TUESDAY, JANUARY 8

On day 3 (after our exciting resupply) we started systematically patrolling specific areas we had charted out over the previous two days, getting a feel for the area and following up on reports from our C-130s, who were continuing to see activity at night, giving us new targets to search for and additional bomb damage assessments (BDA) missions to run the following days.

Walking along a narrow, twisting mountain road, we heard the sound of an approaching vehicle. We quickly formed ourselves into an L-shaped ambush formation, with the longer element stretched out across the road and the shorter, perpendicular element (consisting of Chief Dye and me) parallel to the road, lying hidden with some heavy weapons behind the bushes that lined the road.

As the vehicle came around the bend we could see what it was: a little white Datsun pickup with three guys in it, two in the front and one in the back. As soon as they came face-to-face with our guys lined up across the road, Chris and I popped up out of the bushes with our big guns. By the time they knew what was happening they were locked in a crossfire setup, outgunned, with no avenue of retreat and no options.

These three characters were hardcore and clearly up to no good. The one in the front passenger seat seemed to be in charge. He wore a black turban and a beautiful dark red shawl, a particular kind of earth-colored wrap the Taliban used, that did double duty: It kept him warm and also served as camouflage. *Shit,* I thought, *that looks pretty warm.*

We took their weapons away from them, zip-tied them, and threw them in the back of the truck. Now we had a vehicle.

I knew some basic Arabic, enough to get by on ship boardings ("Get down! Get up!") and order a meal, but that was about it. These guys were not Arabs, though, and my Pashtun was almost nonexistent. Fortunately, we had our interpreter with us: The dude from CTIC was a cryptologist and an accomplished linguist, and he spoke Pashtun. He interrogated them briefly, and they pointed out a village that we had already checked out and thought was abandoned. Turned out this was where they'd just come from.

We went back to the site and looked where these guys directed us. They were caching weapons there. This was SOP for these guys: They would dig hideyholes on the outskirts of abandoned villages and use them to stash weapons and other matériel.

Exactly what we were looking for.

We couldn't take this stuff back with us, so we marked the GPS coordinates and took off, our three prisoners in the back with sacks over their heads. We drove far enough away that we could still see the village location from a safe distance and stopped. Chief Dye called in the coordinates to the platoon so Brad or Eric could call in a CAS (close air support) strike. He pulled the leader's sack off his head a few seconds before the bombs fell, so he got a glimpse of his village blowing up, then slammed it back on again, and we headed back up the mountainside for our camp.

Now, in addition to keeping ourselves alive, we had three prisoners to keep, feed, and guard in our little village. The next day, another squad went out and rolled up two more vehicles (a little pickup and a Daihatsu mini-SUV, both diesel) and a half dozen more guys. Thank God we had the marines to watch them all.

One day back in Kandahar, just before flying up to Bagram, six of us were walking back from the TOC when a marine general accosted us. This particular general was your perfect image of the archetypal hard-hitting, cigar-chomping, no-bullshit marine, like General Patton incarnate. His nickname was Mad Dog.

"Hey, are you guys my SEALs?" he barked at us. Yessir, we told him. "You boys going up north?" Yessir. He pointed over toward the makeshift EPW (enemy prisoner of war) camp we had set up, where there were now several hundred prisoners incarcerated. "You see that EPW camp over there?" Yessir. "I already got enough fucking prisoners there. You get my drift? I don't want any more fucking prisoners coming back here. You get what I'm sayin?" Yessir. It wasn't a subtle message: *You find any guys out there, you take them out. Don't bring 'em back.* He hadn't actually come out and said that (in other words, there was plausible deniability), but the intent was understood.

Now here we were, developing our own little prisoner-of-war camp out in the field. We had nine prisoners we would soon be airlifting back to Kandahar. Mad Dog wasn't going to be happy with us.

WEDNESDAY, JANUARY 9

On day 4 we went out on patrol again and found another village to clear, this one fairly substantial in size. We divided up the platoon, each of us clearing half the village to make sure it was abandoned. It was, and we collected a good amount of both weapons and intelligence, including all sorts of plans and notes. Some we photographed; some we brought with us.

As we were going through this process of rounding up our spoils, we had one of the biggest—and certainly happiest—surprises of our entire deployment. From inside this abandoned village we had just cleared, who should come trotting out toward us but a small, light tan puppy. Last thing we expected to see, that was for sure. I'm a sucker for animals; most of us were. We named him JDAM, and he became our platoon mascot. Cassidy eventually adopted JDAM as his own and brought him back to raise him in the States. Later on we found a second puppy, whom we called CAS, and he ended up with an adopted SEAL home, too.

Finding JDAM was not the only memorable thing about that particular patrol. At one point the group I was with found another of those hidey holes with a cache of weapons in it. Osman and I went down inside, leaving Newman, one of our platoon mates, to stand watch while the others moved on. Osman and I had been in there for a little while, rummaging through passports, money, and various materials, when all of a sudden we heard Newman say, "Hey, guys, come on out here." His voice sounded strained. We crawled out and looked up at him. "What is it, Newman?"

He had his gun raised and pointed, and his eyes were like the proverbial deer in the headlights. We swiveled around to see what he was pointing at. Less than 50 yards away stood four Taliban dudes, heavily armed and staring at us from behind the crest of a hill.

Osman and I immediately drew our weapons, and the four turned and ran back in the direction they'd just come from. They had been walking up the hill toward us and had just started cresting when they'd come to a standstill, so they were still half-concealed by the hill and visible only from the waist up. Now they quickly sank below the ground line again. We got a few shots off but didn't hit them.

Osman and I both turned on Newman. "What the hell is wrong with you? 'Hey guys, come on out here'—and you don't happen to mention that there are four guys with fucking guns out here? What the fuck, Newman?"

We were just about apoplectic with fury. He'd nearly gotten us killed. To this day, I am completely baffled as to why those four didn't simply shoot us in the back as we crawled out of that hole oblivious to their presence.

But there wasn't time to ream Newman out in the manner that he deserved, at least not now. We hopped on the radio and told Cassidy what was going on, then ran over to the hilltop to search out the retreating four Afghans. We glassed them, and sure enough, there they were, tearing for the Pakistan border where we could not pursue. We called in an air strike fast and took them out with a 1,000-pounder before they could get make the border.

Then we went back and unloaded on Newman. I wanted to call in an air strike on him, too.

THURSDAY, JANUARY 10

After the previous day's close call, on day 5 we decided to go out and set up a reconnaissance position so we could have the whole valley in view and watch enemy forces sneaking back and forth along a series of mountain trails that led across the border into Pakistan.

Osman and I took a map and planned the whole thing out. We would go in and insert before dawn, at 3 A.M., driving out on night vision in vehicles that were completely darked out. We'd go in two teams. Four of us—Osman, Patrick, a guy named Mark, and I—would insert at the north end of the valley (where the caves were) and take a position on the northeast corner of the area we were surveilling. A team of six marines would take a position across from us on the northwestern corner, so they could observe the other side of the valley from their vantage point. Two of the marines were first-rate snipers, and they were pretty psyched to get out there and do a sniper op for a change.

By now we knew there was a significant level of enemy activity going on here in this valley. The idea was for these two teams to hide out for the entire day and fill in as many details in our overall picture as possible: who was moving around and where, what they were up to during the day, and where they were laying up at night. We would pass any intel we gathered back to the platoon, who would sort through it all and feed it back to base at Bagram.

Since our resupply, I now had my .300 Win Mag. I felt much better going out on patrol with my proper sniper gun.

Two other guys from the platoon were going to insert us, Jackie and Doug, with Doug driving and Jackie riding shotgun. Osman, Patrick, Mark, and I would ride in the back and quietly slip out when we reached our location at the top of the valley.

In preparation for the mission that night, we each had our specific tasks. Doug and Jackie's job was to tape up all the vehicle lights before we left. There were two reasons for this. First, obviously, was to dark out the vehicle so the enemy couldn't see it. Anyone who happened to be close enough would be able to hear the vehicle, but without any lights showing we'd be invisible, so they wouldn't be able to place us or even know for sure who was driving it. (This was, after all, a vehicle we'd taken from some of their guys.) The second reason was equally important, and that had to do with our ability to see what we were doing. Night vision is so sensitive that any significant source of light renders it useless. Even a vehicle navigation light will flood you with too much illumination and make you as good as blind.

At 2:30 the next morning we were ready, present, and accounted for, our gear assembled and tied in tight. The six of us loaded up our vehicle and climbed in. We were already buzzing with anticipation. This would be a dangerous mission; inserting smack into the midst of armed enemies of unknown number and location is always a relatively freaky thing to do. We had no way of knowing how many hostiles we might encounter, or where, but we were as ready as we'd ever be, and itching to go round up all the intel we could.

Doug switched on the ignition—and all the dash lights came on.

No one had taped them up.

"Jesus," I muttered. Osman leaned over into the front seat and glared at Doug. "Doug, dude, what the fuck?"

"Damn," said Doug. "I thought I told Jackie to tape them up." In the next seat over, Jackie responded with a look that said, *Hey, don't lay it on* me.

I was furious. This had been their one and only job: Tape up the damn lights. It was a mission-critical task. Doug was in charge of making sure this happened—and it didn't.

We clambered out of the vehicle and tried to make a quick job of it, but it was too late. Timing was critical. The sun would be up by five or earlier, and if we were going to do this at all, we had to be out there before then. The marines were waiting on us, because they'd be taking off a few minutes after we did to create a staggered insert (SOP). We couldn't hold things up. We had to make the call: Go now, or cancel the mission. I did *not* want to make that insert with our lights on, but there was a lot riding on this mission. We needed that intel. "Fuck it," we said, "let's go."

We tried driving with our night vision, but it was hopeless; the dash lights made it impossible, as we'd known they would. So of all ridiculous things, we now had to drive out there with our *headlights* on, meaning we could be seen from miles away. *Halloooo, Taliban, anyone out there? Here we are!* Doug drove up the valley while Osman and I did our best to get our rage under control.

We reached our insert point at the northern end of the valley, and the four of us rolled out of the backseats. Doug turned the vehicle around and headed back the way we'd come. We took cover and sat like statues, watching the lights slowly disappear.

The rule of thumb for an insert like this is that once you're dropped off, you immediately rally up in a small perimeter behind cover and then spend your first few minutes motionless and silent, doing nothing but sitting, waiting, watching, and listening. We sat motionless and silent for about fifteen minutes, waiting, watching, listening. We saw and heard nothing.

After a few minutes, we proceeded to make our way up the mountainside as silent as the snow, heading for high ground. We stopped about an hour later when we'd gotten about three-quarters of the way up the mountain, reaching what we call military crest.

This was something we'd all learned way back in Third Phase of BUD/S, in the land nav training. Gaining high ground is one of the most basic tactical advantages known to every military force in history. High ground gives you a better view of your field of engagement, and if you should become embroiled in any direct action it's a lot easier to fight downhill than it is to go up against someone who is above you looking down. On the other hand, you don't want to take position at the very peak of your terrain, called skylining, because there you're more exposed.

Once we reached the ideal elevation (probably at something like 9,000 feet) and found an appropriate hide site, we clipped on some veg and dug into the mountain's flank. We had all three of the conditions we wanted: good concealment, solid cover from potential gunfire, and good eyes on our sector.

Just then the sun started coming up. We called over to the marines on the radio. "ECHO-1," they said, "we're not set. We ran into a little problem on our way out. We're not exactly sure what to do here, over."

"Roger that," we said, "we'll be right there."

Osman and I left Mark and Patrick there and headed back down the mountain to where the marines had stopped. When we reached them we could see that they'd been scared shitless. They described what had happened.

The marines' team had gotten a late start, and by the time they reached their insertion point it was already near sunup. On their way up the mountain to their surveillance location, they had stumbled across a cluster of heavily armed Afghans in rough fighting position. Despite their arms, these characters were disheveled and disorganized; it looked like they'd just woken up and the marines had startled them. Evidently these Taliban guys hadn't realized that the shock and surprise were mutual. They dropped most of their guns and ran. The marines could not believe what they'd left behind: guns, rocket launchers, grenades, a frigging armory. After marking the location, they moved on and were just debating what to do when we called them.

Osman and I told them to go set up on the northwest mountainside according to plan, and we'd go check out the location they'd marked.

We started patrolling back toward the coordinates the marines had given us, which were in the general direction of our insert point. It was daylight by this time, so we had to go slow, using cover all along the way. It took us a while. We finally got to the spot, stopped, and looked around us.

There were rocks stacked up into a fighting position. Clearly this place had been used before. From what we could see, there'd been five guys there. We found one bedroll with about four RPG (rocket-propelled grenades) wrapped in it, a bunch of Chinese hand grenades, a few Enfield bolt action rifles, a few AK-47s, and a bunch of other shit they'd left behind. There was a teapot on their little cookstove. The teapot was still hot.

After thoroughly checking out the site, we started looking around at the surrounding terrain and glanced down the hillside. We both saw it at the same time.

It took an effort to keep my knees from buckling under me.

The spot we were staring at, maybe 150 yards downslope from this heavily armed campsite, was the precise location where we ourselves had inserted four hours earlier, fully lit up and headlights blaring. We had driven practically right into these guys. Our vehicle had to have awakened them up when it drove by. There was no way they would not have heard that thing coming and seen its headlights—and they had the high ground.

Osman and I stared at each other, both in full realization that it was a marvel we were alive. Because we had sat there in silence for fifteen minutes after rolling out of the truck, and had kept ourselves extremely quiet once we did get on the move, these guys had not seen us. If they had, we'd be dead men. No doubt about it.

We examined the campsite again and did our best to work out exactly what they'd been doing there. It clearly was not a makeshift or impromptu site, such as you'd set up if you were passing through and needed to hole up for just one night. It was a planned location, not 150 yards from a road they'd probably seen us traveling before. They were here to ambush us, plain and simple. They knew we were operating in this area and figured one of our daytime patrols would pass by again sooner or later. Only a matter of time. They had dug in a well concealed fighting position on this hilltop and were waiting for us. They just hadn't expected anyone to run into them in the middle of the night.

We worked out the sequence of what must have happened.

Our truck woke them out of a dead sleep at something like 3:00 A.M., then surprised them by turning around abruptly and leaving the area. They shook off their sleep, made some hot tea, and were in the process of setting up for the day—when a team of armed marines on foot stumbled into them. Murphy's Law.

We radioed back to base. Commander Smith happened to be monitoring the radio. We explained the situation and reported that we were sitting on a substantial cache of weapons, as well as a bunch of paperwork and field notes these guys had (incredibly) left behind. What did he want us to do?

"Just take the paperwork," he said, "and leave the weapons there."

Leave the weapons? Why—so these guys could come back and shoot at us the next day? It made no sense. We signed off. Osman and I each took an AK-47 and brought it with us just to have as extra weapons, then carefully dismantled everything else. We hid the rockets, then destroyed the RPG launcher. It took us about an hour to get it all squared away, but there was no way we were leaving all that weaponry there for someone else to use.

After we'd sanitized the place, we made our way back to our hide site up on the northeast face, where we met up with Mark and Patrick and told them what had happened. We spent the day out there, but it was unsatisfying. We saw little, and there was not much to bring back in the way of intel. As much as we'd hoped to chart out the comings and goings of the bad guys we knew were all over the place, we weren't able to see much.

We returned to camp at night a little frustrated—and angrier than ever at Doug. Osman and I wanted to kill him, and he was not happy about being dumped on. But this was the second time in two days that someone's carelessness or laziness had nearly gotten me killed.

Back to that 90/10 rule. Our platoon now consisted of sixteen people, not including the EOD and air force guys and ancillary experts who were with us for this mission. Fortunately, we had jettisoned Gilroy Jones in Oman. (When Harward learned he was in our platoon he said something like—and I'm not quoting directly here but probably close to it—"What? If the guy's a fucking turd, get rid of him!" Harward was my kind of commander: He did not suffer fools lightly. In fact, he didn't suffer them at all.) Even without Gilroy, four of our current sixteen were liabilities, at least from my perspective. Four out of sixteen is 25 percent. We were pushing that 90/10 rule way past its limits.

There had been some tension before, but from this point on a sharp rift developed in the platoon. Osman and I knew this was not a good state of affairs. Of course you want to operate as a team. Of course you want to have harmony among all your forces. We knew that—but damn, we could not afford to tolerate even the tiniest scrap of laziness. We were in the freaking mountains of Afghanistan. Our shit needed to be seriously dialed in tight, and it wasn't, not enough. Not yet.

FRIDAY, JANUARY 11

The next day we went out on another village op. There were genuine bad guys hiding out there, and there were people who were just living up here in the mountains, usually with a wife and couple of kids, living the simple life, farmers wresting their keep from the land. We could usually tell the difference pretty clearly—but not always.

There was a place we'd been watching for a few days now. These people appeared to be farmers, but we were not 100 percent positive. We decided it was time to go out there and see up close. I was set up as sniper over-watch to guard the platoon as they went in to meet the people and talk.

It was morning. I watched as Cassidy and his team made their way up there to where a small group of these guys was congregated in a few buildings. It wasn't like we were storming the place; this was more of a diplomatic mission.

Having dug into my sniper overwatch position, in the kind of well-concealed hide we'd been trained to construct in the stalking phase of sniper school, I used the scope on my .300 Win Mag sniper rifle to get a closer look at these people. The villagers clearly saw Cassidy and the guys approaching. Something was going on there, but I couldn't tell what. They were talking something over, looking a little hurried about it. I caught a glimpse of a few of them running around, as if they were in a rush to get something done. Something felt suspicious about it to me, but it could also be completely innocent.

I relayed my observations to Cassidy on the radio and told him to be on his toes.

As I continued moving my rifle in a small oscillating arc, shifting my view back and forth between Cassidy and his team and the little knot of Afghan farmers, I noticed one guy standing off to the side. He had a gun.

Shit.

The man had his rifle slung casually over his shoulder, and there was nothing threatening about the posture. I couldn't tell if he was a bad actor or an innocent farmer. I was leaning toward farmer—but why was he carrying a gun? Alarm bells were going off in my head.

Cassidy and the team were now close to the house. *Man oh man,* I was thinking, *do I take the shot? Will it put Cassidy in a tough spot?*

The guy was about 600 yards away, slightly more than six football fields. I knew I could take him out in a heartbeat. No problem. I felt my finger against the trigger. *Breathe out . . . focus . . . squeeze . . . pop.* It would be that easy.

But if I did, it would certainly complicate the situation. If I shot the guy and it turned out he was innocent, we'd have quite a scene on our hands. On the other hand, if I didn't and he *wasn't* innocent, the team could be in danger. Even if these guys had more arms stashed close at hand, Cassidy and our guys would clearly outgun them, but you don't want to let things get so far that the question of who outguns whom is your determining factor.

Shit!

What do I do? I had all the information I was going to have. There was no more intel to weigh, no path of logic to make the wiser choice. It came down to pure instinct. *Do I take the shot, or not?*

I breathed out . . . focused . . . squeezed . . .

I decided not to take the shot.

A moment later Cassidy and the guys were there, talking to these Afghan farmers—and suddenly I caught a glimpse of movement way off to my left. Some character in Arab dress, clearly not Afghan, was hightailing it out of there, tearing along a little goat trail up the mountain toward Pakistan for all he was worth.

Motherfucker!

This guy could have been out there on his own, but I didn't think so. They'd been hiding him. That's what I'd been sensing. The Afghan farmer I'd been targeting had been standing sentry, trying very hard not to look like that was what he was doing. They were covering for this al Qaeda dude or whoever he was, and the moment they had Cassidy and his team engaged in conversation, one of them had told him to take off.

I switched to my binos and caught him scurrying up the mountain, closing in on a kilometer away. I couldn't get an accurate shot off in time, and I couldn't go after him, because to do that I'd have to leave my hiding spot and would no longer be supporting Cassidy and the team. I didn't have the radio resources to call in close air support, and in moments that son of a bitch would be over the border.

I got back to Cassidy on the radio and told him what happened. I could see him now, going back and forth with the farmers, who were hotly denying everything. I'd seen enough to know they were lying.

Thinking back over the whole sequence, I didn't see what I would have done differently. With the information I had, giving this farmer the benefit of the doubt still seemed to me the right decision. Yes, these Afghan village people would sometimes harbor other Afghans who were Taliban or Arabs we would call al Qaeda. For the most part, though, they were not bad people; they were just trying to get along and survive, to go on living there in the mountains the way they had been for generations without getting caught in the crosshairs of battle.

When we first arrived, in Kuwait and Oman and finally Afghanistan, we were hyped up and angry and ready to deliver payback. We were coming right off the shock of 9/11, and we had all sorts of people e-mailing us from the States, voicing their support and cheering us on. Underneath that caricature of the white devil and "3 ECHO" on our platoon patch, I'd had a legend stitched that said, EMBRACE THE HATE. That's the mode we were operating in, and our rules of engagement certainly supported that. *When in doubt, take them out.* However, as we got more immersed in the culture and started seeing things from the point of view of the people who lived there, things began to shift a little. I'd been in Afghanistan long enough now to understand that not everyone had to die. I didn't want to shoot anybody who didn't need shooting.

Still, the shot I didn't take sometimes haunts me as much as some of the shots I did.

SATURDAY, JANUARY 12

By day 7 we were starting to wrap up the operation and prepare to return to base. We had now been holed up in this mountain range for a week and had cleared out a ton of enemy resources, taken a handful of prisoners, and racked up dozens of enemy KIA (killed in action), but there were still a lot of bad actors in the area that we hadn't been able to track down. Even our surveillance tactics of a few days ago had had limited success. Sitting in that one spot for the whole day, we weren't able to observe nearly as much as we'd have liked.

Osman and I had an idea. We wanted to get out there on our own, just the two of us, and patrol the area without having to be tied to a whole squad. A two-man mobile surveillance unit.

We pitched the idea to Cassidy. We proposed that the two of us go out, insert at two in the morning, and spend the entire day scouting the area. See what was really going on out there and what we could turn up.

There was a checkpoint we had observed, maybe 5 miles south of our position, a controlled vehicle access point usually manned by two to four guys at any one time. Because of the Army Special Forces incident that had mistakenly taken out a bunch of Karzai's people, we were especially cautious about making sure who these guys were before we took any action. Osman and I had been watching these guys for days, and by now we were clear that they were Taliban. They were facilitators, ground warriors whose primary mission was to run combat supplies back and forth across the Afghanistan-Pakistan border—money, passports, intel, and other tools of the trade. We also knew they'd been surveilling our own platoon. Hell, they'd nearly ambushed us more than once. Now we wanted to go out countersurveilling the guys who were surveilling us.

Cassidy and Chief Dye gave us the thumbs-up. That night we mapped out our route, got our plan together, and packed up our kit.

We headed out early the next morning, about 3:00 A.M. Before leaving we had checked in with Mark, who was our comms guy, and told him what we'd be doing throughout the day and to make sure to check us in with TOC and let that C-130 know they'd have two friendlies out there. We had our IR glint tape on, a special reflective tape like joggers wear at night, except that instead of reflecting visible-range light it reflects infrared. We hoped they'd see that, but it sure wasn't something we'd want to count on. We did *not* want to be little green heat trails in the C-130's video game.

By this point Osman and I were totally garbed out in traditional Afghan gear. We were wearing wool shawls and Afghan roll-up hats; we had water, bullets, a little food, and guns. At a casual glance, we could have passed for Taliban. We'd gotten the lay of the land and were now running around those goat trails, too. As much as it was possible to do, we had become mirror images of the guys we were about to hunt.

We got to the bottom of the hill, humped over to our first observation post, settled in, and waited for the light to come up. Osman looked over at me and said, "Sure hope Mark called that damn C-130." I nodded.

I sure hoped so, too. We were pretty vulnerable out there and had put our lives in Mark's hands.

The cold morning air hung thick in the valley. Each warm exhale of breath briefly fogged the outside corner of my scope as I waited and watched.

There.

I could just make him out: a middle-aged man, wrapped in traditional Afghan dress, darting furtively back and forth and breaking down his makeshift campsite with seasoned efficiency. I noticed a slight crook in his step—an old wound, perhaps a story from the days of the Soviet occupation. The man had been at his clandestine trade for years. He would be at it for less than twenty-four hours more. I saw a faint wisp of smoke from the campfire he had just extinguished, and my brain automatically registered the direction and intensity of the gust of breeze that flirted with the smoke, calculating windage, distance, and elevation. We could take him out right then and there; Cassidy had given us the go-ahead. If we did, though, it would likely be our only kill of the day, because the moment you fire your weapon you've risked compromising your position, and you never know who else is lurking around the corner or somewhere behind you, especially in an environment like this. Besides, we had a bigger strategic goal. We could kill *one* . . . or we could find them all, mark their positions, and they would *all* die.

I've since been deer hunting quite a few times; that's what this was like—except that we didn't expect to shoot anyone. Today it was not our marksmanship we'd be practicing but our stalking craft. As much time, energy, training, and focus as we put into our marksmanship skills, the core skill of the expert sniper is not to shoot. It is to hunt. If intellectual capacity is a sniper's foremost qualification, the number two trait is *patience*. We will take out any enemy we have to when the situation calls for it, whether that means using a rifle, a handgun, a knife, or our bare hands. Yet the sniper's fundamental craft is not killing a person, but being able to get close enough to do so. Osman and I were on a classic sniper stalking mission: track, sneak up, observe, and disappear again, leaving no trace behind.

The man was moving out now, ready to start his day. So were we.

A short while later we found the spot. The man and a few of his cohorts had been using this site to lay up at night: bedroll stash, food and water, some ammo, evidence of a small fire for cooking. Chances were very good they'd be back that night. We marked the GPS coordinates and backed out again, leaving everything exactly as we found it, and moved on.

We spent the day out there, covered a good 10 to 12 kilometers and located about half a dozen sites.

We got back to camp about midnight. After reporting in, we sat down and put our notes together, lining up all the coordinates so we had a tight sequence. By this time we were already familiar with the process of calling these coordinates in ourselves. Brad and Eric had spent so much time over the week calling in air strikes that they'd gotten some of us to spell them at times, just so they could take a break to eat and get some rest. By this point we had already called in a *lot* of ordnance in this valley.

Now, in the middle of the night, they set Osman and me up on the radio, and we called in our sequence ourselves. We had laid a gigantic trap, and now we would be the ones to spring it.

The site we had occupied with Chief Dye that first night at Zhawar Kili gave us an amazingly clear view of the valley below, such that we were able to gaze out with our binos and get an easy visual on all the locations we'd marked during the day. One by one, we saw the barest flicker here, a glint there, telltale flashes as they fired up their cookstoves and campfires signaling us that, yes, this site was occupied again tonight. We called in our coordinates, one by one.

Boom! Boom! Boom!

One after the other, we called in the numbers to our F-18s overhead and sent them all to hell.

SUNDAY, JANUARY 13

After a week of forensic spelunking, and even with all the air strikes we had called in, we knew we still had not come close to destroying all the equipment, weaponry, living supplies, and other matériel that was stashed away in that mountainside. This place was a Fort Knox of war-making wealth. There was no way we could carry all this stuff out with us, and we didn't want these guys coming in here after we left and digging out their stashes of ammo and whatever else they might be able to find. So we choreographed one last hurrah. All the intel we'd gathered over the week was orchestrated into one final bombing session, the largest since the bombing of nearby Tora Bora exactly one month earlier. We pounded that place, and caved in the side of the mountain.

Our twelve-hour mission had turned into a military and political bonanza. In a network of more than seventy caves and tunnels, we'd uncovered nearly a million pounds of ammunition and equipment, along with a ton of intelligence, including extensive papers documenting cross-border traffic and other aspects of enemy tactical plans. More than 400,000 pounds of ordnance was dropped on the targets we flagged. We had destroyed one of the largest terrorist/military training facilities in the country and had taken out a significant number of enemy personnel.

The following day, Monday, January 14, on the ninth day of our twelve-hour mission, we boarded a pair of helos and lifted out of Zhawar Kili, bound for Bagram and Kandahar.

TEN
COALITION

When we arrived back at Kandahar we found a buzz going through the entire camp. Our planned twelve-hour outing had turned into one of the most high-profile missions of the war effort to date, and everyone was fired up about it.

We debriefed with Harward and could tell he was proud of us. It was good for us and our reputation. Some of the other snipers, especially the Danes and Germans, started requesting that Osman and I come over and debrief with them so they could learn more about the terrain and the forces we were up against. The notoriety of our success at Zhawar Kili soon led to a request from the Kommando Spezialkräfte (KSK), the German Special Operations team assigned to Task Force K-Bar. They had been slated to go with the Army Rangers on a direct action mission, but after that disastrous ODA mission went bad they changed their minds and said they would rather join forces with Navy SEALs.

After the attacks on 9/11 the world in general felt a tremendous amount of solidarity with America, and nobody more so than Germany. The German people were horrified at what had happened in New York City, Arlington, and Shanksville, and our KSK buddies were pretty much in the same frame of mind we were: They wanted to get into the action.

The historical significance of the fact that we were going out on a joint raid with German Special Operations was lost on none of us. The last time the Germans were on a battlefield was in World War II, and then we were on opposite sides of the trenches. Ditto in World War I. Hell, there were Hessian mercenaries arrayed against us in the Revolutionary War. This would be the first military mission with German and American forces working together since . . . well, since *ever*.

The Germans were amazingly well trained and extremely solid guys. Most of them also spoke decent conversational English, so communication was not an issue. It was about time we got to work together, and our association was one of the highlights of my experience in Afghanistan.

Our mission briefing started off with the Germans' OIC, Major Mike. (I never learned his last name, and who knew if "Michael" was even his real first name, since most of us were going by nicknames anyway, and they all had fake identities.) Major Mike had developed the mission plan jointly with Cassidy, who would get input from all of us on particulars of helo landing site, insertion points, and other elements of the plan.

This was an HVT mission, meaning high-value target. We were going to descend on an Afghan village called Prata Ghar, a handful of miles northwest of Zhawar Kili, in search of an important al Qaeda higher-up. Prata Ghar was also the site of another cave complex with known al Qaeda ties. The site consisted of one large central building, four stories tall, surrounded by about a dozen smaller buildings. As this was a joint raid, we would divide up the village and field of fire: The Germans would take down the large central building, and we would comb and clear all the others.

We flew up to Bagram in a C-130 (by now my preferred mode of air travel) the day before and prepared for the op. As usual we would be leaving in the middle of the night so we could get on target hours before first light, when anyone in their right mind would be asleep. We needed to hit these guys hard and fast.

Thursday, January 24

We made the brief flight down to Prata Ghar in two Chinook 47s and set down on the far side of a hill, 3 or 4 klicks from the village itself and well out of sight. With its dual rotors and long slender rotor blades, the CH-47 is an extremely agile and maneuverable chopper, the bird of choice for dicey inserts. The moment we stepped out into the snow one of our guys, Forrest Walker, rolled an ankle. Dumb luck. We had to put Forrest back on the chopper and send him home, so we were now down one guy.

We took a head count, rallied up, and moved out. It was still pitch black when we reached the village about forty-five minutes later. We communicated with the German group, moved to our set points, and got ready for the signal. I knew all the other guys were experiencing the same heightened state I was, senses so acutely tuned it felt like the buzz of a high-tension wire. In our briefings we had seen a single photograph of the place, shot from a distance. The interior layout of the individual buildings was a complete unknown, which meant we would be improvising based on what we encountered, and doing so at lightning speed.

"Fifteen minutes," came the word over our comms. We waited, still as statues. "Ten minutes." "Five minutes." "One minute out." Then it was time.

We started taking the place down.

It's an intense experience to bust into a compound like this, knowing that first, you have no idea how the place is laid out inside, second, you'll have only seconds to act in each location if you want to retain the advantage that comes with the element of surprise, and third, the place is packed with highly motivated and determined people who are probably armed to the teeth and will not hesitate to blow your brains out if given half a chance.

Prata Ghar village was pretty big, roughly 2 square kilometers. We had about a dozen buildings to clear, and we would have to play most of it by ear.

We burst into the first room and immediately heard a woman screaming. There on a thin mattress on the floor lay a husband and wife, an infant between them. The baby couldn't have been more than a few weeks old. The woman continued screaming her head off. It wasn't hard to see why. Here she was, safely in bed for the night with her family, and suddenly her door was kicked in and two guys were standing there in balaclavas, pointing weapons at her and shining a SureFire flashlight beam in her eyes. No doubt she was terrified. Of course, that was the idea.

These people were clearly aiding and abetting the enemy. Villages like this one were serving as host-and-resupply stations for Taliban and al Qaeda forces. That's why these guys didn't have to carry around much in the way of supplies. They relied on the hospitality of these villagers to feed them and house them as they roamed around.

Of course, it wasn't like these folks had a whole lot of options. What were they going to do, say no to those guys? Besides, to some extent they were obviously sympathetic to the cause, not only because they shared their Muslim faith but also because these were the people who had helped them fend off the Soviets when they invaded their country. What's more, most were afraid of the mullahs and pressured through fear into helping the Taliban anyway. So we could empathize with them. At the same time, though, they were harboring guys who were plotting to kill as many of us as they could.

We broke into the next room to find one of the most horrifying scenes I've ever witnessed. There in their bedrolls on the floor were a woman and two girls I surmised were her two teenaged daughters. They were just as surprised as the couple in the next room, but they didn't react the same way. Having jumped up at the sound of us busting open their door, now that they saw us enter the room they immediately got back down and lay still. On their backs. The two girls looked terrified; the woman just looked at us stony-faced, betraying no emotion, with an expression that said, *Just do what you came here to do.* For a moment there was no sound in the room but our own ragged breathing and a quiet whimper from the youngest of the three. Osman and I stared at each other for a few seconds as the meaning of the scene sank in. These women assumed we were there to rape them. They thought if they gave no resistance, maybe we wouldn't kill them.

"Jesus," one of us muttered under our breath.

"It's okay," I mumbled to the women in bad Pashtun.

Was it their experiences with the Taliban? No, more likely the Soviets. Lord knows these people had seen enough invaders over the centuries. We moved on to the next room.

We took that place down hard and fast, plowing through room after room, villagers screaming, doors smashing and bursting, us calling out our signals so we could move fast without surprising each other—"Clear left!" "Clear right!" "All clear!" Within less than a half hour we had gone through all the buildings. We wrapped up our search, brought out a few persons of interest, then did a reclear. Now we went through the place like the soldiers in a Vietnam movie poking through rice bags and finding weapons—and there were plenty of weapons for the finding: RPGs, AK-47s, all sorts of bad stuff.

Later, in the course of interrogating our prisoners, we learned that the HVT we were there to capture was gone by the time we arrived. We'd missed him by one day. Still, we had gotten some good intelligence and taken down a significant cache of weapons, and the raid was considered a success overall.

As we regrouped, Cassidy approached me and said, "Listen, the Germans are asking for our assistance. Can you and Osman help them out with something? I trust you guys."

Apparently the Germans had underestimated the terrain and inserted with too much gear. Once they were on the ground, they had decided to stash their big packs as they approached the village. I shook my head. Just like our recon mission to Zhawar Kili all over again: going in too heavy. This was something we'd had to learn the hard way, and the Germans were learning it now, too.

"They're asking if an element from our team can go with one of their guys to retrieve those bags before we exfil."

The sun was already coming up, and we were going out into uncharted territory. I wasn't crazy about this idea, but what could I say? Three of us—Osman, this crazy German guy, Dieter, and I—formed up and commandeered a pickup truck from one of the locals. The plan was simple: Go get everyone's kit and bring it back, fast. We hopped into our "borrowed" truck and took off, Dieter at the wheel.

Within minutes we ran into two Afghan guys with guns. Osman and I hopped out and took them down at gunpoint, zip-tied them, threw them in back of the truck, kept going. We came up over the crest of the mountain, headed for where our KSK buddies had all stashed the gear, and—

"Oh, no," I said.

"*Scheisse,*" murmured Dieter.

"Fuck!" was Osman's comment.

There were four or five Afghans crawling all over the site, looting the Germans' packs like Sunday afternoon yard sale scavengers. We yanked the truck to a stop, got out, and headed down the ridge toward the scene. The looters weren't armed and didn't seem especially dangerous, just a nuisance. We shooed them away and started loading ourselves up with gear. There was no way we'd be able to bring the truck down here into this ravine, so we'd need to haul everything up to the road, maybe 20 feet away and up a significant incline. There were at least forty packs there in the ravine. At four per person, we could carry at most a dozen packs at once between the three of us, so this was going to take a good four trips back and forth. We started hauling.

We got one load to the truck, then came back for load number two, which we hauled up, then repeated the process for load number three, then headed back into the ravine for the last load.

Suddenly we realized we were not alone.

Word had evidently spread to another nearby village that there were some Americans here. Within ten minutes there was a mob there on the road watching us. At least fifty guys, clearly pissed off. With guns. They didn't appear to know exactly what was going on, but whatever it was, they weren't happy about it. Why were we hauling all these packs out of this ravine? And why were two of their compatriots hog-tied in the back of our truck?

One guy who seemed he might be the elder of the group started screaming at us in Pashtun. None of us knew what the hell he was saying. We stood there in the midst of the last batch of packs, trying to figure out what our next move was. They were yards away now, encircling us, and then we were completely surrounded. A bunch of them were still up on the road, and it wasn't hard to see that at any moment one of them would commandeer our vehicle, free the two in back, and drive the thing the hell out of there, leaving us stranded out here. That is, if they didn't shoot us first.

I glanced at Osman, then at Dieter. *Wonderful,* I thought, and I could see Dieter thinking it too. *Wunderbar.* Not only were we outnumbered by something like twenty to one, which is not the kind of odds we like to have, but we also had the low ground. Perfect. All we had to do was get these dozen heavy packs up the ravine and into our truck and drive out of there. Through a mob of fifty or sixty angry, armed, screaming Afghan mountain men.

"Okay, guys," I said, "I think we need to get aggressive with these dudes if we're going to get the fuck out of here."

Nuts, but what other choice did we have?

We started brandishing our weapons at them, shouting and gesturing at our hand grenades, yelling back at them, knowing they wouldn't understand a word of English or German, and knowing that it didn't matter. There is the language of words, sentences, and syntax—and then there is the communication of angry apes in the jungle grunting and bellowing at each other. We may have had an impenetrable language barrier, but they got our message very clearly. They understood very well what we wanted, and what we intended to do about it.

And they were not about to back down.

By now they were on us, screaming in our faces, physically pushing us. The charge in the air was only intensifying. We figured whoever shot off their weapons first would gain the psychological advantage. Time to start shooting.

We fired off a few rounds into the air to show we were serious. It had no effect. We targeted a few of the guys closest to us and fired directly into the ground, inches from their feet, to show that we were *really* serious. *Somebody's gonna get dead if you fuckers don't back off.*

That got their attention. They backed off—just a little, but enough to get our foot in the door. We grabbed those dozen packs and hauled them up into that truck faster than I would have thought humanly possible and then backed that truck out of there like a videotape on fast rewind. We nearly ran over a few of them on our way out.

We made it back to the main group, hoping we hadn't held up the team from extracting, only to learn that the squad of helos that was coming out to get us had been delayed. We would have to wait until nightfall, still many hours away. Nightfall finally arrived, and word came that the helos were delayed some more. We continued to wait, along with our prisoners and our captured intel.

It was probably no more than four hours, but it was so unbelievably, mind-bogglingly cold there in the January snow at Prata Ghar that it felt like an eternity. We had been cold at Zhawar Kili. I'd been cold in survival and resistance training, cold in the land nav portions of BUD/S. Never in my life had I been as bone-numbingly cold as we were here. I remembered Instructor Shoulin in BUD/S saying, "Cold as you are now, trust me, you'll be colder in the teams." We would say, "Yeah, right, whatever." Shit, though, he *was* right. I was truly freezing my nuts off.

An hour or two after sundown, everyone gradually grew silent. It was like that grueling night on the beach of San Clemente Island in BUD/S: no more bitching and complaining, just silent suffering. That's when you know things are really bad, when nobody even talks.

And here was the great irony of it: When we got back to Kandahar the next day, there was a surprise waiting for us. Our shipment of cold-weather gear had finally arrived. We were so happy to see that big crate that we didn't even let ourselves think about the fact that it had been sitting here unopened and unused at the very moment that we were freezing nearly to death up north the night before. So what. We would suffer no more—it was here!

We hungrily tore open the box. I reached in and grabbed at the corner of what was obviously a down sleeping bag. "Oh, man . . ." This was great! I yanked it out of the box, pulled it out of its case, and rolled it out on the floor—and then stared at it, trying to change what I was seeing by sheer force of will.

The thing couldn't have been longer than three and a half feet. And no wonder. It was a sleeping bag made for a child.

I grabbed it and looked it over. Sure enough: ON SALE! There was the frigging REI company sale tag. We knew immediately what had happened: classic military bureaucratic supply thinking. FUBAR. We had submitted a detailed request list all specced with exactly what kind of gear we needed, but the people in supply had decided to save money, so they went out to REI and dug through the sale bin, doing what they could to match up everything on our list with whatever they could find there at better prices.

The whole box was filled with garbage like that. Off-size shoes, off-size gloves. It was all junk, completely useless. We were so irate we all wanted to kill somebody.

Chief Dye fired off an e-mail directly to the team's commanding officer, Captain Adam Curtis. I don't remember the body of the text, but I do remember that it wouldn't have made it through the Motion Picture Association of America's criteria for a PG-rated film, and I recall Chief Dye's closing line:

"Thank you very fucking much, sir, Happy Fucking New Year, enjoy your fucking hot egg nog. Chief Chris Dye, Freezing in Afghanistan."

Not long after Chris dispatched his e-mail, another shipment of cold-weather gear arrived, and this time they had spared no expense.

A few nights after we got back from the mission to Prata Ghar, we had a party to celebrate the successful collaboration of German and American forces. Since the Germans were the only ones on the base with beer, they played host.

This would be the first of a series. Over the following weeks it became commonplace to hear a bunch of SEALs leaving our compound saying, "Hey, we'll be back, we have to go debrief with the Germans." We had a number of parties with the Germans after that first mission, the last of which was quite memorable—although not in a happy sense.

We also went on additional joint missions with the Germans, including one that took us high up in the mountains to Ahmed Kheyl, on the Pakistan border north of Zhawar Kili, to explore another complex of caves. This place was high above the snow line, so we were going to insert by helo and trudge up there on snowshoes to check these caves out. All the intel said it was a fairly benign environment.

Once again, we flew up to Bagram the day before the op and stayed there overnight, departing early the next morning on a few Sikorsky H-53s. This is a big-ass helicopter, much louder than the CH-47, and it puts out such a large rotor wash that you can't really use it for targeted search-and-rescue missions. Stealth was not an important element here, as we were going to be inserting at a friendly checkpoint.

They dropped us off right before sunup, and we immediately sank 3 or 4 feet into the snow. We set a quick perimeter and affixed our snow-shoes. This was the first time I'd ever been on snowshoes. I loved it.

We hoofed up to our checkpoint and checked in with the commander there. This was my first sight of a blond-haired, green-eyed Afghan. Despite his traditional Afghan clothes and hat, with his cheap shades and blond beard he could have easily passed for an American. I thought it must be the Russian influence. I was wrong. In fact, I later learned, there are a lot of Caucasian, blond-haired, green- and blue-eyed Afghans that trace back to an invasion of Europeans led by Alexander the Great. These guys had been defending their turf for a long time.

We hiked up another 3,000 or 4,000 feet in elevation and confirmed the location of the entrance to the caves. It was a big complex, and we explored pretty much all of it. In retrospect, I think of this as a low-key mission, since the intel turned out to be correct and the place was more or less abandoned. But we couldn't be sure of this going in. When you spend hours creeping through thousands of yards of dimly-lit caves and tunnels known to be host to a terrorist enclave, never knowing what you'll find around the next corner (or what will find you), it burns an awful lot of adrenaline.

After we had cleared all the caves, we prepared to hike back down again. I stood and looked out over the valley. Perched up there on that mountain, we could see for miles and miles—a hundred at least. Everything was silent except for the constant flux of the wind wafting through the mountains and crags. It was breathtaking. The snow conditions were unbelievable. *This would make a great place for a ski resort,* I thought. *That is, except for the part about the constant warfare.*

I thought about everything I'd seen in this place. I'd been in Afghanistan now for more than two months, but this location right here seemed to exemplify the place. This was really harsh terrain, extreme altitude, incredibly steep, and incredibly rocky. The ultimate natural impregnable fortress. We were fighting an enemy in an environment where they had the advantage of having been here for generations and generations, back to Alexander the Great and doubtless beyond that. Then it hit me: *You can throw all the technology you want at this place—Predator drones, B52s dropping JDAMs, even teams of the finest Special Operations troops in the world—and they'll just laugh at you. Just ask the Brits and the Soviets. You can't win here.*

I mentioned our parties with the Germans. Two were especially worth noting, and the first of those occurred shortly after our snowshoe trek up to the Ahmed Kheyl cave complex.

The night we went over for this particular shindig, the Germans had already been hitting it pretty hard by the time we got there. As you've no doubt gathered by now, SEALs tend to be a pretty high-voltage, hard-partying bunch. But those KSK guys? They could *drink*.

We arrived to find they had set up a little tent where they were serving the beer. The stereo was turned up loud, and they were singing and marching in circles to the music. Something interesting was going on, but we weren't sure quite what. We stood there watching them. We couldn't understand the music's lyrics and had no idea what the context was.

Major Mike spotted us and headed in our direction. He had heard about our showdown with the angry Afghan mob, and as a result Osman and I had sort of a special standing with these guys, Major Mike in particular. He came over next to me, put his arm around my shoulder, and said, "Hey, please do not be offended by this, I just want you guys to know what this is all about." He proceeded to tell me that a lot of his guys had grandfathers who had served in World War II, and they were very proud of the fact that their ancestors had fought to the death. During those final war years in the mid-1940s, quite a few soldiers in the German army had "gone missing"—in other words, they had deserted and fled. Most of these KSK guys had family members who would never quit and had fought to the end, and they were proud of them.

As he was explaining this we realized what it was we were listening to. These were patriotic German songs from World War II. This was their war music.

By this time all the Americans had gathered around the two of us, listening to what Major Mike was telling me, while all these Germans went on singing and marching to their World War II songs. It was hypnotic.

"Listen," said Major Mike, "if you find any of this in poor taste, please let us know. But we're proud of our heritage. Please understand, we are not at all proud of the Nazi story. The atrocities, it was terrible, all of that should never have happened. Our ancestors, though, all they wanted was to be good soldiers, to fight for their country, to be men of honor—no different than other soldiers.

"In Germany today," he went on quietly, "you can be arrested for drawing a swastika. It is quite taboo. You do not say the word 'Nazi' in public. We all know how horrendous it was, the same as you. But our grandfathers were our grandfathers, and we are proud of them."

It was a bizarre scene. I didn't have any ancestors who fought in World War II, and I don't have any Jewish relatives. But you know, I *could* have had. Any one of us there could have. And if we had, how would this scene have hit us? I glanced around at my guys watching our German brothers singing and marching. These were good men, men we'd fought with side by side; none of them had even been born yet when World War II was happening.

It's a strange thing, war: men of honor, fighting for their country. We see ourselves as the good guys, fighting for a just cause. I know I certainly believed we were the good guys there in Afghanistan, and I still do today. Then again, these guys' grandfathers had thought they were the good guys, too. I suppose we are all heroes of our own story.

In early March we were tasked to work with the Danish Frømandskorpset (Frogman Corps), their elite Special Operations team, to stand QRF watch (quick reaction force) in support of the action that was heating up in Zurmat, a district in Paktia, the province directly west of Khost, as part of Operation Anaconda. The largest ground offensive since the battle of Tora Bora, Operation Anaconda was a massive effort to hem in and wipe out some key HVTs along with an estimated two hundred enemy combatants. That two hundred turned out to be more like a thousand.

Standing QRF is a high-stress, get-ready-and-wait proposition. You and all your gear are prepped to go, your magazines loaded with bullets, everyone in the fighting force and the helo crew ready to take off literally at a minute's notice—and you stand ready like that for hours, days, however long your station lasts. It's something like being a fireman on call at the fire station.

We flew up to Bagram Air Base with the Danes and settled in. Everywhere we went, every minute of the day, we carried radios with us. No matter what we were doing, whether we were sleeping, eating, at the gym, or on the toilet, we were always completely set up and prepared to drop everything and run.

At one point I turned to Osman and said, "Hey, where're our maps? How come we don't have any maps of this area?" We had big country maps, but they didn't show a lot of detail. We were QRF for a very specific region, the district of Zurmat—and we had no area maps for it. Where the hell were they?

We had each been assigned as department head for a different job. If you were assigned to diving, your job was to keep track of all the diving gear. If you were air, you were the one who packed all the air equipment for the platoon, certified it, kept it up, and took care of it constantly. Every one of us had a different specific duty. Mine was air equipment. Who was in charge of intelligence?

Turned out, it was Doug. Damn! There was already a lot of tension between Doug and me because of the taped-out lights that never got taped out at Zhawar Kili. Now I was seriously pissed off. Frankly, intelligence was a pretty easy duty. There was no equipment to be in charge of. All you had to do was make sure we had the maps we needed and that the GPSs were programmed. It was an important job, but not a difficult one by any stretch.

Osman and I found Doug and called him out in front of the other guys. "Doug, where the hell are our maps?"

"Oh," he said, "at the TOC, they said they're out of them right now." This was a bullshit excuse, and we told him so. He was just being lazy, and I did *not* want to get stuck out there in the hostile mountains with no idea where the hell I was. Sure, we had GPS, but that only gets you so far. GPS tells you where you are, in an absolute sense—but it doesn't necessarily give you all the context, what's around you. Especially in that part of the world, where the terrain is so starkly inhospitable, GPS data on its own is practically useless for anything but calling in an air strike or an exfil.

Osman and I said, "Fuck it," and hotfooted it over to the DEVGRU compound (a.k.a. SEAL Team Six), where we explained what we needed.

"Here," they said, and they handed us all the maps we could want. That's how complicated it was. We thanked them, took the maps back to our own compound, threw them down on the table, and said, "Well, there you go, Doug. Appreciate all your hard work getting us the maps."

Doug did not like my attitude, and he let me know it. I let him know it right back. "Look, man," I said, "you almost got me killed once. I'm sure as hell not going to let it happen again." We were toe to toe and almost got into a fistfight right there in the tent.

Later that evening I sat down and thought about what was going on. This was not good. In fact, it was *very* not good, and it had to stop.

I searched Doug out and pulled him aside so we could talk.

"Look," I said, "this isn't personal. I don't want you and me to have this friction going on."

I explained where I was coming from. I didn't apologize for calling him out in front of the other guys. I explained that in GOLF platoon our leaders never let *any* sloppy behavior slide, and they would call us out in front of everyone for the slightest infraction. That's what happened to me when they hazed me for not telling the truth about having gotten married: They let me know that they would not tolerate any lying or withholding of the truth. Honestly, I thought that was the right way to do things. I still do. Get called out in front of your peers, and it shapes you up.

Most people think SEALs are these perfect and infallible warriors, and it's true that SEALs are some of the most dangerous, disciplined, effective fighting machines on the planet. But we're human, too, and as much as there were guys who had their shit together, there were also guys who didn't.

The truth was, Doug was a good guy. He just hadn't been brought up right in his first platoon. As for me, I have the tendency to be a hard-ass and not the most diplomatic when it comes to these things. It's just my nature.

We shook hands and made our peace with each other. From that point on, Doug and I didn't have an issue. What's more, from that day on he was in solid shape.

Later that night a few guys from DEVGRU were flown in to our medical station at Bagram for emergency medical attention. They were in rough shape, really blown to pieces. Word was that their convoy had been hit by a Taliban ambush. The SEALs all survived, but a number of others in the convoy did not. There were guys dying on stretchers as they wheeled them in. It was terrible.

I spent a little time that night with one of the poor bastards from DEVGRU who'd come in to get patched up. He had glass fragments embedded in his skin all over his face. We talked for a bit, and he told me what really happened.

"Man," he said, "that was one of our gunships. No doubt about it."

One of *ours*? Was he saying that the hit that had messed them up so bad, that wasn't Taliban, that was *us*?

He nodded. "We're driving along and *blam!* something explodes in front of the convey, like a howitzer round in the lead vehicle. Then the rearmost vehicle blows up, too, and suddenly we're taking heavy fire. *Holy shit, I'm thinking, this is classic C-130 gunship tactics. Is this a blue on blue?*"

In fact, it *was* a blue on blue, otherwise known as friendly fire. No one likes to believe these things happen, but they do.

The only reason he wasn't dead, he told me, was that when the attack started he managed to get down underneath the engine block of the vehicle he was in. "Man," he said, "when I get back home I'm buying a Toyota—because that thing saved my life."

I don't know whether someone in the convoy hadn't been in touch with air support, or someone made a mistake with their coordinates, or what. Maybe it had been something that at the time seemed no more consequential than Doug neglecting to tape over our dash lights. Whatever it was, something had gone badly wrong. When you're operating in that kind of kill box situation, you better hope the person responsible checked in first with the gunship.

Otherwise, out in those mountain ranges, you're just another heat signature on Murder TV.

First thing next morning we got the call: "Let's get it on!" QRF had been activated. We were going in. Where, or to do what, we had no idea. All we knew was, it was *now*. "Saddle up, you guys," said Cassidy when he showed up at our quarters. "We'll brief en route."

We and the Danes got ourselves loaded up in two Chinook helicopters, Razor 01 and Razor 02—and then sat there on the tarmac. Nothing happened. Minutes ticked by, and still nothing happened. Cassidy was going back and forth on the radio. Why the hell weren't we taking off? Finally we saw some Army Rangers running out toward us. Cassidy sighed and said, "C'mon, guys, we're getting off."

We climbed out of the two birds, and the Rangers got on. Obviously there had been some kind of pissing match between Task Force K-Bar and Task Force Dagger over who was responsible for whom. We sat down on the tarmac and waited for a while to see what would happen next. The Rangers took off. We waited. Finally we went back to our tent and waited there on standby.

Soon we heard people scrambling everywhere. Something heavy had happened, but at first we didn't know what. Then we heard that the Rangers who had replaced us in the two Chinooks were in trouble.

Eventually we got the whole story.

Two teams of SEALs had gone out to insert high up on a nearby mountain called Takur Ghar. Originally they were supposed to insert in the dead of night at two different points in the valley, to provide observation support for an op there, much the way those six marines and four of us had done that day in Zhawar Kili when Doug failed to black out our vehicle. Delays and mechanical problems had forced a change in plans, though, and they were ordered instead to insert closer up toward the peak itself at close to dawn.

A daytime landing in the mountains—not a good idea in Afghanistan. The Taliban knew how to shoot down helicopters. In fact, they'd learned it from us back in the days of the Soviet occupation, using our ground-to-air Stinger missiles. Fortunately the Stingers were no longer operational, but the Taliban were well equipped with RPGs and knew how to use them.

Sure enough, an RPG ripped into one of the SEALs' helos as it went in to land, and one of the team, Neil Roberts—a totally solid guy, a bad-ass who was ready to rock on insert and be first out and on the ground—was hurled through the chopper's open door. The bird was shot to shit and crash-landed a short distance away, where its occupants immediately came under fire. The second helo, carrying the other SEAL team, came in to pick up the remaining personnel from the first chopper and also came under immediate fire. An Air Force Combat Controller was killed. That helo was forced off the peak and requested backup.

That was when a QRF team was dispatched to come get them—which was us, until interbranch political squabbles intervened and we had to exit the helo. The Army Rangers took our place and took off for the ridge, but when they tried to put down they, too, came under fire, killing their door gunner. Moments later their chopper, Razor 01, was shot down by another RPG and crash-landed, just as the previous helo had done, killing three more of their crew. The surviving crew members and the Rangers who made up the QRF took cover, now also under heavy enemy fire.

Back at Bagram they now put us on another set of helicopters and flew us to a refueling station they had set up in the middle of nowhere, maybe fifteen minutes by air from Takur Ghar. We sat there with the Danish Frogman Corps, listening to everything unfold over our comms.

Gunfire, screams, guys dying, pleading for help, and no help arriving. It was brutal.

We heard the Ranger captain, Nate Self, on the radio, begging for reinforcements, but the air force general in charge of the task force, General Gregory Trebon, wouldn't send anyone in. They didn't want to lose another helicopter. "Sorry," the guy on the radio passed the word, "the general says nobody else is going in there, not in daylight."

We begged to get inserted up there, even anywhere close by, so we could go help these guys out. "Go in with F-18s or whatever you have," we said, "and pound the place if you have to first—but put us on the ground."

But it wasn't going to happen.

When you have guys ready and willing to risk their lives to go in there and get their fellow soldiers out of that hell they're in, you let them go do it. If it were me out there, I would want to know that our guys were doing everything in their power to come get me, and come get me *now*. Going into battle you *have* to know that will happen, that your guys will come after you no matter what. That's the psychology you have to have in order to be able to function effectively on the battlefield. "No man left behind" isn't just a catchy slogan, it's the nonnegotiable bedrock of a fighting force's existence.

Do I think it was a bad call? Yes I do. No question in my mind, and morale suffered for sure.

I understand the situation they were in, not wanting to lose another helicopter, but if it were me, I'd take a deep breath, let my guys come up with a solid plan, and execute it. Yes, those first few sorties were kind of fast and loose and got confused, and that's when things can so easily go wrong. Yes, things had fallen apart up there, but that's when you sit back and say, "Okay, time out, let's take stock and plan this out." Then you let the guys who are closest to the action and have a hands-on understanding of what's happening out there make the plan—and then you *go*. That's what should have happened there.

Instead, we sat there all day, the Danes and us, all geared up and ready to go, just a fifteen-minute hop from the spot where our brothers were fighting and dying. It was agonizing, listening to Captain Self's pleas for help all day long, talking about his wounded. Every time he checked back in the casualties were worse—and he'd lose another guy. Ten to twelve hours of daylight went by with no support whatsoever. People died because of it.

Soon after we had relocated to the refueling station, another element of that Ranger QRF did successfully insert, but a good way farther down on the mountainside. We followed their progress on our comms as they struggled up the face of Takur Ghar to link up with the downed helo and Rangers on Roberts Ridge (as the site would come to be called in honor of the downed SEAL), because those guys were being hammered. It took them hours to get up that mountain.

There was also an Australian SAS force nearby, holed up in a reconnaissance outpost on the side of the mountain, observing with long-range optics, providing some situational awareness, and calling in air support. Hats off to the Aussies: They saved some lives that day.

That second Ranger force did eventually succeed in climbing up there with all their kit, fighting their way through, meeting up with the downed QRF group, assaulting that position, and taking it over. There was a huge Taliban force up there that mounted a counterattack, and the Rangers took more casualties, but in the end they got control of the ridge line.

After spending the day sitting on our hands and listening to this whole thing go down, we boarded the helo and flew back to camp. The mood at Bagram was pretty dark. We all felt these guys had died for what appeared to us to be no good reason.

I've thought about this a thousand times, ten thousand times. What would have happened if we had been allowed to leave on those two Chinooks? Would it have just been us who got shot down instead? Or if we had left ten minutes earlier, right when we first boarded the helos, would things have gone differently?

One of the SEALs who was in Neil Roberts's team was a guy known as Turbo. A few years later Turbo and I got to be good friends when we worked as instructors together, and one night over some beers he told me the full story of what happened there on Roberts Ridge.

According to what I remember from Turbo's account, when they were on approach to that ridge, they got the thirty-second call: ready to put down. He was standing right next to Neil. Turbo and Neil were close friends. "Neil was always squared away," Turbo told me, "always had his pack on and ready to go. He was going to be the first one off that 47's ramp."

The ramp went down, they prepared to leap off, and Neil had just lifted one foot off the floor and was half a step out when *boom!* they took that RPG hit. The pilot yanked on the stick and banked the helo abruptly back in the other direction in a desperate bid to escape the volley of gunfire. Before Neil had a chance to catch himself, the inertia of their forward movement hurled him out through the chopper's open door. Turbo reached out and just managed to catch hold of Neil's ruck—but he didn't have a firm enough grip on it to make the critical difference. The ruck tore out of his fingers, and Neil plummeted out of the helo and onto the ridge.

The helo took some further hits and crashed on the hillside, about 4 miles away from where Neil was left behind.

The other chopper swooped in, picked up Turbo and the other guys, and headed back to Bagram. Turbo and his teammates argued with the bird's crew, insisting that they turn around and go back for Neil. The crew had their orders. The team kept arguing and insisting. Finally they practically put a gun to the pilot's head. "Look," they said, "we're going back for our friend. You are going back there and putting this copter down."

The pilot took them back to the same spot on the ridge where they'd lost Neil, and Turbo and his teammates jumped out.

Turbo told me it was the most intense firefight imaginable. "We shot so many of these guys," he said, "and they just kept coming and coming." At one point he was back to back with one of the other SEALs, and he could feel the burn of bullets whipping past. Later he found burn marks all over the sides of his body from the friction of the rounds. Firepower from the enemy was so overwhelming they eventually realized that if they had any hope of surviving, they had to get off the ridge. They stepped off the ridge line and started sliding down the slope.

It was incredibly steep, a 70-degree incline at some points. Predator drones were orbiting the area, and after it was all over I was able to watch this happening on the Predator video footage. It looked like a group of guys shooting down a mountainside on a frigging bobsled.

The moment Turbo stepped off the ledge he took a .762 mm round right through his leg. It blew out his calf, so now he was bleeding badly as he slid hundreds of feet down the hill along with his buddy. Once they came to a stop, he found he couldn't walk. He asked his buddy to leave him there, and when he refused, Turbo insisted—he felt like a complete liability—but the guy would not do it. He put a tourniquet on Turbo's leg and carried him a few miles.

Their OIC was an absolute maniac. The Taliban were pouring down the tree line after Turbo and the rest of them, and this guy held the whole scene together. He'd come back and check on them, then run out to the tree line and lay down a bunch of fire and kill a bunch of guys, then run back again—running back and forth, engaging the enemy and somehow managing to keep them at bay. "He saved all our lives," Turbo said.

Their OIC finally was able to drag Turbo farther away from the firefight, and this was when they made the call for help. The nearby QRF was alerted and boarded a helo to come help them.

That was us. And you know what happened next.

The surviving SEALs spent a lot of time out there in the woods, and Turbo thought it was all over several different times, until he finally lost so much blood that he lost consciousness altogether. Miraculously, they were finally picked up, and Turbo survived.

Seven of our people died there on Takur Ghar: three Army Rangers, Corporal Matthew A. Commons, Sergeant Bradley S. Crose, and Specialist Marc A. Anderson; the two aircrew on Razor 01, Technical Sergeant John A. Chapman and Senior Airman Jason D. Cunningham; Sergeant Phillip Svitak of the Special Operations Aviation Regiment (SOAR); and Petty Officer First Class Neil C. Roberts himself.

After the whole thing was over, the group that had picked up the surviving Rangers went back to survey the scene. There were hundreds of Taliban dead. "We found dozens and dozens of them lying there with multiple shots to the head," they told us later. "That was the SEALs' work."

They could possibly save his leg, they told Turbo when they got him to a hospital, but he'd be crippled for life. Nah, he said, cut it off at the knee, and he would get a prosthetic lower leg. His rehab was unbelievable. What he does even to this day with that prosthetic is insane. You'd never know it was a fake leg.

Ten months from the day he first got back to the States, he was back in theater over in Afghanistan again with his new leg. Turbo is an amazing guy, a true patriot, and an absolute animal.

By late March we knew we were winding down. We had a stellar track record in Afghanistan, but we'd been in this theater of operations for close to six months, and soon it would be time to rotate back home. As it happened, the Germans were about to rotate in a new crew themselves, and the group that was getting ready to leave wanted to have us over for one last get-together before they were gone.

This time the party was held at our compound, around a raging bonfire.

That night the Taliban were shooting mortars at us. They were staged pretty far away and weren't likely to score a hit. There was nothing for us to do about it, anyway; we weren't responsible for camp security, and the army was dealing with it. So we just treated their firepower like fireworks. Every time another mortar went off the Germans would yell, *"Prost!"* and raise their beers in the air. We thought it was pretty hilarious.

Late that night, as we were enjoying ourselves, drinking, listening to the stereo, and laughing every time the Germans raised a toast to another futile Taliban mortar round, I heard a loud voice yell, "Turn that fucking music off!" I looked around and saw that someone's head had popped up over the wall that separated our compound from the one next door.

Uh-oh.

At Kandahar there was a small camp where all the Air Force Combat Controllers hung out. We had Brad and Eric, our two CCTs, living with us, but there was a small contingent of CCTs who were piecemealed out to various other units. Among them were the two young Combat Controllers that Chief Dye had fired in Oman. Even though they were no longer with our platoon, they had still come over to Kandahar and were now living with the other Combat Controllers in this compound—which ironically enough, had ended up being moved right next door to us.

These two guys had not gotten over what happened in Oman. We would see them in passing around the base, and they were clearly copping an attitude and trash-talking our platoon. They had gone to their OIC, an air force major, and given him their story on what went down—who knows how they'd described it—and we could tell he wasn't very happy with us. This major was a big, burly dude, 6'6", looked like he could rip your arms off with his bare hands. We'd heard he was very big in mixed martial arts (MMA) fighting.

The issue got to the point where Brad and Eric went over and talked with this major and gave him their perspective. "Listen," they said, "we've worked closely with this platoon for quite a while now, and these are good guys. We know those two young Combat Controllers weren't happy about what happened in Oman, but there are two sides to every story, and the truth is, those two young fellows have a lot to learn." They came back and told us there shouldn't be any more problems that they'd cleaned up the tension there.

Apparently, though, some tension still remained. The head glaring at us right now over that wall, spitting and fuming and going off on us, belonged to the air force major.

Dave, a SEAL who'd come to Kandahar to augment the DPV group (which I'll get to shortly), started arguing with him. One of the Germans called out some comment, and the major shot back a profanity. The German chucked an empty wine bottle at him. It missed and smashed against the wall.

This thing was escalating fast, and our guys were turning into an angry mob—and then all at once the major was gone and everyone went back to his business. At first it seemed that the whole escalation had reversed itself and things had gotten under control. When I saw Dave stand up and start over toward the CCT compound, I realized what had actually happened. Dave had told the air force major to "come meet me in the alley," and he was going out there now to settle the dispute man to man.

This was not good.

Osman got to his feet and said, "Let's go," and he and two other guys went back out there with Dave. A few minutes later, I followed.

Dave tore out of our compound and, in the pitch blackness, ran straight into a Humvee we had parked there. As Dave recovered from that, the major met up with him and sucker-punched him in the throat—and then looked up and saw the rest of us.

"Help," he started screaming, "the SEALs are ambushing me!" and he turned and ran for the entrance to the CCT compound.

Osman is a street brawler. He grew up in a tough San Diego neighborhood and learned early on how to stand his ground. With Osman there's no foreplay. He doesn't do any trash-talking, chest-thumping, or pushing and shoving. If it's on, it's *on*: He just flips the switch and goes.

Some words were exchanged, but not many. Osman just laid this guy out. Punched him so hard that he broke his nose, knocked him out, and severed a vein. There was blood everywhere. The other air force guys who had joined the major stood there horrified, looking at their commanding officer, this major they all looked up to, this frightening guy with the big reputation as a mixed martial artist, lying on the ground bleeding all over the place. Osman looked at them all and spoke matter-of-factly. "Who's next?"

None of them was next. They were terrified. Not only was Osman standing ready to take out anyone else who moved, but they were also now facing an angry mob of SEALs who looked like they wanted blood. A bunch of us had by now moved from the bonfire out to where this was all happening, and we were standing there ready to back our guys up if necessary.

One of the air force bunch ran to get army security, and the rest just stood there, afraid for their lives.

Suddenly this big German guy, Enne, started pushing through the crowd. "I'm a medic, I'm a medic!" he was shouting. "Let me through." He crouched down with his head lamp over the air force major and started checking him out.

Wait a minute, I was thinking. *Enne's not a medic, is he?*

Enne grabbed the major's nose and started raking it back and forth. The major came to—and found himself lying on the ground with a big German guy tweaking his broken nose. He screamed in pain.

"Oh, yah," Enne said with a completely straight face. "Diss iss definitely broken." He looked over, smiled, and winked at us. I could not believe the audacity of this dude. After a minute Enne let up; the air force guys carried the major off to get him to the medics (the real ones), and we returned to our fading party.

A little later two army MPs came over to our compound to take Osman away. I met them at the gate. "Look, guys," I said, "you aren't taking anybody anywhere." One of them opened his mouth to object—but I stopped him. "Let me explain something," I said. "This is the last place you want to be right now. These guys have been drinking. They're pissed off and they're ready to rip someone's head off. You don't want to come in and try to take anyone out of here right now."

I saw them wrestling with the situation, trying to figure out if they should back down or press their case.

"Look," I said, "we'll sort this thing out tomorrow afternoon with our chain of command, after everyone's had a chance to get some rest."

They could see the logic of that. They backed down and left.

Harward flew back down early the next day from Bagram, and man, was he livid. He reamed our platoon out, no holds barred. It was not pretty. Fortunately for us, when the medics operated on the major's nose that night they could see that he'd been drinking, which meant that everyone involved was culpable and not just us. Technically speaking, nobody was supposed to be drinking on the base. Harward had known we were having parties here and there but had turned a blind eye to that. Until now. Now he had an enlisted man who had struck an officer, and *his* ass was on the line.

Within eight hours Osman and Dave had their bags packed and were on a flight out of there.

I have to admit, it was the right move on Harward's part. Taking Os-man and Dave off the base defused the situation. Now the army couldn't come put Osman in the brig, and the two of them wouldn't be around for the air force guys to run into. He had quickly put a lid on the whole thing.

Later that day the air force major came over and apologized to us all, shaking hands with each one of us in turn. He told us that he'd been drink-ing and he had instigated the trouble. I thought this was a stand-up thing for him to do. At that point the tension had finally gone out of the whole conflict—but the long-term repercussions of the event were still to come.

After this deployment Cassidy put us in for some major awards. Sev-eral of us, including myself, were lined up for a Bronze Star with Valor. Because of the incident with the air force major, Captain Harward knocked all our awards down a notch, and I ended up getting the Navy/Marine Corps Commendation Medal with Valor. If you read the language of the award ("heroic achievement . . . in keeping with the highest traditions of the United States Naval Service"), you can tell that it was originally written up for a Bronze Star and then demoted to a Commendation Medal after the fact.

I suppose Harward did what he had to do. As I said, the guy was an animal, without a trace of sentimentality. Regardless, I was proud to have been nominated for the Bronze Star with Valor.

Our last op in Afghanistan was a mounted direct action mission we would be conducting jointly with the Danish Special Operations forces. We would be taking a convoy about three hours out to an area outside Kandahar City to a village where we knew the people were harboring an HVT. We were going to go take down the whole village in the dead of night.

We also had a DPV (desert patrol vehicle) crew with us. This team (which had included the now-departed Dave) had been flown in to join us while we were out in the mountains of Khost on our nine-day Zhawar Kili mission. I'd also seen these things back when we were first in desert training at Seal Team Three.

Designed by Chenowth, the race car company, the DPV is essentially a dune buggy powered by a souped-up VW engine. In addition to the driver, the thing holds a navigator riding shotgun and a gunner in the back. These babies were designed for open desert, the kind of terrain you see in Kuwait or Iraq. (During Desert Storm, the first U.S. forces to enter Kuwait City were SEALs on DPVs.) They can go up and down all sorts of wild terrain. One of their best features is that you can fit one in the back of an H-53; the helo lands and that little monster comes zipping out of there, fully loaded and ready for action. We'd had a DPV platoon at Team Three and had fun bombing around Coronado on the beach, *Rmmm, rmmm, rmmmm!* They only assigned guys with field experience to the DPV program, though, so we would mostly see the older dudes, some of them combat injured, driving around in these hot vehicles. We called the program Fat Guys in Fast Cars.

Now, I'm no mechanic, but I know that altitude affects performance, and those engines were definitely not designed for the higher altitudes we were seeing in northern Afghanistan. You lose a lot of power at 9,000 feet. Besides, we liked using indigenous vehicles; they worked well with the local terrain, and they could blend in. The DPVs looked like freaking souped-up Baja 1000 racing rigs, and they were definitely going to stand out. From my perspective, these vehicles weren't very useful up north in the Hindu Kush.

For this mission, though, they would be perfect. The DPV crew would be going with us to set a perimeter with their heavy firepower. Once on location we would enter the compound, clear it, and get our high-value target out of there.

I had all the GPS coordinates and worked out our route, planning the whole insertion/extraction sequence. It was a solid mission and sure looked good on paper. Now all we had to do was execute. I was point man for this op, so I felt an added sense of responsibility for everything going smoothly.

We rolled out of there in the dead of night. For the next two and a half hours the trip was silent and uneventful. Serving as navigator, I called the directions at every turn; it wasn't that complicated. We drove in a fairly tight formation, slightly staggered but close enough to keep visual contact. We had two vehicles, the Danish had their two vehicles, and then we had the four DPVs behind us, all loaded for bear.

As we approached our turnoff from the main highway, I radioed the other vehicles to let them know what to expect. "Delta 1," I said, "five out," meaning we were five minutes away from our turnoff.

One of the DPV crew radioed back, "Roger, solid copy. <break> We show twenty out."

I repeated my call. "Negative, four out." We were now almost on top of the turnoff.

They went silent. Then, "We show different."

"Negative," I replied. "We're turning in two."

I don't know if the reset point on their GPS was off, or they'd entered their coordinates wrong, or what, but somehow their data were all screwed up and they were way off.

Navigation is more than a matter of looking at a little dot on a GPS or following a map. You have to look at the sky, at the sun and moon and stars, at the landscape and features on the horizon, at everything available to you; it all helps paint the picture you need. I'd looked at the satellite imagery ahead of time so I'd know what the roads and terrain would be like. I'd been navigating my whole life. I knew for a certainty that this was the goddam turnoff.

I turned to Cassidy and said, "Chris, this is our turnoff."

This was one of those moments that leadership is all about. Cassidy had me in the front seat telling him we had to turn left, and a whole convoy of

DPVs insisting that we had to keep going for another 10 miles. The decision had to be made that instant. We had to turn or go straight—and at least one of those two choices meant completely blowing the mission.

Cassidy didn't hesitate. "Take the turn," he told the driver, and to me he just said, "I trust you."

We turned. For whatever reason, the DPVs decided to keep going and chase down their phantom coordinates. We were now just a few minutes from the compound. We and the Danes were going in there to take down this whole village—*without* the DPVs and our secured perimeter.

We reached the target, came to a halt, and silently slid out of our vehicles, formed up, fanned out, and launched into a sequence we had rehearsed hundreds of time, a classic room-to-room assault-and-clear operation. The big picture would be coordinated by Cassidy, who would also be in constant contact with the Danish assault element, giving and receiving updates, but in the individual assault element, everyone functions as a leader as the thing moves and shifts second to second. You have to be able to flow seamlessly through a building. It's incredibly fluid, and has to be.

As we entered the first building Chief Dye stayed behind us, serving as hall boss and fanning us out with hand signals—two guys this way, two guys that way. If we hit a locked door we might just smash it open if it was flimsy enough, or else blow it with a breacher charge. Whatever it took, we'd blow through and flow through, pushing our way through the house.

Two of us kicked open the door to the first room and tossed in a flashbang—*crash!*—waking two guys out of a dead sleep. They lurched up, blinded and deafened, and made an attempt to grab for the guns they'd had lying next to them as they slept, but they were too late. We were on them and they were zip-tied, hoods over their heads, before they could complete a thought. "All clear! Coming out!" I shouted, and we were down the hall to the next room.

We poured through the entire compound like the unbridled currents of a tsunami flooding through a coastal city's streets and sweeping away everything in its path. Anyone put up even a moment's resistance and *pop!* they got a muzzle strike in the chest. Took the wind right out of them. In movies you'll see assault teams making strikes to the face, but that's Hollywood. Muzzle-strike someone in the face in real life and chances are you just killed him—and that wasn't our aim here. We were here to take these guys alive. They had intel we wanted, intel that could help us snuff out their pals' next operation before it happened.

These were bad, bad dudes, surrounded by tons of weapons and mountains of ammo. Everyone in that compound was as armed and dangerous as armed and dangerous gets. We took well over a hundred guns, grenades, RPGs, you name it. If we'd had any hitches, if they'd had a chance to use any of their arsenal, it could've gone very badly for us. But there were no hitches. Our team coiled through those buildings striking with the speed of a 100-foot-long rattlesnake.

The Danish did an excellent job, too. As with the Germans, it was obvious from the start that these guys were first class, in both conditioning and tactical training. Going into the raid, we never worried for an instant about whether or not they would hold up their end. They did.

The DPV convoy arrived about halfway through the raid and belatedly set up their perimeter. They were embarrassed, but we didn't give them too hard a time. Having to pull off the raid without our planned secure perimeter could have completely thrown us off. But it didn't, not for a moment.

This is something unique about Special Ops forces: We're trained to make decisions on the fly. In a sense, we are *all* trained to function as leaders in the field when necessity dictates. In a conventional unit, all too often when something screws up the whole mission grinds to a halt. In Special Ops we're trained to adjust immediately, to say, "Okay, the thing screwed up, got it—so let's get on with it," and then make whatever executive decisions we have to without hesitation. That's what happened in 2011 in the raid that took Osama bin Laden's compound in Pakistan. The team that went in suddenly lost one of their choppers, which could have been a catastrophic mishap—but it wasn't. They adjusted immediately, blew up the downed copter, completed the mission successfully, and got everyone out of there without losing a single member of the team.

We took more than twenty prisoners that night. They didn't know what had hit them until it was over. We got our HVT, too. If you were following the news at the time, it was a name you'd have recognized. We commandeered a few of their vehicles, threw these guys in back, and headed back to process them into the EPW camp at Kandahar. General Mad Dog wouldn't have been happy, but this was our job.

Not a shot was fired. It was our last op in Afghanistan, and with the exception of the temporary DPV defection it was flawless from start to finish.

A few days before we left Afghanistan, an event occurred that cast a pall over all our victories and triumphs. At the very end of March, some DEVGRU guys from Red Team, the group that would years later be credited with killing Osama bin Laden, went out to Tarnak Farms to do some training. This was exactly the same area we had trained in back when we were still newly arrived in Kandahar.

Back in December, after that episode when we had parked our Humvee on top of a series of live land mines and Brad and Steve had to defuse the entire mess while we stood and waited, we had gone back and given a full report. "Nobody should be going out there," we said. "The area is definitely *not* clear. It was cleared previously by EOD, but it has obviously been visited since then. There's a good chance someone is watching it right now and planting more mines."

We thought our report would handle the problem, that nobody would go out there again. We were wrong. In a classic wartime lack of communications—FUBAR—evidently no one passed the word to Red Team. On March 28, a SEAL named Matthew Bourgeois stepped out of a vehicle at Tarnak Farms and directly onto a land mine. Probably it was very much like the mine I had found there—except that this one wasn't defective. It exploded, instantly killing Bourgeois and injuring a second SEAL.

Later that day I talked to a few of the guys from Red Team. As they were describing the scene to me one of them said, "We were standing right next to a bombed-out blue minivan."

A bombed-out blue minivan. These guys had been standing in precisely the same spot where my buddies and I had been back in December—the spot in that snapshot I still have.

There was no way the mine that killed Bourgeois could have been there a few days after Christmas when we were out there. We were all *over* that area, walking everywhere. Just as we had said in our report, the place had to have been mined after we left.

The people we were up against were devious and fiendishly smart. They kept their swords sharp. No wonder they had fought off the British and Soviets successfully for so many years. How long would we end up being here?

ELEVEN

MY PROUDEST MOMENT

I left Afghanistan with my platoon on Tuesday, April 2, flew a third of the way around the world, grabbed a ride to our little two-bedroom home in Point Loma, California, went inside, and met my five-month-old son for the first time.

Coming face-to-face with Jackson that evening was incredible, even surreal. I don't know what was more amazing to me: the fact that Gabriele and I had produced this little redheaded creature with ten fingers and ten toes, or the fact that I'd made it back from Afghanistan to see him with all *my* ten fingers and ten toes intact, after more close calls than I cared to remember.

The first thing that happened on arriving home was the solid sixty days' leave they gave us to decompress from our six-month deployment, and I spent pretty much all of it with Gabriele and Jackson. It was such a blast hanging out with this little dude, playing with him, watching him learn and grow before my eyes. Later on, when each of our other two kids was born, it would be a replay of the same amazement all over again, but this was the first time, and it knocked my socks off. I was ecstatic. Whatever my expectations of fatherhood had been, this exceeded them. I couldn't get enough of it. Two solid months with this little guy went by as if it were a single day.

Meeting Jackson was the proudest moment of my life—at least in a personal sense. The proudest moment in my *professional* life, my life as a SEAL, was still ahead of me. Before that could happen, though, things would take a few twists and turns I hadn't counted on.

The first thing that happened was that I was suddenly out of the teams.

In truth, I'd been pondering a possible career change for a while. Before 9/11 happened, even as I was trying to get myself assigned to a stint overseas, I was seriously considering what the ideal next move for my career might be, and I wasn't entirely sure it meant staying in the SEALs. A lot of this thinking had to do with the fact that I now had a growing family. As I said, it's not impossible to reconcile family life with life as a SEAL, but it certainly isn't easy. Not too many marriages can survive the kind of fanatical dedication involved in being an active member of the teams. I felt it might soon be time to make a change to a more stable environment, for the family's sake. But if not SEALs, then what?

For some reason flying has been in my blood from as early as I can remember, and I've always been passionate about the idea of going into aviation. Maybe it's just the wanderlust that seems to be a family trait. My dad's sister, Gayle, has always been a world traveler; when we were kids she would pop in periodically with photos and souvenirs she'd picked up from all kinds of exotic places. My parents had their longtime dream of sailing around the world, and they acted on it. My sister, Rhiannon, ended up becoming a flight attendant and has traveled the world just like Aunt Gayle. And Lord knows my career in the SEALs took me to quite a few exotic locales.

In any case, before going to Afghanistan I had been considering finishing my degree and going on to become a commercial airline pilot. The
typical way to pursue this path would be to enroll at Embry-Riddle Aero-
nautical University (a.k.a. "the Harvard of the sky"), a four-year university
heavy in aviation that has a program geared toward helping place ex-
military with the airlines. With my aviation background and field experience, they were willing to give me credits that would have started me out
with more than an associate's degree, putting me well ahead of the game.

But the world had changed while I was in Afghanistan. The airline
industry was in rough shape, and pilots were being laid off. Becoming a
commercial pilot as a way to create more stability for my family suddenly
didn't seem like such a hot idea, so I decided at least to finish out my enlistment, which would run through early 2005.

As it turned out, I didn't have a choice. After the attacks of 9/11 the
navy put a community-wide stop-loss in place, which allowed them to
retain people who were on active duty beyond their official date of separa-
tion. In other words, it was an indefinite suspension of our ability to leave
the service. I couldn't have gotten out even if I wanted to.

Okay, so I was definitely staying with the SEALs for now. Why not
become a BUD/S instructor? That way I could have more consistent time
with my family and at the same time contribute to training the next generation of SEALs.

No such luck. That decision was made for me, too, before I'd even left
Afghan soil. I wasn't going to be a pilot, and I wasn't going to be a BUD/S
instructor, either. The navy had something else in mind. While en route
back to the States I learned I'd been given orders to a newly formed Naval
Special Warfare Group One Training Detachment, TRADET for short.

Change was afoot. With the growing importance of Special Operations
in the warfare of the twenty-first century, the SEAL community was un-
dergoing a comprehensive reorganization. Prior to this, each individual

SEAL team was responsible for its own training. Now they were consolidating all the advanced training under two divisions, one for each coast. TRADET was in charge of developing programs of advanced training, a sort of "continuing education" for SEALs beyond BUD/S and the other basic training courses. It was split up into different training components, including MAROPS (maritime operations), Land Warfare, CQB, Assault, and a handful of others. Since TRADET was brand-new, they badly needed warm bodies to fill their posts, and bodies with experience even more so. Sometimes there was a bit of arm-wrestling in terms of which group got which talent coming in fresh from the field, a little like the competition that happens when top players are drafted onto pro football teams.

When I checked out of SEAL Team Three and into TRADET one sunny day in early June, I was first placed in the Land Warfare office, but that posting didn't stick. Within a few days a request came from another division that set the course of my career for the next several years. The guys running the sniper division said they wanted me, and after a brief political tug-of-war I was out of Land Warfare and had become part of a tiny unit called Sniper Cell, run by a veteran SEAL chief named Jason Gardner.

I felt incredibly fortunate to be recruited into Sniper Cell. For one thing, the group was so small it felt like I could actually make a difference here. It varied as people rotated in and out, but five members was typical. Most of the TRADET training groups were two to three times that size. Also, the East Coast didn't have a dedicated entity focused on advanced sniper training, so our Sniper Cell was unique.

Another reason I felt so fortunate was Chief Gardner himself. Chief Gardner has an amazing résumé of service as a SEAL. He fought in the first Gulf War; he shot a half a dozen guys in Somalia. In Afghanistan he put in more than 340 hours of "troops in contact," meaning under fire, and led his troops in 196 KIA and the capture of six HVT. In 2009 he was awarded the Silver Star. He is the nicest guy you'll ever meet, but you do not want to go up against him in combat. The man is a killing machine. He was also a fantastic boss to work for.

Since TRADET was new, we had to come up with new standardized training methodologies and curricula for the cell. Because of my SAR background and real-world experience as a helo sniper in those ship assaults in the Gulf, Chief Gardner put me in charge of developing a curriculum for the Helo Support block. A separate training for helo support was a brand new concept, and for the most part the curriculum had to be created from scratch. And it had to be done fast. We had new teams with new snipers coming up who needed to be trained for the realities of combat conditions. The war in Afghanistan wasn't over—and it didn't take a crystal ball to see that hostilities in Iraq might be just over the horizon. (In fact, the U.S. Joint Resolution authorizing use of force in Iraq was then only a few months away, and the invasion itself followed just five months later.) There wasn't a moment to waste.

Fortunately, I had an excellent ally in this project: my old friend Eric Davis, the same guy who'd been with Osman and me that freezing cold night on the beach of San Clemente Island. Eric had arrived at Sniper Cell just before I did, and our reunion was a harbinger of great things to come.

Eric is a superstar instructor, one of the best guys on the podium I've ever seen. I would sit in on one of Eric's classes and at the end find myself saying, *Damn, I don't want that guy to stop!* I'd get so engaged listening to him teach that I'd blink and an hour had gone by. And he wasn't just a good lecturer; he also genuinely cared about the students. I couldn't have wished for a better partner in the work we were about to undertake— work that, as it turned out, would stretch into several years.

Chief Gardner gave us free rein to put together whatever we thought made the most sense for the new Helo Support block, and we threw ourselves into the task. I talked to every sniper I could find with significant helicopter experience to get their input and make sure I had the latest crew communication language, and I wrote, wrote, and wrote some more. I was responsible for coordinating airspace, air assets (always challenging), live-fire ranges, boats, air flow out to San Clemente Island (where the bulk of our training was conducted), and the actual training of the platoon snipers. It was an insane flurry of activity, and it felt a little like jumping out of a plane at 20,000 feet—exhilarating and terrifying.

Everyone had always complained that helicopter assets were next to impossible to come by for training purposes. I was determined that this was not going to be a problem for our course. I had strong relationships in the helicopter community; I figured I should be able to get us live resources, and from my perspective, this was essential. Simulators are fine, as far as they go, but anytime you can get your guys into a real helicopter, show them how to rig up their weapons in the door, give them live-fire training at some real target on the ocean's surface, both daytime and nighttime with night-vision gear and lasers, you're going to have really superior results. When Air Operations scheduling reported that there were no assets available for us, I made it happen anyway. I refused to compromise. Sometimes we'd have helo assets come pick us up and fly us out to San Clemente Island, and sometimes we'd take our guys on a quick plane ride and meet the assets out there. Whatever it took, I would not take no for an answer, and we always had the genuine article for our training exercises—*always*. The guys taking the course were stoked.

Something else that had always bugged me about operations that involved helo support was the lack of a clearly integrated, efficient communications protocol. With a handful of different procedural standards being thrown together into the mix of an op, sometimes it was almost like trying to work in metric and inches at the same time. That had to change. I developed a new system of standardized operations and communications procedures between pilots and snipers. In terms of long-term impact, this was my biggest accomplishment while running the Helo Support block. In an eval I received later, the chief warrant officer reviewing my work wrote:

> These streamlined procedures have greatly reduced communication clutter between pilots, HELO-borne pilots and ground assault forces, and have significantly contributed to safer and more dynamic target assaults.

It was a crazy task; we were inventing everything on the fly (literally!), but I loved the challenge. In about a month I had a complete curriculum developed and ready to teach. Now all I had to do was start teaching it.

Damn! I thought, *I've never* taught *before.*

I remembered my own sniper training and how there were teachers who could teach and others who couldn't. I was determined to be one of those who could, so I got myself put through Instructor Training School, a four-week program offered at Thirty-second Street by the San Diego Bay. I can't say enough good things about this school. All the public speaking and teaching I've done ever since has been tremendously influenced by the experience of those few weeks. They put us up in front of a classroom and videotaped us while we taught, then played the tapes back to us. There is nothing like watching yourself teach on videotape. We would sit there staring at ourselves on screen and hearing ourselves say "Uh" and "Um" and "Y'know" ten, twelve, fifteen times a minute. It was brutal. If you've never done this, I highly recommend it—and if you have any intention of teaching or being in any kind of leadership position, it is something you *have* to do.

Guys would watch in horror as they saw themselves cursing in the middle of their sentences, saying things they would have sworn they never said until they saw the hard evidence. Talk about shock and awe. It was embarrassing—or it would have been if the instructors had stopped and rubbed our noses in it. But they had a job to do, and they got on with it. They would count up all the *uhs, ums,* and *whatevers,* all the *shits* and *fucks* and *damns,* then run us through it again. They drummed all the verbal tics out of us.

They taught us how to work off a curriculum, how to structure a class, how to gauge how the different students were doing and support slower ones in picking up the pace without browbeating them. They taught us it was okay to pause and gather our thoughts without filling in the empty space with an "Um"; how to ask questions without shotgunning or drilling students to the point where we'd embarrass them or make them uncomfortable; how to encourage students to ask their own questions and get them thinking so they absorbed material instead of just parroting it back.

They taught us how to *teach.* In terms of practical life skills, it was one of the best schools I've ever experienced. Back when I was in sniper school, the only SEALs who were put through Instructor Training School were the BUD/S instructors. This was about to change. Today they put *all* their instructors through that program.

Once Eric and I had the Helo Support block up and running, Chief Gardner asked me to assist him with the redesign of Urban Sniper Training, which he had been putting together based in part on his experiences in Somalia. We did this right in San Diego in some old buildings that were owned by the Naval Training Center. Urban is all about trying to cover as many angles as you can and using cover effectively as you move through a village or city. We took our guys through our urban scenarios as two-man units, showing them how to set up urban hides—instead of going up on the rooftops where everyone expects you to be, find a basement where you can get eyes on your target—and how to disguise their hideout sites so that no one could see into them, but they could shoot out of them with a clear line of sight.

While I was at Sniper Cell, Chief Gardner led the charge on updating the basic optics we used community-wide and eventually SOCOM-wide, replacing our Leupold scopes with a new Nightforce scope. The U.S.-made Nightforce pieces were much better optics, and they had a feature I especially loved: Pull out a little knob and suddenly the reticles become illuminated, so that in low-light conditions or an urban nighttime environment we now had crosshairs lit with a faintly glowing red light.

I had to smile the first time I sighted through that tiny, precision-manufactured glowing reticle. There it was again: my red circle.

As we got these curricula up and running, we started pulling snipers aside while their platoons were going through their workups and running them through the Helo and Urban courses. Soon word started to spread and we heard that SEALs in the teams were saying to each other, "Man, you *have* to go through that Helo Support block and Urban block." Back in Afghanistan, when snipers from the other countries' Special Operations teams were asking Osman and me over to debrief them after Zhawar Kili, I'd befriended a very sharp Danish sniper named Henning, from the Danish Frogman Corps. Now Henning was running the sniper training in Denmark, and he flew over to the States, went through our advanced courses, then took what he'd learned and implemented it in Denmark.

We ran another block called Rural Training, where we brought guys who'd been through all the other training up to Bull Hill Ranch in Washington state, right up against the Canadian border, and took them out hunting whitetail deer and elk. Tracking Taliban hideouts out in Zhawar Kili with Osman had reminded me of deer hunting, and I now found the comparison worked both ways: Taking students out for some actual deer hunting was a great way to train them in the realities of combat.

Hunting deer is typically much harder than hunting people. People get lazy. Not so with wild animals; their instincts are honed to a razor's edge. Taking our snipers out into the wild, having them stalk a live animal, get it on target, and stop a beating heart for real—it was phenomenal training, and one of my favorite parts of everything we did. There were some bear up there, too. One of our instructors, Matt Hussian (who later took over my courses when I left Sniper Cell), grew up in Texas hunting deer with a .22 to put food on the table for his mom and little brother. Hussian would go out and disappear for a few days, and next thing you knew he'd come walking out of the woods dragging some big bear he'd taken down.

We would hunt in the mornings, hold classes in the afternoons, long-distance shooting courses and things like that, then hunt again in the evening. (Our students blew the minds of some local hunters, too, because we were nailing deer at distances like 600 to 800 yards.) At the five-star lodge where we stayed, we'd come in from hunting at ten in the morning to a full country breakfast spread. At night we'd come back from hunting and dress out our deer or whatever we'd caught, wash up, and then sit down to an amazing dinner.

Everyone in the cell was a pretty damn good cook, with the exception of my buddy Eric and one other guy, Bill. I'm not sure who started it, but soon we were taking turns making lunch for each other. Here we were, a bunch of trained killers, trying our level best to outdo each other in the kitchen and arguing over who had the best recipe. It would have made a great reality television show. We had fantastic kitchen action and great food, only instead of the usual boring cooking-show banter, our lunch hour was filled with X-rated stories that would make a hooker blush. (This show would have to go on cable.) We were as competitive as Navy SEALs can be, too. It didn't matter if we were trying to kick the shit out of each other on a swim, a training run, or in the effort to come up with the best recipes, we were always in it to come out on top. I never had a bad meal the whole time I was there.

Chief Gardner, our senior member and veteran of Somalia and the Gulf War, made one of the best tri-tip marinades on the West Coast.

Johnny, another instructor, was a great hunter and fisherman. He was the biggest, loudest, most boisterous character in Sniper Cell, but he was also one of the few guys in the cell not to have any combat experience, at least not at the time. Naturally we reminded him of this several times a day, and it drove him nuts. He had always been one step behind the action, in a few cases literally missing the boat when some serious action was about to go down. I think we would have left it alone, but it made him so crazy that we just had to give him massive hell for it. One day I put together a Rainbow Coalition Medal for him (completely spurious, of course), and we held a formal ceremony to award him this citation, which singled out "his innate cowardice and keen ability to avoid combat action at all costs." We had quite the laugh at his expense. To Johnny's credit, he proudly displayed the award up to the day he left the cell. He went on to become one of the most accomplished combat SEALs from the West Coast.

Johnny was famous for his hickory-bacon-wrapped venison with jalapeño peppers.

Bill was a very quiet guy and extremely professional in everything he did, a very solid sniper, instructor, and stand-up guy. However, Bill could not cook worth a damn, and we reminded him of this with great frequency. He tried to cobble together some sort of dish once, but whatever it was turned out to be such an abomination that he threw in the towel and never tried again.

Eric is as terrible as a cook as he is excellent as a friend. He has trouble microwaving popcorn without burning it. Even today, at his own back-yard cookouts, I have to man the grill for him.

And me? I became famous (within the cell, at least) for my homemade mango salsa; I even grew my own peppers. My salsa, combined with white albacore tuna salad sandwich, was very tasty. When it was my turn to cook I'd whip up my mango salsa, maybe grill some yellowtail and serve it with steamed rice and some sort of homemade sauce. If they gave med-als for cooking, I'm pretty sure a few of us would have been contenders.

Of course, they didn't give medals for cooking—but there was a promotion coming, and one I wasn't expecting. Every year, at the end of the year, they would traditionally give one person in the entire command a meritorious promotion. I knew very well that in this command, I was surrounded by superstars. Chief Gardner had put me in, though, and to my great surprise, at the end of 2002, after six months at Sniper Cell, I was selected for early advancement and meritoriously promoted to petty officer first class, E-6. It was one of the proudest moments of my navy career.

But not *the* proudest moment. That was still to come.

As much fun as we were having at Sniper Cell, there was one dark cloud over those months in late 2002. Shortly after I arrived, it became painfully clear that something was up with Senior Chief Seth Carver.

I knew Senior Chief Carver from sniper school in 2000 when he took over the course from his predecessor, Master Chief Jordan. Now, in addition to being master chief of the West Coast sniper school, he was also department head of the West Coast TRADET Sniper Cell. Chief Gardner was in charge of the day-to-day operation of the cell, but it was ultimately Seth's command, and it was he who interacted with the rest of TRADET and the navy command structure—and this was becoming a problem.

TRADET would hold morning meetings that Chief Carver attended, representing our cell. I started seeing him roll in barely five minutes before that day's meeting, his hair all messed up, and grab a scrap of paper out of the trash can to jot some hasty notes before dashing into the meeting. *What the hell's going on with Chief Carver?* I thought. *He's a mess!*

None of this behavior computed. I remembered Chief Carver as a 100 percent hardcore professional back at sniper school just a few years earlier. Now he seemed a complete train wreck. What was the deal?

A few of the guys pulled me aside and told me what was happening.

In the few years that had elapsed since I'd gone through Chief Carver's sniper course, he'd had a rough time of it. Some thorny family problems had spiraled out of control, and Chief Carver ended up in an acrimonious divorce contest that was tearing him apart. Soon he was drinking heavily and God knows what else.

By that winter it got so bad that something was going to blow. Chief Gardner was doing his best to keep this all under wraps, but Chief Carver was teetering close to the edge of being thrown out of the navy. Finally Chief Gardner got us all together and we staged a full-blown intervention, after which the navy put him through rehab—and he managed to pull it out and get himself back on track.

Chief Carver had nineteen years in at that point, one year from retirement. If he'd been in the regular navy and this whole drama had gone down, he would almost certainly have been tossed out with a "Sorry, hate to see ya go" and maybe some kind of rehab at the VA if he was lucky, but no retirement: screwed, nineteen years down the tubes. But with the help of his SEAL buddies he was able to put in one more functional year and salvage his retirement.

That's how it is with our community. SEALs take care of their own. If you had an attitude, if you were a persistent screwup who threatened to pull the standards down for the rest of us, they were merciless. However, if you were a good guy who had the misfortune to go through some adversity or other, they wouldn't just toss you aside. If you had earned some respect and proven yourself as a good operator, they would do everything they could to take care of you and keep your career alive. And that's exactly what we did with Chief Carver.

In the summer of 2003, after I'd been at TRADET for a little over a year, Chief Gardner came to Eric and me one day and told us that the guys who ran the basic SEAL sniper school had come to him for some help.

"They're completely redoing the course," he said, "and they need a few experienced guys to go through a pilot version with them, decide which parts of the curriculum to lock down. I thought we could loan you two out for a few months."

Eric and I both felt honored to be asked and psyched at the prospect. Rewriting the basic sniper school course, from the ground up? Talk about having an impact on the future of the U.S. military!

The year before, soon after I arrived at Sniper Cell, I'd been selected by WARCOM, the parent command for all the SEAL teams, to represent the entire SEAL community at Spec Ops Command in a review-and-selection process for the new SOPMOD kit's weapon upgrade. SOPMOD stands for Special Operations Peculiar Weapons Modification; the SOPMOD kit consists of everything that goes with the M-4, our basic assault rifle—flashlight, laser (visible and infrared), hand grips, scope, night sight, some ten items in all. I flew out to the East Coast, to Virginia and North Carolina, sat on a board with my corresponding representatives from the army and the air force, reviewed vendors' presentations (i.e., pitches), tested out all sorts of weapons and other equipment, and determined what equipment the next generation would be using. The SOPMOD kit we put together there was what all our Special Ops guys used in Iraq and are still using today in Afghanistan. It was a huge responsibility—and an incredible honor.

And now we would be having a similar input into the SEAL sniper course curriculum. This was the chance of a lifetime.

The only thing we were not entirely thrilled about was the location where this would be happening. At the time there were still two sniper schools, one for the West Coast and one for the East, and this pilot program was happening at the latter. The East coast ran their school at Camp Atterbury, a massive World War II–era training facility. The two of us would have to spend three months far from home smack in the middle of hot, humid, uninteresting Indiana.

Now, if you happen to be from Indiana (or Illinois or Ohio or anywhere around there), please don't be offended. I'm sure your homeland has much to offer and many wonderful features but we weren't from there, and it wasn't where we wanted to be, especially in the middle of the summer. Still, that's where the new course was being launched, so off to Indiana we went.

There's always been a slightly weird dynamic between the East Coast and West Coast teams; not outright hostile, and not exactly competitive. Maybe "suspicious" is the best word. There's a perception that on the West Coast it's all surfing and suntans, while on the East Coast they really work. If I were to drop in on an East Coast SEAL team they might say something like "Oh hey, what's up, Hollywood?" Coming into this situation as two guys from the West Coast, there as experts to weigh in on their East Coast course—this could have felt a little strained. But it didn't, not even slightly, and the main reason for that was Master Chief Manty, the East Coast division officer. A born leader, Master Chief Manty was extremely intelligent and a very solid guy; he brought us in and made us feel right at home. We also met and worked with the West Coast division leader, Senior Chief Nielson. Both had done their last tours with DEVGRU, and both were phenomenal to work with.

It's incredibly rewarding to be part of a team where you're valued for your experience and where you're able to genuinely influence change. That was the atmosphere we encountered out at Camp Atterbury. Eric and I showed up in Indiana in early August and worked our asses off for the next three months. Master Chief Manty had introduced some fascinating and powerful changes to the course (more about that shortly), and we both clicked with his ideas immediately. We worked like crazy to nail down that pilot course, redesigning things on the fly just as we had with the elements of the advanced courses at TRADET a year earlier. It was an all-out ninety-day sprint.

When the pilot course finished, we returned to our posts at TRADET, where we resumed teaching our training blocks, and life went back to normal—but not for long. Shortly after we got back from that stint in Indiana, Chief Gardner came to talk to Eric and me again.

"Okay, guys," he said, "here's what's happening. Senior Chief Nielson wants you down at the sniper school full-time to continue reworking the course."

Apparently Senior Chief Nielson had been selling this idea hard to our command. It had taken some finagling, because I was supposed to be halfway through a three-year commitment to TRADET, and it was pretty much the same for Eric. Yet he managed to swing it. Now that he'd sold it to TRADET, he had to sell it to us, too.

In fact, I'd been strongly thinking about trying to transfer over to the Naval Special Warfare Center (NSWC) to work as a BUD/S instructor. After a solid year and a half at Sniper Cell, I figured I'd probably had whatever impact I was going to have there, and BUD/S was an attractive job. I'd be working four days a week, with plenty of time off to be with my family. Our daughter, Madison, had been born that January, so I now had a wife and *two* kids, and they deserved a dad who was there at least a decent amount of time out of the week. On the other hand, I didn't see how I could say no. In effect, Senior Chief Nielson was offering us an opportunity to write a bit of military history. How could we resist?

Thus began another intense period of redesign, much like our first few months at TRADET except that now, as we picked up where we'd left off just weeks earlier, we were shaping the basic core training of all future SEAL snipers—shooting, stalking, the whole thing.

It was an incredibly creative time. We would roundtable our ideas, make decisions, and implement them the next day. We started going through everything we'd experienced when we went through the course ourselves and addressing whatever weak spots we'd seen. Before long we were completely overhauling the course, updating all the existing classes and adding some new ones.

For example, we began aggressively integrating technology into the training. At the time, sniper students were still being taught to survey their target terrain with binos and then sketch it out by hand—just like we'd been doing since Vietnam. Hey, when the last U.S. helicopter airlifted out after the fall of Saigon, I was not quite one year old! Wasn't it about time to get with the times? We stopped the hand sketches and started showing our guys how to shoot and crop digital photos with Nikon cameras. We taught them how to use DLT-3500 software (the military version of Photoshop) to adjust levels and enhance a photograph's readability and clarity, and how to annotate their field intelligence on a laptop, compress and encrypt the data, and send it via satellite back to the base. This turned into a mandatory two-week program called PIC (photographic intelligence course) that new students now went through just prior to starting the regular scout/sniper school.

We introduced ballistic software programs and focused on making sure these guys had a thorough understanding of external ballistics (what happens from the moment the bullet leaves the barrel until it hits the target). In the old course we were basically taught to call the wind and shoot well, period. Now we started digging into the subject and turning these guys into ballistics experts.

We used technology to get more exacting with our weapons as well. When I entered the course back in 2000, I had been stuck with a faulty sight that could have gotten me washed out, if I hadn't insisted on having the rifle tested. Too often, I had seen similar problems tripping up great shooters. Now we had the technology to solve these problems before they happened. We taught our students how to use a chronograph, a device that measures the muzzle velocity in fps (feet per second) of each specific rifle.

Let's say you have two identical .300 Win Mag bolt action rifles, both from the same manufacturer and even from the same manufacture batch.

One could still be as much as several hundred fps slower than the other. For that matter, there are even variances in individual lots of ammunition. Granted, these variances will typically affect accuracy only to a minute degree, but add them all together, especially when you're shooting at very long ranges, and it can make a critical difference. Perhaps we will eventually reach a level of manufacturing precision where that margin decreases to the point of insignificance. Perhaps. Right now, though, these individual variances are a fact of life, and we decided it was time to deal with it.

A chronograph can also help gauge the condition of the barrel. As I mentioned before, these rifles have a certain barrel life: Put your .300 Win Mag through a few thousand rounds and the barrel will start to go, which means your bullets will become troublingly inaccurate. We shot each student's rifle through a chronograph to find out quickly whether or not its barrel had gone beyond its useful life.

Eric transformed the KIM (keep in memory) class by pioneering a whole new way of teaching memorization skills. Rather than relying on pure rote memory, with its endless repetition, he employed some impressive techniques that involved linking the objects or numbers you wanted to memorize with a systematic sequence of objects or sounds in your mind.

Eric was a master at this. Just before teaching his first class of a new KIM session, he would look at the student roster and in five or ten minutes code all their data and store it into his memory. Then he'd walk into class, look at the assembled students, point to one at random and say, "Okay, you over there, what's your name?" The guy would tell him his name, and Eric would nod and say, "Right, your Social Security number is . . ." and rattle off the guy's social and phone number. Then he'd do the same thing with everyone else in the room. I watched him do this over and over, and it never failed to blow the minds of everyone in the class. Mind you, Eric didn't have any natural gift of photographic memory. This was *trained* memory, and he trained all our guys to have that ability, too.

For my part, I pushed hard on shifting the curriculum so that all our students would come out of the course knowing how to deploy independently, as solo operators. The way it was before, you'd have one student who happened to be a little better on the spotting scope, while his partner might be a little weak on ballistics but be a crack shot. To me, that was a recipe for breeding weakness into our graduates. It seemed to me we needed to make sure that every one of these guys we graduated had a complete command of every piece of the picture and could deploy by himself. Practically speaking, in most of the jobs they would be doing out in the field they *would* be called upon to act as lone gunmen. How could you graduate a competent sniper who didn't have a complete grasp of spotting?

I developed tests to make sure these guys *knew* ballistics—that if the shot went high, they knew in a split second how many minutes of angle they'd have to correct to have a center-mass, on-target hit the very next shot. I wanted to put each student through a whole range of scenarios where he would have to make these calculations himself and not rely on a spotter. The idea was to develop the complete package in every single sniper, with the full gamut of skills and no deficiencies. My December '04 eval, a year after Eric and I started working consistently with the course, referred to this:

> Devised a practical test that evaluates student wind calling and spotting abilities; simple and extremely effective.

Now we were graduating guys who were going out into the field and being absolutely deadly, whether in pairs or operating on their own.

We also introduced a new structural element that had the effect of raising the student-instructor relationship to a whole new level: We divided the class into pairs and assigned each pair to a specific instructor as their personal mentor. In effect, this created a kind of competition among the instructors. You didn't want one of your pairs to be the pair who failed the course, because that would reflect poorly on you as an instructor. Suddenly each of us had ownership of these specific students, which created an incentive for all of us to really get in there, spend some extra time with these guys, and make sure they knew what the hell they were doing. When I went through the course in 2000 we had some instructors who didn't give a shit if we passed or not, and at least one who was almost trying to get us to fail. Now we had built into the system an intrinsic motivation for every instructor to be working with students that they strongly wanted to succeed. In all my time there, I only had one student fail. All the others passed—because I'd be damned if *my* guys were going to wash out!

Our instructors were teaching better, and our students were learning better. The course standards got harder, if anything—but something fascinating happened: Instead of flunking higher numbers of students, we started *graduating* more. Before we redid the course, SEAL sniper school had an average attrition rate of about 30 percent. By the time we had gone through the bulk of our overhaul, it had plummeted to less than 5 percent.

In that same December eval, my commanding officer wrote:

> Primary instructor for Sniper COI [course of instruction]. Graduated highest percentage of qualified snipers in Naval Special Warfare Center (NSWC) history.

For the first few pilot courses, we had constantly changed things around and experimented, designing and implementing improvements and refinements on the fly. By the end of 2004, after we'd been doing this for about a year straight, we settled on a finalized curriculum that we then continued to teach without much change—but we also built into it the idea of continuous improvement from that point on. Today the course goes through an annual review to make sure it continues adapting to changes on the battlefield and to new developments in technology.

Earlier I said that intellectual capacity was the first trait we look for in a sniper, that physical ability, as important as it is, is only 10 percent of the game. Of all the changes we made in the course, the one that felt most significant to me and that I was proudest of was our system for *mental management*.

When we first encountered the concept of mental management it was being taught exclusively to instructors as a way to help us coach and teach more effectively. In essence, it was all about where we as instructors focused a student's attention.

Say you're doing batting practice with a kid and you notice he's standing with his knees buckled in, shoulders misaligned, hands spread wide apart on the bat. Your impulse might be to start telling the kid everything he's doing wrong. If you focus his attention on all these wrong things, though, what you're really doing is imprinting them into the poor kid's mind, with the result that they start becoming ingrained habits. If you say, "Hey, you're *flinching*. Every time the ball comes at you, you're *flinching! Stop flinching,*" then what the hell's that little kid thinking about? He's thinking about flinching!

If instead you say, "Hey, put your hands closer together, like this, and look: feet apart." Then you're showing him what to do rather than focusing his attention on what *not* to do.

A beginner typically starts out very focused on everything that's going on. He'll tend to absorb whatever is thrown at him. He is, in other words, highly programmable. The question is, as an instructor, what are you going to feed that rapt attention: bad habits or good habits?

This translated directly to instruction on the sniper course. In the old days instructors would bark at us for everything we did wrong. "Stop! You're putting your finger on the trigger wrong! When you pull the trigger, you're flinching! You're jerking the barrel! You're fucking up!" Suddenly we'd be thinking, *Holy shit, there're twenty things I'm doing wrong!* Instead, we learned we could give a student three *positive* commands, three things he could do to correct those errors, and now he'd be developing good habits from day 1.

I have to admit, I was not completely on board with the whole concept of mental management when I first bumped into it, and I had to overcome my own skepticism. Shortly after Eric and I checked into NSWC to start working with the basic sniper course, we and a handful of other instructors were brought out to Scottsdale, Arizona, for a one-week course taught by a champion marksman named Lanny Bassham, one of the pioneers of mental management. I was pretty dubious. Mental management? What, like some positive-thinking guru? Oh boy. "Great," I said to Eric, "when is Tony Robbins gonna come in and blow smoke up our asses?"

My attitude didn't last long. Bassham is such an amazing, down-to-earth guy—and what he taught us was nothing short of incredible.

"I wasn't good at sports," Lanny told us. "I was kind of this weak, goofy kid. My dad said, 'Hang in there, we're going to find something for you. Everyone has a talent.'"

Lanny found his talent when he got into competitive shooting. After college he joined the army and was assigned to their marksmanship unit, which is comprised of the best match shooters in the world. By the time he went to shoot in the 1972 Olympics in Munich at the age of twenty-five, Lanny was famous, the youngest world champion in the sport, and everyone expected him to shoot gold.

"I was on the bus with a bunch of competitors from different countries," he said. "I heard some Russians in the seat behind me talking about how much pressure I must be under, with the entire reputation of the United States on my shoulders, and how they were glad they weren't me—and they started getting in my head."

By the time he stepped off the bus, Lanny was completely rattled. "I shot the worst match of my life," he said. This being Lanny, the worst match of his life meant he came in second—but he was devastated. He came back to the States and visited with a handful of sports psychologists to see if he could understand what had happened to him, and they all said the same thing: "Hey, it's okay to be number two. Olympic silver is a great achievement, Lanny. You should be satisfied with that."

Lanny said, "Screw that. I don't think so!"

He spent the next few years interviewing dozens of gold-medal champions and recording all the specific traits he could identify in his interviews. They gave him an earful; you don't get to be a gold medalist without doing an awful lot of self-examination and studying best practices and key practice/performance tactics and strategies. Out of everything he heard, he found there were two specific traits they all shared in common.

First was *complete and total confidence*. Not arrogance or cockiness, but an absolute, unshakable confidence in their ability to perform regardless of adversity. Here's how Lanny described this trait:

> If I'm a champion tennis player, playing a championship game, it doesn't matter if the strings start popping off, or my favorite racket breaks in the middle of the game. I'll pick up a piece of plywood, tape it to a stick, and I'll still beat you on the tennis court.

It's an attitude that says, *I will win no matter what*. These people didn't just want to win, they *expected* to win. When they went out to compete, they had *already* won in their minds.

We've all seen people who have the talent and skill to win, but at the last minute something goes wrong: their favorite bat breaks, or a golf swing misses, or something in their environment distracts them—the way Lanny was psyched out by the Russians' taunts—and their game just unravels. It didn't unravel because the bat broke, Lanny was saying, or because the pitch went wild, or because of the other teams' taunts. It unraveled because *it was vulnerable.*

For champions that doesn't happen. Their game is invulnerable. That's the kind of confidence Lanny was talking about—and that was the kind of confidence we wanted to instill in our sniper course graduates.

The other common trait was that they all did some kind of *mental rehearsal*—closing their eyes and practicing their winning game in their heads, over and over again.

Lanny told us about a navy pilot he met in the seventies named Captain Jack Sands. Captain Sands was shot down while serving in Vietnam and spent seven years in a prison camp in Hanoi, confined in isolation with no physical activity. In order to preserve his sanity, he decided to practice his golf game. Of course, he couldn't physically play golf—but the $5' \times 5'$ cage he was in couldn't prevent him from creating a course in his mind. In his imagination he evoked an image of a beautiful country club course, placed himself there, and let himself experience it all in great detail. He saw himself dressed in golfing clothes, smelled the trees and grass, and felt himself making each stroke as he played. Every day, for seven years, Captain Sands played a full eighteen holes in his mind while his body sat in his cage. He played it perfectly, never hooking, slicing, or missing a single shot or putt. Hey, he was making it all up, right? Why not make it perfect?

Here was the amazing part. Before joining the navy, Captain Sands was an average weekend golfer, barely breaking 100. After he was finally released from his captivity and made his way home, he eventually got out onto a real grass-and-air golf course, and his first day out on the green he shot a stunning score of 74. He had taken more than twenty strokes off his game—without once laying a hand on a club. (By the way, some have claimed this story is an urban legend and there was no such person. It's no urban legend: Lanny sat next to the guy on a seven-hour flight to a world championship match they attended together.)

The point, said Lanny, was that your reality is defined by your mind, not your external environment. Jack Sands's golf game changed so dramatically because that was how he had programmed his brain to see it.

Lanny went on to tell us about a national shooting championship he participated in. As part of his preparation, he had spent time mentally rehearsing the moment when he would be kneeling there and suddenly realize, *Holy shit, I'm about to shoot a perfect score.* What so often happens in a high-stakes situation like this? The realization that you are on a roll knocks you off balance. It's that *Uh-oh, I'm so close, what if I screw up now?* moment that can come with asking someone out on a first date, taking your first driver's test, asking for a raise, or doing anything risky and important in life. We're not ready for this place of victory and don't know how to react now that we *are* here—so we choke. Not Lanny. He'd rehearsed that moment so many times that it was now as familiar to him as coming home.

"When I hit that moment in that championship," he said, "I recognized it like an old friend. Just like I'd done every time I'd rehearsed it, I took two deep breaths, said to myself, *I'm shooting the next three shots perfectly,* then took my time. *Boom. Boom. Boom.*"

He shot a perfect score.

Lanny returned to the Olympics in 1976, and this time, using his mental management system, he took the Olympic gold. Over the following years he dominated the field, winning twenty-two world individual and team titles and setting four world records on top of the gold medal he took in Montreal. Lanny incorporated what he'd learned into a whole mental management program, which he wrote about in his book, *With Winning in Mind.* His system became so popular that other coaches and athletes started having him come train them.

We hired Lanny to help us apply his methods to our sniper course—not just for the instructors but for the *students.* We also went and studied what the British and the army and Marine Corps were doing and consulted with coaches on a wide range of championship athletes, collating and discussing everything we learned. We ran a few pilot courses, experimenting in our live laboratory, trying out different techniques and seeing how each one affected the students. Eventually we developed an entire system of mental management and integrated it into our marksmanship class.

The first time I started teaching the mental management material as part of our course, some of the students were just as skeptical as I had been at first. I had a pair of Team One guys, Brant and Lieberman, as my personals. We issued Lanny's book to the whole class, but these two guys were *my* guys, so I also made them listen to Lanny's CDs. Every night, Brant and Lieberman would be out in the car listening to these CDs, and the other guys would ride them unmercifully. "Hey, you guys, you gonna go make out in the car again tonight?"

The two guys ignored them and kept listening. The others kept taunting, too—but not for long. When that class's first shooting test came up, a snaps and movers test, Brant and Lieberman both shot perfect 100s. We had *never* had a pair shoot perfects 100s. In the second part of the test, Brant shot another 100 and Lieberman shot a 95.

It was the highest score in U.S. Navy SEAL sniper course history.

Talk about people swallowing their pride: Suddenly all the other guys were begging to borrow Brant and Lieberman's CDs and burning copies for themselves. Before we knew it, the whole parking lot must have turned into a make-out session—because every night the parking lot was full of pairs of guys in their rental cars listening to those CDs.

* * * *

Despite all the progress we were making, throughout the year a darkening cloud hung over our work at the sniper course. It was a problem that made the issue with Chief Carver the year before seem like a summer vacation, and it kept getting worse.

Barely a month after Eric and I had checked into NSWC, Senior Chief Nielson pulled me into his office one day and said, "Brandon, I'm retiring."

I didn't know whether to be shocked or pissed. In truth, I was both. "What do you mean, retiring? Who's replacing you?"

He paused, then looked me square in the eye and said, "Master Chief Harvey Clayton."

Clayton had a reputation, and it wasn't good. I barely knew him, just enough to say hi as we passed in the halls, but it's a small community. I knew he had run the course many years earlier. I also knew he'd spent most of his time in the fleet navy and had really absorbed that culture—not usually a good mix with SEALs. What's more, while he was a very good match shooter, Harvey had never done any kind of operational tour.

He also had the reputation of being a real prick to work for.

"Harvey? Are you serious? I just signed up for a couple of years here, and now you're sticking me with *Harvey Clayton*?"

Senior Chief Nielson shook his head. He knew exactly what I was talking about. "Look, I'm sorry—but listen, you're the most experienced guy here, and I'm setting you up to be course manager."

That latter point was no small thing. To put it in perspective: The sniper school was taught by course instructors, typically E-5 and E-6 petty officers, who reported to the course manager, usually a chief, who managed the curriculum and ran the whole course. The course manager in turn reported to the division officer (Senior Chief Nielson, soon to be Master Chief Harvey Clayton), who ran interference between the course itself and the parent command. I was still an E-6, and teaching this course was my first LPO (leading petty officer) billet. By making me course manager, Senior Chief Nielson was saying he would be giving me an E-7 billet—in essence, setting me up to make chief petty officer the moment I became eligible.

Advancement to chief petty officer (E-7 and above) is a big deal in the navy. It's more than just a pay raise. Chief petty officers are considered a breed apart, a community within the community. And making chief after being in just over ten years? That would be a *seriously* big deal. A lot of guys go through their whole careers without making chief.

I understood what Senior Chief Nielson was saying and what it meant—but, man oh man, I did *not* want to work for this guy.

As it turned out, working for Harvey Clayton was not as bad as I'd expected. It was worse. Of all the leaders good and bad, all the bosses I've had throughout my entire career, from Petty Officer First Class Howard in boot camp to Chief Clarin in HS-6 to Commander Smith in Afghanistan, Master Chief Harvey Clayton was the worst.

Harvey was not much enamored with technology, or progress, or change. He was not interested in whatever improvements and new developments we wanted to bring to the course. He was too insecure to hear new ideas from anyone. If he had supported us the way Senior Chief Nielson had done, or even just stayed out of the way and let us do what we were there to do, he could have taken credit for all of it, and we would have been happy to let him do it. He couldn't get his own ego out of the way long enough to see that. Instead, he just wanted to rewind everything and have it all go back to the way it used to be. He also was quite clear that he was in charge; it was his show, and if he said no, that meant no.

One afternoon we were out at Coalinga teaching a course and one of our instructors, Arty, had pulled a group of students aside to give them some coaching on elevation. Arty was a very smart guy and especially sharp with technology; he could write code and had a reputation (deserved) as an Internet technology guru. Whenever Arty talked about anything technological, I made sure to listen.

"So, you adjusted your elevation when you shot this morning," he was explaining, "but now that you're shooting in the afternoon, you'll find that when you shoot at 200 yards your existing 200-yard adjustment is an inch too high. That's because it's a good 20 degrees warmer now than it was this morning, and as the temperature increases your chamber pressure also increases, which translates into higher muzzle velocity. So now you have to bring your elevation down an inch to compensate—"

"Stop!" Suddenly there was Harvey, striding out onto the range and interrupting Arty right in the middle of his class. "Stop, stop, *stop*! You guys, listen, you just trust your dope." (*Dope* meaning "data on personal equipment," the elevation data from a data book.) "Trust your dope. Don't start changing your settings and messing everything around. Trust your dope!"

I felt the blood drain from my face. Everything Arty was saying was spot-on accurate, of course. Even if it hadn't been, though, the last thing you want to do is start contradicting your instructor in front of the students. If one of your instructors does screw up, you pull him aside afterward and talk to him in private, but *never* in front of the students. Do that and everybody loses credibility.

As soon as I could I pulled Harvey aside and said, "Harvey, you're killing me here. You can't do things like this to my instructors." This wasn't the first time he'd done this; he was becoming infamous for it. The students weren't stupid, between Harvey and Arty, they could clearly see which one knew what he was talking about. Harvey's behavior was undermining the whole concept of respect for leadership—not only privately, among the instructors, but also among the students.

At the end of Arty's course we had everyone in the class fill out critiques, as we did with every course. The students absolutely hammered

Harvey. They had their certificates at this point, so they must have figured they had nothing to lose, and they just told the truth. "Unprofessional," said some of the critiques. "Hurting credibility." "A clear weak point." "You need to know," wrote one, "that Master Chief Clayton is an idiot."

When Harvey read the critiques he was furious and declared he would order the students to redo them.

"I'm sorry, Master Chief," I said, "but it doesn't work that way. You can't do that."

He started getting drunk after hours and picking on students. "Hey, you," he'd say, "Mister So-and-So, get over here. I don't like you. You can't shoot for shit." He would be truly mean to these guys. No matter what authority you have, you just don't treat people that way. I can be hard on my own people, but I'm always careful to be fair. Harvey didn't seem to give a damn about being fair.

I had recently gotten my private pilot's license. Senior Chief Nielson had let me take enough time off to do the fourteen-week course, which I started in April and finished by mid-July. The drive from San Diego up to Coalinga was about seven hours, but I could fly there in two, and I would sometimes round up a group of students, fly them up there, and take them out for steaks at a nearby ranch that had its own private runway.

Harvey hated it. He hated the fact that I flew. I think he hated my having any kind of autonomy.

Soon everyone was coming to me, complaining about the latest thing Harvey had done. It was a nightmare, and I didn't know what any of us could do about it. I started worrying that the course's reputation would suffer, and if that started happening, it could unravel everything we were working so hard to accomplish.

One Friday toward the end of 2004, we had a staff meeting to go over a course we were starting the following Monday and weigh whether we were going to approach the subject using minutes of angle, mil dots, or exactly what. As so often happens with a discussion like this, the best idea came to the surface, and we all agreed to do it a certain way. That weekend I spent some hours prepping the course, redoing it and getting all the materials together so I'd be ready to go. On Monday morning, about an hour before the class was scheduled to start, Chris, one of our chiefs, came over to talk to me with a hangdog expression on his face. *Uh-oh,* I thought, *what is it now?*

"Hey, Brandon," said Chris, "Harvey wants you to teach it the other way."

What? I stared at Chief Chris in disbelief.

"Yeah," he said. "He told me to come tell you. He wants it taught the other way."

I lost it. "No fucking way," I said. "You go back and tell him to get his ass in here right now." As a chief, Chris outranked me (as did Arty, who was also a chief), but he knew I was course manager and this was my terrain. This was my course Harvey was dicking around with.

A few minutes later Harvey showed up, and I reamed him out, right in front of the other instructors.

"You son of a bitch," I said. "I'll tell you what, Harvey, if we were on a pirate ship at sea right now I would shoot you in the back, toss your sorry ass over the side, and declare mutiny."

I know, I know: This is not the recommended manner for addressing one's superior officer. I value respect as much as any SEAL, and I don't lose my cool very often. This was one of those rare moments, and master chief or no, I tore him a new one.

He tucked his tail between his legs and left, and I taught the course the way we'd agreed to teach it the Friday before. I knew this was the beginning of the end, though. For close to a year I'd done my best to be loyal to the guy and work things out, and the situation had gone from bad to worse. Morale on the course was in the can, and the place was starting to feel like it was going to fall apart if something drastic didn't happen, and happen soon.

At the time, we had instructors who were newly minted chiefs with us while waiting to ship out to leadership posts: Arty (the instructor Harvey had so boorishly upstaged), Joe, and Chris. I went to all three of them and said, "Guys, something has to be done about Harvey. You guys are the chiefs. You've got to take some kind of action!"

All three understood that while I was in charge of the course, my hands were tied. They all outranked me, and any initiative here would have to come from one or all of them. Understandably, though, all three were extremely reluctant to take any action. In the military, there is hardly anything you can do to screw up your reputation worse than going up the chain of command to complain about a superior. Whether you're talking army, air force, marines, or navy, I don't care what division or what force, ratting on your superior officer is tantamount to taking your life in your hands, reputationally and professionally speaking. In a situation like this, it's far easier and safer to take the path of least resistance: Wait it out. Suck it up. Grin and bear it. But we'd been sucking, grinning, and bearing for close to a year.

It was Chief Chris who finally decided to do something. He went to our command's master chief and complained about Harvey.

I don't know exactly how he did it, and I don't know exactly what he said, but whatever he did, it didn't work. Nothing happened to Harvey—and Chief Chris got demoted. In the pecking order of chiefs in our command, he went from the number two spot to the last in line, and they pulled him from the course. You don't recover from something like that. From this point on, Chris effectively had no hope of ever making master chief. It was a career-destroying move.

Not surprisingly, Arty and Joe, the two remaining chiefs, were now completely intimidated, and they certainly weren't going to make any moves against Harvey. Not *ever*.

So it was up to me.

I knew it could be the end of my career in the navy—the unfortunate fate of Chief Chris had made that abundantly clear—but we couldn't keep operating like this. Harvey was screwing up the course. You go out into the jungle and mess with a lion cub, and you will hear about it from the lioness. The sniper course was my cub, and as long as there was breath in my body I was not going to let anyone compromise the integrity of what we had all worked so hard to build. Not even if it meant my career.

I started carefully documenting all his bad behavior, every incident I could think of, from his contradicting Arty in front of the class to the students' terrible critiques to his arbitrary changes in the course to the student complaints about his drinking and verbal abusiveness—everything. I didn't editorialize, comment, or draw conclusions. Just put down the facts in black and white. I gathered up my sheaf of documents and proceeded over to the office of Harvey's boss, a warrant officer named Len Marco, sat down with him, and spelled out the entire situation.

"This is what's happening with Harvey," I said, "and it's a problem. You can fire me from the course and send me anywhere you want me to go. I would rather stay. But someone needs to shed some light on the damage this guy is doing."

I took a deep breath and waited to see what would happen. Had I just committed career suicide?

Len was silent for a few moments, looking at the papers I'd put in front of him as I spelled out the whole story. Then he looked up at me. "Come with me. We need to go talk to Master Chief Jordan."

Master Chief Jordan wasn't just the next higher-up on the navy food chain; he was the master chief in charge of the entire Naval Special Warfare Center. As it happened, he was also the very same Master Chief Jordan who'd been running the sniper course when I enrolled in it two and a half years earlier, before Chief Carver took over. I took this as a good sign: At least he knew me well enough to know that I wasn't some weenie jerk-off making trouble just because I had a bad attitude.

On the other hand, he was also the very same master chief who had shit-canned Chief Chris when *he* told the same story I was about to tell. I took this as a bad sign.

A very bad sign.

But what could I do? There was no backing out now. Besides, I wouldn't have backed out if I could. For the course, for the guys, and for myself, this was the right thing to do.

Len started the meeting by explaining in the broadest terms why we were there and then turned it over to me. I went through what I had to say, detailing the worst of Harvey's offenses, and Len, to his considerable credit, backed me up. Chief Jordan listened without comment, then nodded slightly and said, "We'll look into this."

We were dismissed.

The next day Harvey started packing. Orders had come down. Apparently there was something of an emergency situation developing in Bahrain where they needed a master chief. Harvey had been assigned to station there unaccompanied for a year.

Instead, he put in for his retirement papers. Within a few weeks Harvey was gone—and suddenly I was not only running the course but also serving in the role of division officer, at least until another interim division officer could be assigned.

In an evaluation Harvey had written up not long before he left, he had said of me, "Promote ahead of his peers!" Ironically, his advice was acted on—after he was gone. In February 2005, just weeks after Harvey left, I made chief petty officer my first time up.

With Harvey gone and our new curriculum in place, the sniper course started soaring, and we were graduating guys who were absolutely deadly.

Suddenly our graduates were in big demand in the field, and I was getting phone calls from other branches of the service. "Major So-and-So wants to come out and observe your course." Our guys were gaining such a reputation in combat overseas that these officers were saying, "What are these guys doing that we're not doing—and how can we change our course so we start getting our guys to this level?" We were happy to give them all the help we could.

Everything I'd experienced in the navy up to this point, from those early days as an aircrew search-and-rescue swimmer to BUD/S and STT through deployment on the USS *Cole*, in the Gulf, and in Afghanistan, all of it had gone into our work in revamping and refining this sniper course, and we were now turning out some of the most decorated snipers in the world.

There is no better example of this than Chris Kyle.

Like Matt Hussian, Chris is a Texan who had been shooting since he was a kid, and like a lot of guys who grew up hunting, he knew how to stalk. He was also a champion saddle-bronc rider; in fact, the first time he applied to the navy he was flat-out rejected because of pins in his arm, the result of a serious accident he'd had while in the rodeo ring. The navy later relented and actually sought him out for recruitment. Good thing for our side, as it turned out.

Chris was not one of my personals—Eric had him as his student. He immediately made a big impression on all the staff and obviously had great potential, although it didn't jump out and bite you at first. Chris is a classic example of a Spec Ops guy: a book you definitely do not want to judge by its cover. A quiet guy, he is unassuming, mild-mannered, and soft-spoken— as long as you don't get him riled. Walk past Chris Kyle on the street and you would not have the faintest sense that you'd just strolled by the deadliest marksman in U.S. military history, with more than 150 confirmed kills.

Like me, when it came time for assignment to the teams, Chris had chosen SEAL Team Three as his top pick, and gotten it, too. For his first deployment, he was one of the SEALs on the ground in Iraq with the first wave of American troops at the commencement of Operation Iraqi Freedom in March 2003. While he was there, Chris saw some serious action; it was a helluva place to have your first deployment.

Upon rotating back home, one of the first things Chris did was to go through our sniper course. After graduating, he shipped right back out to Iraq, where he fought in the Second Battle for Fallujah, which turned out to be the biggest and bloodiest engagement in the entire Iraq war. Since the largely unsuccessful First Battle for Fallujah seven months earlier, the place had been heavily fortified, and we had big army units going in with small teams of our snipers attached to help give them the edge they needed. Our snipers would sneak in there, see enemy insurgents (sometimes snipers themselves) slipping out to try and ambush our guys, and just drop them in their tracks. It was no contest.

Our guys were not only expert shots, they also knew how to think strategically and tactically, and they came up with all kinds of creative solutions on the battlefield. For example, they would stage an IED (improvised explosive device) to flush out the enemy. They would take some beat-up vehicle they'd captured in a previous op, rig it up with explosives, drive it into the city, and blow it, simulating that it had been hit by an IED. Meanwhile, they would take cover and wait. All these enemy forces would start coming out of the woodwork, shooting off guns and celebrating, "Aha, we got the Americans!" and the snipers would pick them all off like proverbial goldfish in a bowl. You didn't hear about this on the news, but they did it over and over, throughout the city.

Chris was in the middle of all this. In his first deployment he racked up close to 100 kills, 40 of them in the Second Battle for Fallujah alone. He was shot twice, in six separate IED explosions, and received multiple frag wounds from RPGs and other explosives.

The insurgents had a sniper there from the Iraqi Olympic shooting team, who was packing an English-made Accuracy International, about $10,000 worth of weapon. This guy was not messing around. Neither were Chris and our other snipers. They shot the guy and took his rifle. Al Qaeda put a bounty on Chris's head—but nobody ever collected. You can read about Chris's exploits in his book, *American Sniper: The Autobiography of the Most Lethal Sniper in U.S. Military History.*

As remarkable as he is, Chris Kyle is quick to point out that he was not unique on that battlefield. There was a whole lineup of SEAL snipers in Iraq at the time who were cutting a wide swathe through the hotbeds of insurgency, providing clear zones for our marines and army forces to operate without being picked off by enemy snipers themselves or being ambushed by IEDs.

It's easy to have an image of these guys as trained killers—mean, ruthless men who think nothing of ending other people's lives. Maybe even violent and bloodthirsty. The reality is quite different.

Think about the various ways we have gone about winning wars in the past. Think about American planes firebombing Tokyo and Dresden during World War II, which burned to death hundreds of thousands of civilians. And that's an awfully painful way to go. Or consider what it's like to take out a high-value target by leveling the city block where he's located at the moment with a targeted JDAM strike. Imagine being someone he's located in that building, slowly crushed to death under the rubble.

Now think about a trained Navy SEAL sniper like Chris, waiting, sighting, and finally squeezing the trigger of his .300 Win Mag. The supersonic round reaches its destination in less than a second—the man is gone before the rifle's report reaches his ears.

The reality is that the death that comes with the sniper's strike is typically clean, painless, and as humane as death can be. A cleaner death, if we're really going to be honest with ourselves, than most of us will experience when we come to the end of our own lives. The sniper is like a highly skilled surgeon, practicing his craft on the battlefield. Make no mistake: War is about killing other human beings, taking out the enemy before he takes us out, stopping the spread of further aggression by stopping those who would perpetuate that aggression. However, if the goal is to prosecute the war in order to achieve the peace, and to do so as fast and as effectively as possible, and with the least collateral damage, then warriors like Chris Kyle and our other brothers-in-arms are heroes in the best sense.

One of our better students was Marcus Luttrell, another Texan and author of *Lone Survivor*, his account of Operation Redwing in Afghanistan. I mentored both Marcus and his twin brother, Morgan, who came through the course about half a year before Marcus did.

Marcus and Chris Kyle are actually good friends as well as fellow Texans—and they couldn't be more different. Where Chris blends in and wears his strength inconspicuously, Marcus is the dictionary definition of "conspicuous"—a big strapping hunk of a guy, colorful, rambunctious, entertaining as hell, and larger than life in every way. If Chris Kyle and Marcus Luttrell had been alive in the Old West, Chris would have been the quiet one in the corner that you didn't notice (at least, not until the gunplay started). Marcus would have been the gunslinger they ended up making the subject of Hollywood films.

Unfortunately, for a sniper, *conspicuous* is not necessarily an asset. Like Morgan, Marcus was a first-rate SEAL, but he did not pass through our sniper course without incident. While he was a crack shot, he had a tough time meeting the course minimum requirements for stalking, where we were teaching the students how to use camouflage, the terrain, and stealth skills to sneak up to an enemy position.

I vividly remember the first practice stalk we did with Marcus's class. We were giving them a bunch of practice outings first so they could get the lay of the land and get their stalking feet under them. Once we'd gone through these we would start a series of ten graded stalks, on which the students had to score an 80 or above—meaning you could miss a maximum of two out of the ten, or you were out of the course.

On these practice stalks we gave the students time to clip off bits and pieces of natural vegetation to put all over their ghillie suits and hats so they would be fully camouflaged, and then hide themselves, at which point we would scan the field to judge how well they were hidden, in other words, whether or not we could detect them. We got the sign that everyone was fully vegged up and hidden, I put my binos to my eyes and started scanning— and right away found myself staring at this odd-looking ice plant.

As I watched, that odd-looking ice-plant monster got to its feet and stood up.

Here was the problem: Ice plant doesn't grow six feet tall, and it also doesn't suddenly haul itself up to a standing position. Sure enough, it was Marcus, covered with wilting scraps of vegetation. He looked like an ice-plant Sasquatch.

"Oh, man," I remember saying more than once during the course of those practice stalks, "it's Marcus again."

Marcus and his shooting partner were one of my two pairs in that course, and I often took them out on the course after hours, quizzing them and working with them, doing whatever I could to make sure they were getting this down. This was exactly why we'd set up this mentor system: so that the instructors would take ownership of their pairs and have a vested interest in their success.

As much as we all put into it, though, it wasn't enough: Marcus didn't make it. He was crushed, and so were we; he was an excellent shooter and as solid a SEAL as they come, and we all badly wanted to pass him— but we hadn't succeeded in getting him through that concealment and stalking phase.

So what did he do? He turned right around and went through the course a second time, the whole damn three months of it. This is a guy who does not know the meaning of the word "quit."

The second time through the course, Marcus was partnered with a BUD/S friend of his named Tej, who was even bigger (and even louder) than Marcus. Easily the biggest guys in the class, these two were so outrageous and boisterous I nearly had to separate them. At the same time, they kept that class in line. We had one student who was a career complainer, and more than one who tried to give us a hard time—but whenever someone started piping up or getting out of line, Tej and Marcus would shut them down. They were rowdy, hilarious, impossible, and two of the most standup guys we'd ever had.

Once again, Marcus and his partner were my personals, and once again, I was determined to see him succeed. Of course, we wanted every one of our students to succeed, but Marcus was so damn likable and such a good guy that we *really* wanted him to make it. He knew he'd have to get through on his own merits, but I'd be damned if I wasn't going to do everything I could to make sure that happened.

When it came to the stalking portion he started having a rough time again—but at a certain point it just clicked for him, and from then on he did really well. This time around, he graduated with flying colors. I don't know who was happier about it, Marcus or us. I'd say we were all pretty fired up.

Just as he was graduating, Marcus approached me to ask a favor. "Hey," he said, "I'm about to deploy to Afghanistan, but we've got this big family event happening in Texas. Is there any way I could not do that FTX?"

Normally after graduating the course you could take up to thirty days' leave to spend time with your family, but Marcus had already sacrificed his leave time to get himself placed immediately into the sniper course for his second go at it. Now the only way he could see his family before deploying would be if we let him out of the FTX, or final training exercise, which would normally add about one more week's time on the course.

The FTX was a graded mission, so theoretically it was mandatory, but hell, Marcus had clearly made it through at that point, so I worked it out for him to skip it and have that week with his family.

The week after that family event he was on a plane to Afghanistan.

What happened next is the subject of his book. Marcus and three teammates—Matt Axelson (Morgan Luttrell's best friend), Danny Dietz, and Michael Murphy—went out on a reconnaissance mission in northern Afghanistan, not far from the area where we had run so many missions with ECHO platoon. The mission went bad, and soon the four were scrambling across the brutal Afghan terrain under heavy fire. Marcus watched as his teammate and brother's best friend died in his arms. Murphy and Dietz were killed, too, as were all sixteen of the men (eight SEALs and eight Army Airborne "Night Stalkers") dispatched as a QRF to rescue Marcus's team. It was the worst U.S. loss of life in a single event in Afghanistan—a grisly record of tragedy that was broken only six years later when a Chinook helo was shot down in August 2011.

We were devastated when we heard the news. I'd lost other friends before, but this was the worst. I'd gotten close to all those guys during the course and had especially come to know Marcus and Axelson really well. As far as we knew, Marcus had died, too. That was what almost everyone believed (although Morgan insisted that he *knew* his twin brother was still alive). It wasn't until five days later that we learned Marcus had miraculously pulled through.

Badly wounded and with all his buddies gone, this big Texan who had failed stalk after stalk when he first landed in our course had managed to walk and crawl undetected through some 7 miles of hostile terrain, somehow evading capture and killing 6 more Taliban fighters along the way, until he made it to an Afghan village that shielded him until he could be rescued.

Marcus was the only one out of the entire operation who made it home alive.

The next time I saw Marcus was more than a year later, in the late summer of 2006, on the deck of the USS *Midway* off San Diego where the navy was holding a big fund-raiser. He and his coauthor, Patrick Robinson, had just finished writing *Lone Survivor*, although it would not come out on the bookstands until the following summer. I spotted him at the event and went over to talk with him.

"Hey, Marcus," I said.

"Hey, Brandon," he replied.

We embraced each other, then quickly caught each other up on what was going on in our lives. There was quite a crowd around us, and we both knew we wouldn't have more than a minute to talk. He grabbed me by both shoulders and said, "Brandon, listen. You need to know, that stalking course? That saved my life. If you hadn't pounded that training into me, I wouldn't be standing here today."

His voice choked, and I saw tears in his eyes. I was getting pretty emotional myself.

"You saved my life, man," he repeated, "and I want you to know that, and I want to thank you for it."

I thought about all he had been through in Afghanistan, watching his friends die one by one, the long days and longer nights hidden away in that Afghan village while the Taliban hunted for him, not knowing whether he would make it out alive. I flashed on all the time we'd spent in the course, the hours we put in together long after the day's studies were officially over, shaping him into a first-class stalker. I thought about the hours Eric and I and the rest of us had put in crafting and refining that course, the strain on our families while we were away, even the long months of enduring the reign of Harvey Clayton . . . and knew that this made it all way, way past worthwhile.

That was my proudest moment as a SEAL.

CONCLUSION

SEPTEMBER 2006, WHEREABOUTS UNKNOWN. Even now, I couldn't tell you the exact day. All I know is this: I had gone into this building with an assault team and now found myself standing alone in what looked like an abandoned warehouse, a dimly-lit clear-span space about the size of an average high school gymnasium. And I was *in* it, deep. Whoever the anonymous characters were who occupied this place, I knew their mission was to break me down to my constituent parts. I was pretty sure I would be more useful to them alive than dead. But you can never be completely sure about these things.

In the faint light I began surveying my surroundings.

The walls were painted black, lending an even darker aspect to the intimidating pall of my new digs. Loud rock music blared from oversized speakers, adding to the sense of confusion and disorientation. At my feet I could make out a large red circle painted crudely onto the floor, as if I were standing in the middle of a target where I was the bull's-eye. I smiled briefly. *My old friend, the red circle.* Maybe this wasn't a simile or metaphor. Maybe this *was* a target. Maybe I *was* the bull's-eye. All I knew was that a world of hurt was coming my way, and I'd be damned if I was going to give ground. They could attack me, hurt me, even try their level best to kill me, but I wasn't about to cave in or back down.

I was going to hold this damned red circle no matter what came at me.

As I stood there thinking these thoughts, there was motion behind me and a hood suddenly came down over my head and I was pitched into blackness. Didn't hear him coming. Whoever this sonofabitch was, he had already impressed me. Of course, with those speakers filling the room with their godawful din it wasn't all *that* hard to stay under the sound radar. Still, my hearing is pretty damn good—and I hadn't heard a thing.

Whatever came next, it was going to be serious. The people who brought me here were doing everything they could to throw me off balance. I knew they expected me to panic, but I would not be giving them that satisfaction—or that advantage. My SEAL training taught me to prepare for situations and moves like this. I had already rehearsed a range of worst-case scenarios in my head and was ready for whatever they might throw at me.

Let the punishment begin.

Nothing happened.

I continued standing there, blinded inside my hood, reflexes ready, senses as acute as I could muster. My ears strained to hear past the distorted cacophony of hyperamplified rock; my nostrils flared to pick up any scent I could through the thick cloth. Who was out there beyond the confines of this dark hood? Hostiles, clearly. How many? Empty seconds ticked by. Despite myself, I started to relax ever so slightly—and the instant I did so my unsensed enemy yanked the hood off my head and punched me square in the face, hard.

My head snapped back, and I was temporarily blinded by the brilliant light that invariably follows a strong blow to the head. My training kicked in faster than any conscious thought process. My body had been trained to stand in a way that protects posture and ensures a balanced stance, and—to their surprise, I hoped—I did not lose my balance. Instead my head jerked back upright and my vision returned, and I instantly took in my situation: There was one immediate threat in front of me (the guy who had just clocked me in the face) and two more at a slight distance, coming at me from the far end of the room, both armed.

I saw that my quick recovery from his frontal blow had caught Target Number One by surprise, slowing his reaction time by the barest fraction of a second, and I used that fractional gap to my immediate advantage. Instantly I slammed the guy, delivering a quick muzzle strike with my M-4 that put him down on the floor, prying open my advantage another two seconds—two seconds I was fully prepared to use with lethal finality. I snapped my rifle into position and unloaded two rounds to his head. Target One down and out.

Now Target Two and Target Three were running at me full tilt, 10 feet and closing fast. No time to think. I shot the closest one first, two rounds to the head—but as I squeezed the trigger to put a third round into him, something screwed up. It was the kind of glitch you hope never happens, but you know that if it does, it will be at the worst possible moment: My M-4 malfunctioned.

No time to curse, not even time to think.

In situations like this you can't afford to stop and deal with the malfunction. The M-4 was already gone from my mind as my fingers let go of it, my focus shifting single-mindedly to Target Three. The M-4 was slung in a way that caused it to swing down and to the left, out of the way of my secondary weapon, a Glock 17 holstered at my right side. As the rifle dropped and swung, my right hand had already drawn the pistol. I pumped four rounds into the last guy coming at me, and he, too, went down. As he fell he got off one shot, and it clipped my right forearm. It barely registered. My total focus was on Targets Two and Three, making sure they were down— all the way down. They were.

Then there was nothing but stillness around me and the sound of hard, slow panting, a sound I realized was coming from me. I was hit but still standing. Breathing hard with sweat dripping down my face, I felt the salt sting in my eyes. I wiped my forehead, looked down—and smiled.

I'd held my red circle.

After another few moments the three men I'd taken down began to stir. Gradually they got back to their feet. They were, obviously, not dead. We'd been using simulated ammunition. Still, while not lethal, these were high-velocity rounds. When one of these things hits you, you're hit, and you know it. These guys would be sore for a while.

It was good to have completed my first scenario, especially good that I'd acquitted myself well. The scenarios to follow would get increasingly more difficult, designed to induce the maximum amount of stress.

I was no longer in the U.S. Navy SEALs. I was on my own, in a facility somewhere in or around D.C. participating in a one-week refresher course in close-quarters battle. Soon I would be driving the streets of Iraq, providing mission support for an intelligence unit, part of an outfit that we referred to only as the Client. Whatever I might be called upon to do there, whoever I'd be working with and whatever situations, operations, or emergencies I might face, I knew one thing: I would stand my ground and hold whatever red circle I was given to hold.

I should back up a little.

After running the SEAL sniper course for two and a half years, I finally decided in mid-2006 to leave the service and go into the private sector. The entrepreneurial impulse was as much in my blood as aviation, maybe more so, and I decided to follow a dream that had been bubbling up throughout my SEAL years: To create a private facility that would help us train the finest fighting forces anywhere on earth, whether military combat units, Special Ops teams, or civilian law enforcement personnel. I knew from experience that all of the above suffered from a perennial shortage of excellent training grounds, and I wanted to do something about it.

I needed two things. The first was a certain kind of experience. In my thirteen years of service I'd seen the military from almost every angle—but I had no experience of the world of private contractors. The name Blackwater had made this kind of shadow forces infamous, yet they were a far more crucial element in the big picture than most civilians realized. There are a handful of intelligence agencies in the United States who help to keep us safe while we sleep, and most of them require the skills of highly trained Special Operations personnel for their work. Since they don't have the capacity to produce their own operators, these personnel are almost without exception privately contracted. I needed to know what that world was like.

The second thing was, frankly, finances. As I contemplated my options, I happened to run into a good friend who was doing some work for an OGA (other governmental agency) and told me what he was earning for relatively short-term deployments overseas. I calculated that in a fairly short time, I could go a long way toward bankrolling at least the early phases of my entrepreneurial venture.

A buddy of mine happened to work in that same intelligence network coordinating job applications. My application got fast-tracked, and by the time I officially left the service I already had a package approved and a deployment date set with the Client.

I wasn't about to jump without a backup chute.

Gabriele was nearing the end of her third pregnancy when I officially left the navy on July 6, 2006. Our second son, Tyler, was born the last day of August. By September I was standing in an abandoned warehouse somewhere in the D.C. area, holding on to my red circle and putting three guys onto the floor.

That fall I deployed to Iraq, where I provided mission support services for the Client. While I was there I rewrote the entire security plan for one of their remote sites in Iraq (it was a joke when I got there, two pages long and useless) and developed a complete training program for our Kurdish Peshmerga security force (who'd had basically no training up to that point). I also ran missions that ranged from the mundane to the bizarre, including delivering attaché cases full of American cash to intel assets (in case you've ever wondered how much $1.5 million in cash weighs, I can tell you: a lot), grabbing double-agent informers in the middle of the night and hauling them in for questioning, arranging and coordinating clandestine meeting points with locals-turned-intel-assets, driving like hell through the city losing Iranian tails, and anything you might imagine from everything you've seen in the movies. I was never ambushed at any of our checkpoints or meeting spots, but it was known to happen. One group got into a firefight on the road to Kirkuk and had to blast their way through. At another checkpoint, a few of our guys realized too late that the officials on hand were not acting as friendly as they should have been; they got lit up by machine-gun fire and never made it out of there.

There was an incident late in 2006 where several key Iranian diplomats were caught spying in Baghdad and several high-level assets suddenly had to be smuggled into Iraq. I was in the middle of that mess, driving a vehicle through the city with stolen Iraqi plates and trying to calm a case officer who was bawling her eyes out because our assets had suddenly changed our rendezvous point and her commander was screaming at her on a cell phone. (FUBAR.) I had to pull the car over in the middle of the op, turn around in my seat, and yell into her face to break through and keep the op moving. Training, training. We got the assets and made it out alive. (You don't want to know who they were or what intelligence we got from them.)

By the end of 2007 I was out of Iraq and back in the States, and with the help of my investors I had purchased the raw land for the site of my new facility: about a thousand acres of California desert out in Imperial County—and where? Right across the Salton Sea from my old friend Niland, of course. Where else? I called the facility Wind Zero, a precision shooting term that refers to the practice of precisely tuning your weapon to a point of perfect balance and neutrality.

It took a good four years to raise the full financing and secure the zoning and other legal go-aheads to get Wind Zero under way. There was a shocking amount of resistance to the plan from some local environmentalists and other forces resistant to change (which I had a hard time not thinking of as incarnations of the spirit of Harvey Clayton). By that time, though, we had the support of the local law enforcement community, the fire department, public safety personnel, and everyone else in the community who had a grip on common sense. Besides, it wouldn't matter if it took twice that many years. Whatever red circle I'm given to hold, I'll stand my ground.

My dad did well for himself eventually. Not long after I joined the navy he started another company doing spec homes and custom housing, bought some land on the outskirts of Jackson Hole along the Idaho-Wyoming border and developed it, then sank his profits into properties that provided him his retirement. He built a house down in Cabo San Lucas, where he lives in the winter, fishing off the beach and playing drums in a local band. He's sixty-two now and still plays music every day—and he has a 42-foot boat. Our relationship still has that bit of edginess to it. But he's my dad.

My mom and I are still very close, and I see her often. A good number of the memories from the first chapter of this book come from her. To this day my parents still talk regularly, and if you asked either of them, I think they would describe themselves as good friends.

I can say much the same for Gabriele and me. Despite our best efforts, our marriage did not survive the intensity and long separations of the SEAL years; in 2009 we separated, and she and our three kids took up residence in a nice property within a half-day's drive. We managed it all in as friendly and collaborative a way as anyone could hope for, and we remain committed to having a good relationship, both for the kids' sake and out of respect for ourselves and for each other. I wish it would have worked out better for us, but I've seen friends do far worse. I make the five-hour drive out there several times a month to spend time with Tyler, Madison, and Jackson, and it's always amazing to see them, every time. The marriage may not have made it, but the family is forever. That, too, is part of my red circle.

I see quite a few of my old SEAL buddies, too, from my Sniper Cell friend Eric to Chief Dan from the GOLF platoon days. I may not be an active member of the teams now, but the community is more like a family than a job, and once you're an intrinsic part of it, that never goes away. Glen, my shooting partner and best friend from sniper school, is a partner with me today in Wind Zero; not long ago we wrote a book together, *The 21st-Century Sniper*.

Our quiet community was thrust into the public spotlight in April 2009 when a coordinated team of three SEAL snipers took out three Somalian pirates in a perfectly coordinated trio of shots, rescuing Captain Richard Phillips of the *Maersk Alabama*. Soon my phone was ringing off the hook, and before I knew it I was standing before the CNN cameras explaining to Anderson Cooper the practically impossible logistics involved in pulling off such a mission and the lengths to which those three covert warriors had gone in training for it.

Two years later that spotlight grew more intense when a team of SEALs staged a covert raid on a compound in Pakistan and killed Osama bin Laden, America's Public Enemy No. 1 for the past decade and the man credited with orchestrating the 9/11 attacks. Once again I found myself on CNN and other media outlets providing viewers some insights into what had just happened. That sense I'd had back in 2000, standing on the deck of the crippled USS *Cole* off the coast of Yemen, that the nature of our modern military was tipping upside down and covert ops forces would soon become the vanguard of twenty-first-century warfare, has proven out. Yet I'm not sure the American public fully grasps what that looks like from the inside.

Three months after the bin Laden raid, in August 2011, enemy forces shot down an American helicopter over Afghanistan, killing thirty American Special Ops troops, including seventeen SEALs. It was the highest number of casualties in a single incident in the now ten-year-old war in Afghanistan, higher even than the devastating losses of Operation Redwing, the op Marcus Luttrell had so narrowly survived. For me, this latest tragedy touched equally close to home. My good friend Heath Robinson, one of the strongest members of our team at ECHO platoon, was one of those seventeen SEALs who died in that helo crash. So was Chris Campbell, a BUD/S classmate of mine. By this time the bin Laden raid had long left the headlines, and most of us in the States were on to other hot news of the day. But the SEALs are not like a sports team who goes off to celebrate and take the season off after winning the Super Bowl. The guys who took out bin Laden were back to work the next day.

Not long ago I was sitting at the barber's in San Diego getting a haircut when the guy in the next chair looked over at me and said, "Brandon?" I recognized him immediately, but it took me a minute to come up with the name: Chris Ponto. Chris was one of the kids I hung out with in the harbor at Ventura in my teens, when we were all aimless and hadn't yet figured out what the hell we were going to do with our lives. When I made my decision to get out of there and join the navy, I'd lost touch with them. It was great to catch up. Chris was doing okay, had a boat service going in Ventura. We got to talking about the old days, and after a few minutes I asked him about a guy named Jake who'd been my best friend in those days.

"Jake," said Chris, his eyes dropping to the floor in an unconscious gesture. "Yeah. He's homeless now. Totally addicted."

I asked about the girl Jake used to hang out with; I couldn't bring up her name. Neither could Chris. "They're still together," he said. This surprised me. Jake's girlfriend was from a wealthy family and had a trust fund. I'd always wondered if they'd stayed together and hoped that maybe she had pulled him out of that scene, helped him get on some positive track. Turned out, the opposite had happened. Jake had dragged her down. They were both still hanging around the harbor now, eking out a wretched existence.

Neither Chris nor I said it, but I know we were thinking the same thing. *That could so easily have been me.*

I've thought long and hard about why I am writing this book and what I want it to say. I think the message I want my story to get across boils down to two words:

Excellence matters.

Throughout my time with the navy and within the SEAL community, I've seen poor leadership and exceptional leadership. I've seen training that was simply good, training that was great, and training so transcendingly amazing it blew my mind. I've seen the difference it makes.

In political matters I have always been a down-the-middle-line person. When it comes to leaders, I care less about their party affiliation and more about their character and competence. I don't care how they would vote on school prayer or abortion or gay marriage or gun laws. I want to know that *they* know what the hell they're doing, and that they are made of that kind of unswerving steel that will not be rattled in moments that count, no matter what is coming at them. I want to know that they won't flinch in the face of debate, danger, or death.

I want to know that they excel at what they do.

A free society looks like it rests on big principles and lofty ideals, and maybe it does for much of the time. But in the dark times, those times that count most, what it comes down to is not reason or rhetoric but pure commitment, honed over time into the fabric of excellence.

Why am I telling you this? Because it *matters*.

You may never shoot a sniper rifle. You may never serve as part of an assault team, or stand security in combat, or board a hostile ship at midnight on the high seas. You may never wear a uniform; hell, you may never even throw a punch in the name of freedom. I'll tell you what, though. Whatever it is that you do, you are making a stand, either for excellence or for mediocrity.

This is what I learned about being a Navy SEAL: it is all about excellence, and about never giving up on yourself. And that is the red circle I will continue to hold, no matter what.

ACKNOWLEDGMENTS

Writing this memoir has been very personal for me. Exposing your skeletons in the closet and baring your soul to the world can be both humbling and frightening. It reminds me of checking into BUD/S and gazing up at the life-sized "Creature from the Black Lagoon" statue, gift of some graduating BUD/S class or other, that stands on the quarterdeck greeting all newcomers with its green-mouthed, red-eyed stare. The sign around its neck reads, SO YOU WANNA BE A FROG-MAN. Not a question, just posing a dare.

So you wanna write a MEMOIR. . . .

The first time I sat down to discuss this project with my agent, the legendary Margret McBride, in her office in La Jolla, California, she gave me a crucial piece of strategic advice. "Nobody writes his or her own memoir, Brandon," she said. "You're a good writer, but you need a *great* coauthor to help you out."

I didn't get great; I got incredible. Thank you, John David Mann. Having you as my "swim buddy" on this book project was like having one of my trusted teammates covering my six (navyspeak for "watching out for my backside") in the field. You took all my scattered notes, napkin files, threads of memories, and countless hours on the phone, and then you turned it all into something truly special. For that I thank you tremendously. We have many sayings in the SEALs. One of them goes, "That guy is solid; I'd take a bullet for him any day," and that's how I feel about John Mann.

The support of so many people goes into any book project, far too many to identify each by name here, but at the top of my list are the following family and friends who will always hold a special place in my heart. Thank you:

To my mother, Lynn, for not giving me up for adoption in those early years in Canada (!) and for always being there for me, rain or shine.

To my dad, Jack, for being there for those early-morning sporting events; it meant a lot to me.

To my sister. You're the best!

To my ex-wife, for being a great friend, coparent, and mom to our wonderful kids.

To my family in Canada.

To Glen "Bub" Doherty, my sniper-school shooting partner and lifelong friend. No one makes a better right-hand man.

To Eric Davis, for your friendship and hard and innovative work at the SEAL sniper course.

To the men of SEAL Team Three GOLF and ECHO platoons; you know who you are.

To Travis Lively, for proving that brotherhood still exists.

To Thomas Frasher, for always being there when it counted. You're a true brother.

To Johnny "Tsunami" Surmont, one of the most creative SEALs I know, always inventing something new. You've been a great friend, Johnny—keep making great things!

To Billy Tosheff, my friend and fellow aviator and hell-raiser; thanks for everything, brother. Not too many friends will show up at 2:00 A.M., no questions asked!

To Alex Tosheff, for believing in my site and the business potential of SOFREP.com. You are Tier One IT, my friend!

To Master Chief Manty, for teaching me what it means to be a chief.

To Master Chief Jason Gardner, for your support and knowledge in all things sniper.

To Sally Lyndley, for your amazing muselike support, love, and friendship. You're the world's best fashion stylist, in my opinion. Apparently a whole lot of important people agree with me.

To fellow teammate Rob Smith and his lovely wife, Nicole. It never ceases to amaze me how creative guys in our SOF community are. Rob, your handmade RESCO instruments are incredible, and I've gladly put my Rolex out to pasture in favor of my new RESCO. Thanks for keeping the brotherhood alive and working with me on the signature "Red Circle" RESCO watch.

To Bill Magee, owner of the dive boat *Peace*. Some of my fondest childhood memories are of time on that boat with you and the crew.

To Marc Resnick, our editor at St. Martin's, for believing in this book before it even existed, and to our literary agent, Margret McBride, for helping to make it happen.

To Marcus Luttrell and his wife, Melanie (I know who's in charge). Thanks for that great foreword, brother.

To the WindanSea Surf Club, for welcoming me into their clan.

Finally I want to acknowledge the following fallen SEAL teammates who touched my life in both training and combat. You guys will live in my memories forever: Matt "Axe" Axelson, Mike Bearden, Chris Campbell, Jason Freiwald, Mike Murphy, Tom Retzer, Heath Robinson, Jon "JT" Tumilson, John Zinn, and honorary teammates Mike Dahan and Paulo Emanuele.

See you on the other side, gents.

Brandon